the **tantra** experience

Extemporaneous talks given by Osho at
the OSHO International Meditation Resort, Pune, India

the **tantra** experience

Evolution through Love

ON *THE ROYAL SONG OF SARAHA*

OSHO

Previously published as *Tantra Vision*, Vol. 1

This book is a series of original talks by Osho, given to a live audience. All of Osho's talks
have been published in full as books, and are also available as original audio recordings.
Audio recordings and the complete text archive can be found via the online OSHO Library
at www.osho.com/library

Osho comments in this work on excerpts from: *The Royal Song of Saraha: A Study in the
History of Buddhist Thought,* translated and annotated by Herbert V. Guenther (1968). All
rights reserved. Permission granted by Dr. Ilse Guenther.

OSHO MEDIA INTERNATIONAL
New York • Zurich • Mumbai
an imprint of
OSHO INTERNATIONAL
www.osho.com/oshointernational

Distributed by Publishers Group Worldwide
www.pgw.com

Library of Congress Catalog-In-Publication Data is available

Printed in India by Manipal Technologies Limited, Karnataka

ISBN 978-0-9836400-3-5
Also available as eBook 978-0-88050-321-1

contents

preface

Tantra acceptance is total; it doesn't split you. All the religions of the world, except Tantra, have created split personalities. All the religions of the world, except Tantra, have created schizophrenia. They split you. They make something bad in you and something good. And they say the good has to be achieved and the bad denied, the Devil has to be denied and God accepted. They create a split within you and a fight. Then you are continuously feeling guilty, because how can you destroy the part that is organically one with you? You may call it bad, you may call it names; it doesn't make any difference. How can you destroy it? You never created it. You have simply found it; it was given. Anger is there, sex is there, greed is there; you have not created them; they are given facts of life, just like your eyes and your hands. You can call them names, you can call them ugly or beautiful or whatsoever you like, but you cannot kill them.

Nothing can be killed out of existence; nothing can be destroyed.

Tantra says a transformation is possible, but destruction, no! And a transformation comes when you accept your total being. Then suddenly everything falls in line, then everything takes its own place; then anger is also absorbed, then greed is also absorbed. Then without trying to cut anything out of your being, your whole being rearranges itself. If you accept and say yes, a rearrangement happens, and whereas before there was a noisy clamor inside, now a melody – music is born, a harmony comes in.

Osho
Tantra: The Supreme Understanding

CHAPTER 1

learning through action

The Royal Song of Saraha:

I bow down to noble Manjusri,
I bow down to him who has conquered the finite.

As calm water lashed by wind
turns into waves and rollers,
so the king thinks of Saraha
in many ways, although one man.

To a fool who squints,
one lamp is as two.
Where seen and seer are not two, ah, the mind works
on the thing-ness of them both.

Though the house lamps have been lit,
the blind live on in the dark.
Though spontaneity is all encompassing and close,
to the deluded it remains always far away.

Though there may be many rivers, they are one in the sea.
Though there may be many lies, one truth will conquer all.

When one sun appears,
the dark, however deep,
will vanish.

Gautama the Buddha is the greatest master who has ever walked on the earth. Christ is a great master, so is Krishna, so is Mahavira, so is Mohammed, and many more, but Buddha still remains the greatest master. Not that his achievement of enlightenment is greater than anybody else's – enlightenment is neither less nor more. He has attained to the same quality of consciousness as Mahavira, as Christ, as Zarathustra, as Lao Tzu. There is no question of any enlightened man being more enlightened than anybody else. But as far as his being a master is concerned Buddha is incomparable because through him thousands of people have attained to enlightenment.

It has never happened with any other master. His line has been the most fruitful line; his family has been the most creative family up to now. He is like a big tree with so many branches – and each branch has been fruitful, each branch is loaded with many fruits. Mahavira remained a local phenomenon. Krishna fell into the hands of scholars and was lost. Christ was completely destroyed by the priests. Much could have happened, but it didn't happen; Buddha has been tremendously fortunate in this. Not that the priests have not tried, not that the scholars have not tried; they have done all that they can do – but somehow Buddha's teaching was devised in such a way that it could not be destroyed. It is still alive. Even after twenty-five centuries a few flowers come on his tree, it still blooms. Spring comes, and still it releases fragrance, it still bears fruit.

Saraha is also a fruit of the same tree. Saraha was born about two centuries after Buddha; he was in the direct line of a different branch. One branch moves from Mahakashyapa to Bodhidharma, and Zen is born – and it is still full of flowers, that branch. Another branch moves from Buddha to his son, Rahul Bhadra, and from Rahul Bhadra to Sri Kirti, and from Sri Kirti to Saraha, and from Saraha to Nagarjuna – that is the Tantra branch. It is still bearing fruit in Tibet. Tantra converted Tibet, and Saraha is the founder of Tantra just as Bodhidharma is the founder of Zen. Bodhidharma conquered China, Korea, Japan; Saraha conquered Tibet.

These songs of Saraha are of great beauty. They are the very foundation of Tantra. You will first have to understand the Tantra attitude towards life, the Tantra vision of life. The most basic thing about Tantra is this – and very radical, revolutionary, rebellious – the basic vision is that the world is not divided into the lower and the higher, but that the world is one piece. The higher and the lower are holding hands. The higher includes the lower, and the lower includes the higher. The higher is hidden in the lower – so the lower has not to be denied, has not to be condemned, has not to be destroyed or killed. The lower has to be transformed. The lower has to be allowed to move upward and then the lower becomes the higher. There is no unbridgeable gap between the Devil and God: the Devil is carrying God deep down in his heart. Once that heart starts functioning, the Devil becomes God.

That is the reason why the very root of the word *devil* means the same as *divine*. The word *devil* comes from *divine*; it is the divine not yet evolved, that's all. Not that the Devil is against the divine, not that the Devil is trying to destroy the divine – in fact the Devil is trying to find the divine. The Devil is on the way toward the divine; it is not the enemy, it is the seed. The divine is the tree fully in bloom, and the Devil is the seed – but the tree is hidden in the seed, and the seed is not against the tree. In fact the tree cannot exist if the seed is not there. The tree is not against the seed; they are in deep friendship, they are together. Poison and nectar are two phases of the same energy, so are life and death – and so is everything: day and night, love and hate, sex and superconsciousness.

Tantra says: never condemn anything – the attitude of condemnation is a stupid attitude. By condemning something you are denying yourself the possibility that would have become available to you if you had evolved the lower. Don't condemn the mud, because the lotus is hidden in the mud; use the mud to produce the lotus. Of course the mud is not the lotus yet, but it can be. The creative person, the religious person, will help the mud to release its lotus so that the lotus can be freed from the mud.

Saraha is the founder of the Tantra vision. It is of tremendous import – and particularly for the present moment in human history because a new man is striving to be born, a new consciousness is knocking on the doors, and the future is going to be that of Tantra because now dual attitudes can no longer hold man's mind. They have tried for centuries; and they have crippled man and they have made man guilty They have not made man free; they have made man a prisoner. They have not made man happy either, they have made man very miserable. They have condemned everything: from food to sex they have condemned everything, from relationship to friendship they have condemned all. Love is condemned, the body is condemned, the mind is condemned. They have not left a single inch for you to stand on; they have taken away all, and man is hanging, just hanging. This state of man cannot be tolerated any longer.

Tantra can give you a new perspective; hence I have chosen Saraha. Saraha is one of my most-loved persons; it is my old love affair. You may not even have heard the name of Saraha, but Saraha is one of the great benefactors of humanity. If I were to count on my fingers ten benefactors of humanity, Saraha would be one of those ten. If I were to count five, then too I would not be able to drop Saraha.

Before we enter into these songs of Saraha, a few things about Saraha's life. Saraha was born in Vidarbha. Vidarbha is part of Maharashtra, very close to Pune. He was born when King Mahapala was the ruler. He was the son of a very learned brahmin who was in the court of King Mahapala; the father was in the court, so the young man was also in the court. He had four brothers; they were all great scholars, and he was the youngest and the most intelligent of them all. His fame was spreading all over the country by and by, and the king was almost enchanted by his superb intelligence. The four brothers were also very great scholars, but nothing compared to Saraha.

As they became mature, the four got married. The king was willing to give his own daughter to Saraha – but Saraha wanted to renounce all, Saraha wanted to become a sannyasin. The king was hurt; he tried to persuade Saraha – he was so beautiful and he was so intelligent and he was such a handsome young man. His fame was spreading all over the country, and because of him Mahapala's court was becoming famous. The king was very worried and he didn't want this young man to become a sannyasin. He wanted to protect him; he wanted to give him all comfort possible, he was ready to do anything for him. But Saraha persisted and the permission had to be given. He became a sannyasin, he became a disciple of Sri Kirti.

Sri Kirti is in the direct line of Buddha: Gautam Buddha, then his son Rahul Bhadra, and then comes Sri Kirti. There are just two masters between Saraha and Buddha; he is not very far away from Buddha. The tree must have still been very, very green; the vibe must have still been very, very alive. Buddha had just left; the climate must have been full of his fragrance.

The king was shocked because Saraha was a brahmin. If he wanted to become a sannyasin he should have become a Hindu sannyasin, but he chose a Buddhist master. Saraha's family was also very worried; in fact they all became enemies: this was not right. And then things became even worse – we will come to know about it.

Saraha's original name was Rahul, the name given by his father. We will come to know how he became Saraha – that is a beautiful story. When he went to Sri Kirti, the first thing Sri Kirti told him was, "Forget all your Vedas and all your learning and all that nonsense." It was difficult for Saraha, but he was ready to stake anything. Something in the presence of Sri Kirti had attracted him; Sri Kirti was a great magnet. He dropped all his learning, he became unlearned again.

This is one of the greatest renunciations. It is easy to renounce wealth, it is easy to renounce a great kingdom, but to renounce knowledge is the most difficult thing in the world. In the first place, how to renounce it? It is there inside you. You can escape from your kingdom, you can go to the Himalayas, you can distribute your wealth – how can you renounce your knowledge? And then it is too painful to become ignorant again. To become ignorant again, innocent like a child, is the greatest austerity there is.

But Saraha was ready. Years passed, and by and by he erased all that he had known. He became a great meditator. Just as he had started to become very famous as a great scholar, now his fame started spreading as a great meditator. People started coming from far and away just to have a glimpse of this young man who had become so innocent, like a fresh leaf, or like dewdrops on the grass in the morning.

One day, while Saraha was meditating, suddenly he saw a vision – a vision that there was a woman in the marketplace who was going to be his real teacher. Sri Kirti had just put him on the way, but the real teaching was to come from a woman.

Now this too has to be understood: it is only Tantra that has never been male chauvinistic. In fact to go into Tantra you will need the cooperation of a wise woman; without a wise woman you will not be able to enter into the complex world of Tantra. He saw a vision: a woman there, in the marketplace – so, first a woman, second in the marketplace. Tantra thrives in the marketplace, in the thick of life. It is not an attitude of negation, it is utter positivity.

Saraha stood up. Sri Kirti asked him, "Where are you going?" And he said, "You have shown me the path. You took my learning away; you have done half the work, you have cleaned my slate. Now I am ready to do the other half." With the blessings of Sri Kirti, who was laughing, he went away. He went to the marketplace and he was surprised, he really found the woman that he had seen in the vision. The woman was making an arrow; she was an arrowsmith woman.

The third thing to be remembered about Tantra: it says the more cultured, the more civilized a person, the less is the possibility of his tantric transformation. The less civilized, the more primitive, the more alive a person is. The more you become civilized, the more you become plastic; you become artificial; you become too cultivated, you lose your roots in the earth. You are afraid of the muddy world. You start living away from the world, you start posing as though you are not of the world.

Tantra says: to find the real person you will have to go to the roots.

So Tantra says those who are still uncivilized, uneducated, uncultured are more alive, they have more vitality, and that's the observation of the modern psychologists too. A Negro is more vital than the American – that is the fear of the American. The American is very afraid of the Negro. The fear is that the American has become very plastic, and the Negro is still vital, still down-to-earth.

The conflict between the Blacks and the Whites in America is not really the conflict between black and white, it is the conflict between the plastic and the real, and the American, the white man, is very afraid. Basically he is afraid that, if the Negro is allowed, he will lose his woman, the white American will lose his woman. The Negro is more vital, sexually more vital, more alive; his energy is still wild. And that is one of the greatest fears of civilized people: to lose their women. They know that if more vital persons are available, they will not be able to hold their women.

Tantra says in the world of those who are still primitive, there is a possibility of starting to grow. You have grown in a wrong direction; they have not grown yet, they can still choose a right direction, they have more potential. They don't have anything to undo, they can proceed directly.

An arrowsmith woman is a low-caste woman, and for Saraha – a learned brahmin, a famous brahmin, who had belonged to the court of the king – going to an arrowsmith woman is symbolic. The learned has to go to the vital, the plastic has to go to the real. He saw this woman – a young woman, very alive, radiant with life – cutting an arrow-shaft, looking neither to the right nor to the left but wholly absorbed in making the arrow. He immediately felt something extraordinary in her presence, something that he had never come across. Even Sri Kirti, his master, paled before the presence of this woman. Something so fresh and something from the very source...

Sri Kirti was a great philosopher. Yes, he had told Saraha to drop all learning, but still he was a learned man. He had told Saraha to drop all Vedas and scriptures, but he had his own scriptures and his own Vedas. Even though he was anti-philosophical, his anti-philosophy was a sort of philosophy. Now here was a woman who was neither philosophical nor anti-philosophical, who simply did not know what philosophy was, who was simply blissfully unaware of the world of philosophy, of the world of thought. She was a woman of action and she was utterly absorbed in her action.

Saraha watched carefully: the arrow ready, the woman – closing one eye and opening the other – assumed the posture of aiming at an invisible target. Saraha came still closer... Now there was no target, she was simply posing. She had closed one eye, her other eye was open and she was aiming at some unknown target: invisible, it was not there. Saraha started feeling some message. This posture was symbolic he felt, but still it was very dim and dark. He could feel something there, but he could not figure out what it was.

So he asked the woman whether she was a professional arrowsmith, and the woman laughed loudly, a wild laugh, and said, "You stupid brahmin!

You have left the Vedas, but now you are worshipping Buddha's sayings, the Dhammapada. So what is the point? You have changed your books, you have changed your philosophy, but you remain all the time the same stupid man." Saraha was shocked. Nobody had talked to him that way; only an uncultured woman can talk that way. And the way she laughed was so uncivilized, so primitive – but still, something was very much alive. He was feeling pulled; she was a great magnet and he was nothing but a piece of iron.

Then she said, "You think you are a Buddhist?" He must have been in the robe of the Buddhist monk, the yellow robe. She laughed again and she said, "Buddha's meaning can only be known through actions, not through words and not through books. Is not enough, enough for you? Are you not yet fed up with all this? Do not waste any more time in that futile search. Come and follow me!" And something happened, something like a communion. He had never felt like that before. In that moment the spiritual significance of what she was doing dawned upon Saraha. Neither looking to the left, nor looking to the right had he seen her – just looking in the middle.

For the first time he understood what Buddha means by being in the middle: avoid the excess. First he was a philosopher, now he had become an anti-philosopher – from one extreme to another. First he was worshipping one thing, now he was worshipping just the opposite – but the worship continues. You can move from the left to the right, from the right to the left, but that is not going to help. You will be like a pendulum moving from the left to the right, from the right to the left. And have you observed? When the pendulum is going to the right it is gaining momentum to go to the left; when it is going to the left it is again gaining momentum to go to the right. And the clock continues… And the world continues. To be in the middle means the pendulum just hangs there in the middle, neither to the right nor to the left. Then the clock stops, then the world stops. Then there is no more time; then the state of no time…

He had heard it said so many times by Sri Kirti; he had read about it, he had pondered, contemplated over it; he had argued with others about it: that to be in the middle is the right thing. For the first time he had seen it in an action: the woman was not looking to the right and not looking to the left – she was just looking in the middle, focused in the middle. The middle is the point from where the transcendence happens.

Think about it, contemplate on it; watch it in life. A man is running after money, is mad, money-mad; money is the only god.

One woman was asking another, "Why have you left your boyfriend? What happened? I had been thinking that you were engaged and that you were going to be married – what happened?"

The woman replied, "Our religions are different and that's why we have broken up."

The questioner was puzzled because she knew that both were Catholics, so she asked, "What do you mean by saying that your religions are different?"

The woman said, "I worship money, and he is broke."

There are people whose only god is money. One day or other the god fails – it is bound to fail. Money cannot be the god. It was your illusion that you were projecting. One day or other you come to the point where you can see that there is no god in it, that there is nothing in it, that you have been wasting your life. Then you turn against it, then you take an opposite attitude: you become against money. Then you leave money, you don't touch money. You are continuously obsessed now; now you are against money, but the obsession remains. You have moved from the left to the right, but your center of consciousness is still the money.

You can change from one desire to another. You were too worldly, one day you can become otherworldly. You remain the same, the disease persists. Buddha says: "To be worldly is to be worldly and to be otherworldly is also to be worldly." To be for money is to be mad after money, to be against money is to be mad after money; to seek power is foolish; to escape is also foolish.

To be just in the middle is what wisdom is all about.

For the first time Saraha actually saw it there – he had not even seen it in Sri Kirti. It was really there. The woman was true; she said, "You can only learn through action – and she was so utterly absorbed that she was not even looking at Saraha who was standing there watching her. She was so utterly absorbed; she was so totally in the action. That is again a Buddhist message: to be total in action is to be free of action.

Karma is created because you are not totally in it. If you are totally in it, it leaves no trace. Do anything totally and it is finished; you will not carry a psychological memory of it. Do anything incompletely and it hangs with you, it goes on – it is a hangover. The mind wants to continue and do it and complete it. Mind has a great temptation to complete things. Complete anything and the mind has gone. If you continue doing things totally, one day you suddenly find there is no mind. The mind is the accumulated past of all incomplete actions.

You wanted to love a woman and you didn't love her; now the woman is dead. You wanted to go to your father and you wanted to be forgiven for all that you had been doing, for all that you had been doing in such a way that he was feeling hurt; now he is dead. Now the hangover will remain, now the ghost… Now you are helpless – what to do? Whom to go to? And how to ask forgiveness? You wanted to be kind to a friend but you could not be because you became closed. Now the friend is no longer there, and it hurts. You start feeling guilt; you repent. Things go on like this.

Do any action totally and you are free of it and you don't look back. The real man never looks back because there is nothing to see. He has no hang-overs; he simply goes ahead. His eyes are clear of the past, his vision is not clouded. In that clarity one comes to know what reality is.

You are so worried with all your incomplete actions – you are like a junk-yard: one thing is incomplete here, another thing is incomplete there; nothing is complete. Have you watched it? Have you ever completed anything, or is everything just incomplete? You go on pushing aside one thing and you start another thing, and before it is complete you start another. You become more and more burdened. This is what karma is; karma means incomplete action.

Be total, and you will be free.

The woman was totally absorbed. That's why she was looking so lumi-nous, she was looking so beautiful. She was an ordinary woman, but the beauty was not of this earth. The beauty came because of total absorption. The beauty came because she was not an extremist. The beauty came because she was in the middle, balanced. Out of balance comes grace. For the first time Saraha encountered a woman who was not just physically beautiful, but who was spiritually beautiful. Naturally, he was surrendered. The surrender happened.

Absorbed totally, absorbed in whatsoever she was doing... He understood for the first time: this is what meditation is. Not that you sit for a special period and repeat a mantra, not that you go to the church or to the temple or to the mosque, but to be in life – to go on doing trivial things, but with such absorp-tion that the profundity is revealed in every action. He understood what medi-tation is, for the first time. He had been meditating, he had been struggling hard, but for the first time meditation was there, alive. He could feel it. He could have touched it, it was almost tangible, and then he remembered that closing one eye and opening the other is a symbol, a Buddhist symbol.

Buddha says – psychologists will agree with him now; after two thousand and five hundred years psychology has come to that point where Buddha was, so long before – Buddha says half the mind reasons and half the mind intuits. The mind is divided into two parts, into two hemispheres. The left hemisphere is the faculty of reason, logic, discursive thought, analysis, philosophy, theology: words and words and words, and arguments and syllogisms and inferences. The left-side mind is Aristotelian. The right-side mind is intuitive, poetic: inspi-ration, vision, a priori consciousness, a priori awareness. Not that you argue – you simply come to know. Not that you infer – you simply realize. That is the meaning of a priori awareness: it is simply there. The truth is known by the

right-side mind. Truth is inferred by the left-side mind. Inference is just inference, it is not experience.

Suddenly he realized that the woman had closed one eye. She had closed
one eye as symbolic of closing the eye of reason, logic, and she had opened
the other eye symbolic of love, intuition, awareness. And then he remembered the posture.

Aiming at the unknown, the invisible, we are on the journey to know the
unknown – to know that which cannot be known. That is real knowledge: to
know that which cannot be known, to realize that which is unrealizable, to attain
that which cannot be attained. This impossible passion is what makes a man a
religious seeker.

Yes, it is impossible. By impossible I don't mean that it will not happen; by
impossible I mean that it cannot happen unless you are utterly transformed.
As you are it cannot happen. But there are different ways of being, and you
can be totally a new man, then it happens. It is possible for a different kind
of man. That's why Jesus says: "Until you are reborn, you will not know it."
A new man will know it.

You come to me – *you* will not know it. I will have to kill you, I will have
to be drastically dangerous to you; you will have to disappear, and the new
man is born, a new consciousness comes in because there is something indestructible in you which cannot be destroyed; nobody can destroy it. Only the
destructible will be destroyed and the indestructible will be there. When you
attain to that indestructible element in your being, to that eternal awareness in
your being, you are a new man, a new consciousness. Through that the impossible is possible, the unattainable is attained.

So he remembered the posture. Aiming at the unknown, the invisible, the
unknowable, the one – that is the aim. How to be one with existence? The nondual is the aim: where subject and object are lost, where I and thou are lost.

There is a very famous and great book of Martin Buber: *I and Thou.* Martin
Buber says the experience of prayer is an I-thou experience. He is right. The
experience of prayer is an I-thou experience: God is the thou; you remain
the I and you have a dialogue, a communion with the thou. But Buddhism
has no prayer in it, and Buddhism goes higher. Buddhism says even if there
is an I-thou relationship, you remain divided; you remain separate. You can
shout at each other, but there will be no communion. The communion happens only when the I-thou division is no longer there, when subject and object
disappear, where there is no I and no thou, no seeker and no sought, when
there is unity, unison.

Realizing this, seeing into this woman's actions and recognizing the truth…
The woman called him Saraha. His name was Rahul; the woman called him

Saraha. *Saraha* is a beautiful word. It means he who has shot the arrow: *sara* means arrow, *ha* means have shot. Saraha means one who has shot the arrow. The moment he recognized the significance of the woman's actions, those symbolic gestures, the moment he could read and decode what the woman was trying to give, what the woman was trying to show, the woman was tremendously happy. She danced and called him Saraha, and said, "Now, from today you will be called Saraha, you have shot the arrow. Understanding the significance of my actions, you have penetrated..."

Saraha said to her, "You are not an ordinary arrowsmith woman. I am sorry to have even thought that you were an ordinary arrowsmith woman. Excuse me, I am tremendously sorry. You are a great master and I am reborn through you. Till yesterday I was not a real brahmin, from today I am. You are my master and you are my mother and you have given me a new birth. I am no longer the same. So right you are – you have dropped my old name and you have given me a new name."

You ask me sometimes, "Why do you give new names?" To drop the old identity, to forget the past, not to be any more in any attachment with the past, a clean break is needed. You have to become discontinuous with the past. Rahul became Saraha.

The legend has it that the woman was nobody but a hidden buddha. The name of the buddha given in the scriptures is Sukhnatha: the buddha who had come to help the great potential man, Saraha. The buddha, a certain buddha of the name Sukhnatha, took the form of a woman. But why, why the form of a woman? Because Tantra believes that just as a man has to be born out of a woman, so the new birth of a disciple is also going to be out of a woman. In fact all the masters are more mothers than fathers. They have the quality of the feminine. Buddha is feminine, so is Mahavira, so is Krishna. You can see the feminine grace, the feminine roundness; you can see the feminine beauty. You can look into their eyes and you will not find the male aggressiveness.

So it is very symbolic that a buddha took the form of a woman. Buddhas always take the form of a woman. They may be living in a male body, but they are feminine – because all that is born, is born out of the feminine energy. Male energy can trigger it but cannot give birth.

A master has to keep you in his womb for months, for years, sometimes for lives. One never knows when you will be ready to be born. A master has to be a mother. A master has to be tremendously capable of feminine energy so that he can shower love on you; only then can he destroy. Unless you are certain about his love, you will not allow him to destroy you. How will you trust? Only his love will make you able to trust, and through trust, by and by, he will cut you limb by limb. One day suddenly you will disappear. Slowly, slowly,

slowly... And you are gone: *Gate, gate, para gate* – going, going, going, gone. Then the new is born.

The arrowsmith woman accepted him. In fact she was waiting; a master waits for the disciple. Old traditions say that before a disciple chooses the master, the master has chosen the disciple. That's exactly what happened in this story. Sukhnatha was hiding in the form of a woman waiting for Saraha to come and be transformed through him.

It seems more logical too that a master should choose first – because he is more aware, he knows. He can penetrate to the very possibility of your being, the very potentiality. He can see your future; he can see that which can happen. When you choose a master you think *you* have chosen. You are wrong. How can you choose a master? You are so blind, how can you recognize a master? You are so unaware, how can you feel a master? If you start feeling him, that means he has already entered in your heart and has started playing with your energies – that's why you start feeling him. Before a disciple ever chooses a master, the master has already chosen him.

She accepted. She was waiting for Saraha to come. They moved to a cremation ground and started living together. Why to a cremation ground? Because Buddha says unless you understand death you will not be able to understand life. Unless you die, you will not be reborn.

Many Tantra disciples have lived in the cremation ground since Saraha; he was the founder. He lived in a cremation ground; people would be brought, dead bodies would be brought and burned, and he lived there, that was his home. He lived with this arrowsmith woman, they lived together. There was great love between them, not the love of a woman and a man, but the love of a master and a disciple, which is certainly higher than any man-woman love can ever reach; which is more intimate, certainly more intimate because a man-woman love affair is just of the bodies. At the most sometimes it reaches to the mind, otherwise it remains in the body. A disciple and a master is a soul love affair.

Saraha had found his soul mate. They were in tremendous love, great love, which rarely happens on the earth. She taught him Tantra. Only a woman can teach Tantra. Somebody asked me why I have chosen Kaveesha to be the group leader for Tantra – only a woman can be a Tantra group leader, it will be difficult for a man. Yes, sometimes a man can also be, but then he will have to become very, very feminine. A woman is that already, she has already those qualities, those loving, affectionate qualities; she naturally has that care, that love, that feeling for the soft.

Saraha became a Tantrika under the guidance of this arrowsmith woman. Now he was no longer meditating. One day he had left all the Vedas, scriptures and knowledge. Then he left even meditation. Now rumors started spreading all over the country: he no longer meditates. He sings, of course, and dances too, but no longer any meditation. Now singing was his meditation, now dancing was his meditation, now celebration was his whole lifestyle.

Living in a cremation ground and celebrating! Living where only death happens and living joyously! This is the beauty of Tantra: it joins together the opposites, the contraries, the contradictories. If you go to the cremation ground you will feel sad; it will be difficult for you to be joyous. It will be very difficult for you to sing and dance where people are being burned, and where people are crying and weeping, and every day death and death, day and night, death. How will you rejoice? But if you cannot rejoice there, then all that you think is your joy is just make-believe. If you can rejoice there, then joy has really happened to you. Now it is unconditional. Now it doesn't make any difference whether death happens or life, whether somebody is born or somebody is dying.

Saraha started singing and dancing. He was no longer serious. Tantra is not – Tantra is playfulness. Yes, it is sincere, but not serious; it is very joyous. Play entered his being. Tantra is play because Tantra is a highly evolved form of love, and love is play.

There are people who would even not like love to be a play. Mahatma Gandhi says: "Make love only when you want to reproduce." Even love they change into work: reproduction. This is just ugly! Make love to your woman only when you want to reproduce – is she a factory? *Reproduction* – the very word is ugly. Love is fun! Make love to your woman when you are feeling happy, joyous, when you are at the top of the world. Share that energy. Love your man when you have that quality of dance and song and joy – not for reproduction! The word *reproduction* is obscene. Make love out of joy, out of abundant joy. Give when you have it.

Play entered into his being. A lover always has the spirit of play. The moment the spirit of play dies you become a husband or a wife; then you are no longer lovers, then you reproduce. The moment you become a husband or a wife, something beautiful has died. It is no longer alive; the juice no longer flows. Now it is just pretension, hypocrisy.

Play entered his being, and through play true religion was born. His ecstasy was so infectious that people started coming to watch him dancing and singing. And when people would come and watch, they would start dancing, they would start singing with him. The cremation ground became a great celebration. Yes, bodies were still being burned, but more and more crowds started gathering around Saraha and the arrowsmith woman, and great joy was created on that cremation ground.

And it became so infectious that people who had never heard anything about ecstasy would come, dance and sing, and fall into ecstasy, go into *samadhi.*

His very vibration, his very presence, became so potent that just if you were ready to participate with him, it would happen: contact high. Those who came around him... He was so drunk that his inner drunkenness started over-flowing to other people. He was so stoned that others started becoming stoned and more stoned.

But then the inevitable... The brahmins and the priests and the scholars and the so-called righteous people started vilifying and slandering him – that I call the inevitable. Whenever there is a man like Saraha the scholars are going to be against him, the priests are going to be against him, and the so-called moral people, puritans, self-righteous people. They started spreading abso-lutely biased rumors about him.

They started saying to people, "He has fallen from grace; he is a pervert. He is no longer a brahmin, he has given up celibacy, he is no longer even a Buddhist monk. He indulges in shameful practices with a low-caste woman and runs around like a mad dog in all directions." His ecstasy was just like a mad dog to them – it depends how you interpret. He was dancing all over the cremation ground. He *was* mad but he was not a mad dog, he was a mad god! It depends on how you look.

The king was also told these things – he was anxious to know exactly what was happening. He became worried, more and more people started coming to him. They knew him, they knew that the king was always deeply respectful toward Saraha, that he wanted to appoint him as his councilor in the court, but Saraha had renounced the world. The king had much respect for his learning, so they started coming to the king.

The king was worried. He had loved the young man and respected him too, and he was concerned. So he sent a few people to persuade Saraha and tell him, "Come back to your old ways. You are a brahmin, your father was a great scholar, you yourself were a great scholar. What are you doing? You have gone astray, come back home. I am still here; come to the palace, be part of my family. This is not good."

The people went and Saraha sang one hundred and sixty verses to those people who had come to convert him. Those one hundred and sixty verses... And those people started dancing and they never came back. The king was even more worried. The king's wife, the queen, was also always interested in the young man. She wanted the young man to marry her daughter, so she went there. Saraha sang eighty verses to the queen, and she never came back. Now the king was much puzzled: "What is happening there?" So the king himself went there – and Saraha sang forty verses and the king was converted. He started dancing in the cremation ground like a mad dog!

So there are three scriptures available in the name of Saraha. First, *The People's Song of Saraha* – one hundred and eighty verses; second, *The Queen's Song of Saraha* – eighty verses; and third, *The Royal Song of Saraha*, which we are going to meditate upon – forty verses. One hundred and sixty verses for the people, because their understanding was not great; eighty for the queen – she was a little higher, her understanding was a little higher; forty for the king, because he was really a man of intelligence, of awareness, of understanding.

Because the king was converted, the whole country by and by was converted, and it is said in the old scriptures that a time came when the whole country became empty. *Empty* – it is a Buddhist word. It means people became nobodies, they lost their ego trips. People started enjoying the moment. The hustle and bustle, the competitive violence disappeared from the country. It became a silent country. It became empty, as if nobody was there; the men as such disappeared from the country. A great divineness descended on the country. These forty verses were at the root of it, the very source of it.

Now we enter into this great pilgrimage: *The Royal Song of Saraha*. It is also called *The Song on Human Action* – very paradoxical because it has nothing to do with action. That's why it is also called *The Song on Human Action*. It has something to do with the being, but when the being is transformed, action is transformed. When *you* are transformed, your behavior is transformed – not vice versa. Not that first you change your action and then your being changes, no. Tantra says first change your being and then your action changes automatically, of its own accord. First attain to a different kind of consciousness, and that will be followed by a different kind of action, character, behavior.

Tantra believes in being, not in action and character. That's why it is also called *The Song on Human Action* – because once being is transformed your actions are transformed. That is the only way to change your actions. Who has ever been able to change his actions directly? You can only pretend.

If you have anger in you and you want to change your action, what will you do? You will suppress the anger and you will show a false face; you will have to wear a mask. If you have sexuality in you, what will you do to change it? You can take the vow of celibacy, of *brahmacharya,* and you can pretend, but deep down the volcano continues. You are sitting on a volcano which can erupt any moment. You will be constantly trembling, constantly afraid, in fear.

Have you not watched the so-called religious people? They are always afraid – afraid of hell, and always trying somehow to get into heaven. But they don't know what heaven is; they have not tasted it at all. If you change your consciousness, heaven comes to you, not that you go to heaven. Nobody has ever gone to heaven and nobody has ever gone to hell. Let it be decided once and for all: heaven comes to you, hell comes to you. It depends on you; whatsoever you call, it comes.

If your being changes, you suddenly become available to heaven – heaven descends on you. If your being does not change you are in a conflict, you are forcing something which is not there. You become false and false and more false, and you become two persons; you become schizophrenic, split. You show something, you are something else. You say something; you never do it, you do something else, and then you are continuously playing hide-and-seek with yourself. Anxiety and anguish are natural in such a state – that's what hell is.

Now the song:

> *I bow down to noble Manjusri,*
> *I bow down to him who has conquered the finite.*

This word *Manjusri* has to be understood. Manjusri was one of the disciples of Buddha, but he was a very rare disciple. Buddha had many rare disciples; they were rare in different ways. Mahakashyapa was rare because he could understand the message not delivered in words, and so on and so forth. Manjusri was rare because he had the greatest quality of being a master.

Whenever somebody was too much of a difficult problem, somebody was a problematic person, Buddha would send him to Manjusri. Just the name of Manjusri and people would start trembling. He was really a hard man, he was really drastic. Whenever somebody was sent to Manjusri, the disciples would say, "That person has gone to Manjusri's sword." It has become famous down the ages – the sword of Manjusri – because Manjusri used to cut off the head in one stroke. He was not a slow-goer; he would simply cut off the head in one stroke. His compassion was so great that he could be so cruel.

So by and by the name of Manjusri became a representative name – a name for all masters because they are all compassionate and they all have to be cruel. Compassionate because they will give birth to a new man in you; cruel because they will have to destroy and demolish the old.

So when Saraha bows down first before starting his song, he says: *I bow down to noble Manjusri* – the master of all masters – *I bow down to him who has conquered the finite.* And he bows down to Buddha who has conquered the finite, and who has become the infinite.

> *As calm water lashed by wind*
> *turns into waves and rollers,*
> *so the king thinks of Saraha*
> *in many ways, although one man.*

Visualize a lake, a placid, silent lake with no waves. Then there comes a great wind and it starts playing on the surface of the lake, and the lake is disturbed, and a thousand and one ripples and waves arise. Just a moment before the reflection of the full moon was there in the lake; now it is no longer there. Now the moon is still reflected, but in a thousand and one fragments. It is all over the lake. The whole lake is silvery because of the reflection, but you cannot catch hold of the real reflection: where the moon is, how it looks. It is all distorted.

Saraha says this is the situation of the worldly mind, of the deluded. This is the only difference between a buddha and a non-buddha. A buddha is one whose wind is no longer blowing. That wind is called *trishna:* desire.

Have you watched, observed? Whenever there is desire, there are a thousand and one ripples in your heart; your consciousness is disturbed and distracted. Whenever desire stops, you are at ease, at peace with yourself. So desire is the wind that distorts the mind, and when the mind is distorted, you cannot reflect the reality.

As calm water lashed by wind turns into waves and rollers, so the king thinks of Saraha in many ways, although one man. Saraha says two things. First he says: your mind is too disturbed by the rumors; so much wind has blown over the surface of your mind. You will not be able to see me, though I am one, but your mind is reflecting me in a thousand fragments.

This was true. He could see through and through the king. The king was puzzled. On one hand he respected the young man, on one hand he had always trusted the young man – he knew that he could not be wrong. But so many people, so many so-called honest, respectable people, rich, learned, came to him and they all reported, "He has gone wrong, he has become almost mad, he is a maniac, he is a pervert. He lives with an arrowsmith woman of low caste. He lives in the cremation ground – this is not a place to live. He has forgotten all old rituals, he no longer reads the Vedas; he no longer chants the name of the god. He is not even heard to meditate, and he is indulging in strange, ugly, shameful practices."

Tantra looks shameful to people who are very sexually repressed. They cannot understand: because of their repressions they cannot understand what is happening. So all these things are like a great wind in the mind of the king. One part of him loves and respects; one part of him is in deep doubt.

Saraha looked directly and he said: *...so the king thinks of Saraha in many ways, although one man.* Although Saraha is one man... I am just like the full moon, but the lake is in turmoil. So please, if you want to understand me, there is no way to understand me directly. The only way to understand me is to stop this wind which is blowing on the surface of your mind. Let your consciousness

be at ease, then see! Let all these waves and the rollers stop, let your consciousness be a placid pool – and then you see. I cannot convince you of what
is happening unless you are able to see it. It is happening, it is here. I am here
standing before you. I am one man, but I can see into you – you are looking at
me as if I am a thousand men.

> *To a fool who squints,*
> *one lamp is as two.*
> *Where seen and seer are not two, ah, the mind works*
> *on the thingness of them both.*

And then he takes similes, metaphors. First he says, "Like a lake you are in
turmoil." Then he says: *To a fool who squints, one lamp is as two* – he cannot
see one, he sees two.

I have heard…

Mulla Nasruddin was teaching his son the ways of being a drunkard. After
a few drinks Mulla said, "Now let us go. Always remember, this is the rule
when to stop: when you start seeing that one person is looking like two, then
go home – it is enough."

One person looking like two, but the son asked, "Where? Where is that
one person?"

Mulla said, "Look, there are two persons sitting at that table."

And the son replied, "There is nobody!" He had already drunk too much.

Remember: when you are unconscious things don't look as they are.
When you are unconscious, you project. Tonight, looking at the moon, you
can press your eye with your finger and you can see two moons. And when
you are seeing two moons, it is very difficult to believe that there is one – you
are seeing two. Just think, somebody is born with a natural defect, his eye
has that pressure which makes one thing look like two; he will always see two
things. Wherever you see one, he will see two. Our inner vision is clouded with
many things, so we go on seeing things which are not, and when we see, how
can we believe that they are not? We have to trust our own eyes, and our own
eyes may be distorting.

*To a fool who squints one lamp is as two. Where seen and seer are not
two…* Saraha says to the king: "If you are thinking me and you are two, then
you are unconscious, then you are a fool, then you are drunk, then you don't
know how to see. If you really see, then I and you are one, then the seer and
the seen are not two. Then you will not see Saraha dancing here – you will see

yourself dancing here. Then when I go into ecstasy, *you* will go into ecstasy. That will be the only way to know what has happened to Saraha, there is no other way."

What has happened to me? If you want to know, the only way is to become a participant in my being. Don't be a watcher. Don't stand aside and just become a spectator. You will have to participate in my experience; you will have to lose yourself a little bit into me. You will have to overlap my boundaries. That's what sannyas is all about. You start coming closer, you start losing your boundaries into me. Only then, one day, through participation, when you fall *en rapport* with me, something will be seen, something will be understood. You will not be able to convince anybody else who has just been a spectator because your visions will be different. You have participated, and he has only been observing; you are living in two different worlds.

> *Though the house lamps have been lit...*

Listen to this beautiful saying of Saraha:

> *Though the house lamps have been lit,*
> *the blind live on in the dark.*
> *Though spontaneity is all encompassing and close,*
> *to the deluded it remains always far away.*

He says: Look! I have become enlightened. *Though the house lamps have been lit...* my innermost core is no longer dark. See! There is great light in me, my soul is awakened. I am no longer the same Rahul you used to know. I am Saraha; my arrow has reached the target.

Though the house lamps have been lit, the blind live on in the dark. But what can I do? Saraha says: "If somebody is blind, even when the house lamps are lit he goes on living in darkness. Not that the lamps are missing, but his eyes are closed. So don't listen to blind people. Just open your eyes and look at me, see me – who is standing in front of you, whom you are confronting. The blind live on in the dark, though the house lamps have been lit."

Though spontaneity is all encompassing and close... And I am so close to you; the spontaneity is so close to you, you can already touch it and eat it and drink it. You can dance with me and you can move into ecstasy with me. I am *so* close – you may not find spontaneity so close again!

...to the deluded it remains always far away. They talk about *samadhi*, and they read the Patanjali sutras; they talk about great things, but whenever that great thing happens they are against it. This is something very strange

about man. Man is a very strange animal. You can appreciate Buddha, but if
Buddha comes and just confronts you, you will not be able to appreciate him
at all – you may go against him, you may become the enemy. Why? When
you read a book about Buddha, everything is okay – the book is in your hand.
When an alive buddha has to be confronted, he is not in your hand – you are
falling into *his* hand. Hence the fear, resistance; one wants to escape, and the
best way to escape is to convince yourself that he has gone wrong, something
is wrong with him. That is the only way: if you prove to yourself that he is
wrong. And you can find a thousand and one things in a buddha which can
look wrong because you are squinting and you are blind and your mind is in
a turmoil. You can project anything.

Now this man has attained to buddhahood, and they are talking about the
low-caste woman. They have not looked into that woman's reality. They have
only been thinking that she is an arrowsmith woman, so low-caste, sudra,
untouchable. How can a brahmin touch an untouchable woman? How can
the brahmin live there? And they have heard that the woman cooks food for
him. This is a great sin; this is a great fall – a brahmin eating food cooked by
a sudra, by an untouchable, by a low-caste woman?

And why should a brahmin live on the cremation ground? Brahmins have
never lived there. They live in the temples, they live in the palaces. Why on the
cremation ground? A dirty place – skulls and dead bodies all around. This is
perversion! But they have not looked into the fact that unless you understand
death you will never be able to understand life. When you have looked deep
into death and found that life is never dead, when you have looked, penetrated deep into death and found that life continues even after death, that death
makes no difference, that death is immaterial… You don't know anything about
life; life is eternal, timeless. So only the body dies, only the dead dies; the alive
continues.

But for this, one has to go into deep experimentation – they will not look at
that. Now they have heard that he is going into strange practices. They must
have gossiped and exaggerated; things must have got out of hand. Everybody
goes on multiplying the gossip, and there are Tantra practices which can
be gossiped about. In Tantra the man sits in front of the woman, the naked
woman, and he has to watch her so deeply, to see her through and through,
that all desire to see a woman naked disappears. Then man is free from the
form. Now this is a great secret technique – otherwise you go on continuously
seeing her in your mind. Each woman that passes by on the road, you want to
undress her – that is there.

Now suddenly you see Saraha sitting before a naked woman – how will
you interpret? You will interpret according to yourself. You will say, "So okay,

what we always wanted to do he is doing, so we are better than him, at least we are not doing it. Of course we visualize sometimes, but it is only in thought, not in deed. He has fallen." And you will not miss the opportunity.

But what is he really doing? It is a secret science. By watching – for months together the Tantrika will watch the woman, meditate on her body form, meditate on her beauty; will look at everything, whatsoever he wants to look at. Breasts have some appeal – he will look and meditate on the breasts. He has to get rid of the form, and the only way to get rid of the form is to know it so deeply that it no longer has any attraction.

Now something just the opposite is happening from what the gossipers are saying. He is going beyond. Never again will he want to undress a woman, not even in the mind, not even in a dream will that obsession be there. But the crowd, the mob, has its own ideas. Ignorant, unaware, they go on talking about things.

Though spontaneity is all encompassing and close,
to the deluded it remains always far away.

Though there may be many rivers, they are one in the sea.
Though there may be many lies, one truth will conquer all.
When one sun appears,
the dark, however deep,
will vanish.

And Saraha says: "Just look at me – the sun has risen. So I know howsoever deep is your dark, it is going to vanish. Look at me – the truth is born in me. You may have heard thousands of lies about me, but one truth will conquer them all."

Though there may be many rivers, they are one in the sea. Just come close to me. Let your river drop into my ocean, and you will have my taste.

Though there may be many lies, one truth will conquer all. Truth is one. Only lies are many, only lies can be many – truth cannot be many. Health is one, diseases are many. One health conquers all diseases, and one truth conquers all lies.

When one sun appears, the dark, however deep, will vanish. In these four verses Saraha has invited the king to enter into his inner being, he has opened his heart. He says, "I am not here to convince you logically, I am here to convince you existentially. I will not give any proof and I will not say anything in defense of myself. The heart is just open – come in, go in, see what has happened – so close is spontaneity, so close is godliness, so close is truth; the sun has risen. Open your eyes!"

Remember, a mystic has no proof. He cannot have any proof by the very nature of things. He *is* the only proof, so he can bare his heart to you.

These verses, these songs of Saraha, have to be meditated on deeply. Each song can become the opening of a flower in your heart. I hope these forty verses will become forty flowers in your being, as they became in the being of the king. The king was liberated – so can you be. Saraha has penetrated the target. You can also penetrate the target. You can also become a Saraha: one whose arrow is shot.

Enough for today.

transformation is
a consequence of understanding

The first question:

Osho,
Is there any difference between the approaches of Shiva and Saraha toward
Tantra?

Not really, not essentially. But as far as the form is concerned, yes. Religions differ only in the form; religions differ only in their methodology. Religions differ as far as the door into the divine is concerned, but not existentially. There are only two basic formal differences: that of the path of devotion, prayer and love; and the path of meditation and awareness. These two basic differences persist.

Shiva's approach is that of devotion, it is that of prayerfulness, of love. Saraha's approach is that of meditation, awareness. The distinction is still formal because when the lover and the meditator reach they arrive at the same goal. Their arrows are released from different angles, but they reach the same target. Their arrows are released from different bows, but they reach the same target. The bow does not matter finally. What type of bow you have chosen does not matter if the target is attained. These are the two bows because man basically is divided into two: thinking and feeling. Either you can approach reality through thinking or you can approach reality through feeling.

The Buddhist approach – the approach of Buddha and Saraha – is through intelligence. It is basically through the mind that Saraha moves, but it is the mind that has to be left behind. Of course the mind has to be left behind, by and by the mind has to disappear into meditation. It is the mind that has to disappear; it is the thinking that has to be transformed, and a state of no-thought has to be created. But remember, it is a state of no-thought, and that can be created only by slowly, by and by dropping thoughts. So the whole work consists in the thinking part.

Shiva's approach is that of the feeling, of the heart. The feeling has to be transformed. Love has to be transformed so that it becomes prayerfulness. On Shiva's way, the devotee and the deity remain, the *bhakta* and *bhagwan* remain. At the ultimate peak they both disappear into each other.

Listen to it carefully: when Shiva's Tantra reaches to its ultimate orgasm, I is dissolved into thou, and thou is dissolved into I; they are both together, they become one unity.

When Saraha's Tantra reaches to its ultimate peak, the recognition is: neither you are right, nor you are true, neither you nor I exist, both disappear. There are two zeros meeting, not I nor thou. Two zeros, two empty spaces dissolve into each other because the whole effort on Saraha's path is how to dissolve thought, and I and thou are parts of thought. When thought is utterly dissolved, how can you call yourself "I"? And whom will you call your God? God is part of thought; it is a thought creation, a thought construct, a mind construct. So all mind constructs dissolve and *shunya,* emptiness, arises.

On Shiva's path you no longer love the form, you no longer love the person; you start loving the whole existence. The whole existence becomes your thou, you are addressed to the whole existence. Possessiveness is dropped, jealousy is dropped, hatred is dropped; all that is negative in feeling is dropped, and the feeling becomes purer and purer. A moment comes when there is pure love. In that moment of pure love, you dissolve into thou and thou dissolves into you. You also disappear, but you disappear not like two zeros; you disappear as the beloved disappears into the lover and the lover disappears into the beloved.

Up to this point they are different, but that too is a formal difference. Beyond this, what does it matter whether you disappear like a lover and a beloved, or you disappear like two zeros? The basic point, the fundamental point, is that you disappear, that nothing is left, that no trace is left. That disappearance is enlightenment.

So you have to understand it: if love appeals to you, Shiva will appeal to you, and *The Book of Secrets* will be your Tantra bible. If meditation appeals to you, then Saraha will appeal to you. It depends on you. Both are right, both are going on the same journey. With whom you would like to travel, is your choice. If you can be alone and blissful, then Saraha; if you cannot be blissful when you are alone, and your bliss comes only when you relate, then Shiva... This is the difference between Hindu Tantra and Buddhist Tantra.

The second question:

Osho,
I always agree with whatsoever you say – then why is my life not changing?

Maybe it is because of the agreement. If you agree with me, or if you disagree with me, your life will not change. It is not a question of agreement or disagreement, it is a question of understanding, and understanding is beyond both agreement and disagreement. Ordinarily, when you agree you think you have understood me. If you have understood me then there will be no question of agreement and disagreement. How can you agree with truth – or disagree? The sun has risen – do you agree or do you disagree? You will say the question is irrelevant.

Agreement, disagreement, is about theories, not about truth. So when you agree with me you are not really agreeing with me; you start feeling that I agree with your theory that you have already been carrying with you. Whenever you feel, "Osho is in agreement with me," you feel, "I agree with Osho." Whenever I am not in agreement with you then there is trouble, then you don't agree with me. Or you don't listen to that, you don't hear that. You simply close yourself when I am saying something which does not agree with you.

It is not a question of agreement and disagreement. Drop that! I am not here in search of any converts. I am not trying any philosophy; I am not here proposing any theology. I am not seeking followers, I am seeking disciples – and that is a totally different thing, utterly different. A disciple is not one who agrees; a disciple is one who listens, who learns. The very word *disciple* comes from *learning, discipline*.

A disciple is one who is open to learn. A follower is closed. A follower thinks he has agreed; now there is nothing and no need to remain open – he can close, he can afford to close. A disciple can never afford to close; there is so much to learn. How can you agree or disagree? And a disciple has no ego, so who will agree and who will not agree? A disciple is just an opening, there is nobody inside to agree or not agree. Your very agreement is creating the trouble. Nobody is ever transformed through agreement. Agreement is very superficial, very intellectual.

To be transformed one needs understanding. It is always understanding that transforms, that mutates. When you understand, you are not to do anything;

the understanding will start doing things. It is not that first you understand then you practice, no. The very understanding, the very fact of understanding, goes deep into your heart, sinks, and there is transformation.

Transformation is a consequence of understanding.

If you agree, then the problem arises: now what to do? I have agreed, now something has to be practiced. Agreement is very stupid, as stupid as disagreement. And the mind is very cunning: you never know what you mean by agreement.

A few scenes, first:

The boy's mother had died when he was an infant, and his father had worked hard to raise him properly. Finally the boy went away to college. His first letter was a disappointment to his father. It was a disappointment, but the old man did not know exactly why. Surely there was nothing to despair of in the content. Perhaps something in the tone bothered him. The letter read, "Dear Dad, everything is fine. I like it here at college. I'm on the football team. I'm in the best fraternity on campus. I got an 'A' on my first algebra exam…"

After some thinking, the father was able to put his finger on the difficulty. He wrote back, "Look, son, I don't want to seem to be a silly old man, but there is something which would make me very happy. It isn't that I think you're ungrateful in any way, but I've had to work very hard to raise you and send you to college and I never had a chance to go to college myself. What I mean is this: it would mean a lot to me if you would say, '*We* did this and *we* did that,' instead of '*I* did this and *I* did that.' It would help me to feel as if I had a part in it all."

The boy understood immediately and thereafter letters came in the form, "Well, Dad, we won this big game last Saturday. We've got a date with a swell girl. We're going to get an 'A' in history." The old man took earnest pleasure in this sharing of experience. Days were sunny for him.

One day a telegram arrived: "Dear Dad, We got the dean's daughter in trouble. She had twins – mine died. What are you going to do with yours?"

The mind is very cunning. Watch! When you agree with me, do you really agree with me or do you find that I am agreeable to you? And then the mind is very legal, the mind is a lawyer; it can find ways to agree and yet remain the same. Not only that, when you agree, you start feeling as if: "Now it is Osho's duty to transform me." What more can you do? You are agreeing; you have done your part. What more can you do? You have agreed, you have become a sannyasin; you have surrendered. What more can you do? Now if nothing is happening you start getting angry with me.

Then when I say something to you, it is not exactly the same thing that you hear. You hear in your own way, you hear with all your interpretations. You hear through your past, through memories, through knowledge, through your conditionings. You hear through the mind, and the mind gives a color to everything that you hear. It immediately jumps on it, changes it, makes it agreeable to you, drops a few things, exaggerates a few other things, fills the gaps. Only part of what I have said remains in it, and the part can never transform, only the whole can. But the whole can remain whole only when you are not making any effort to agree or disagree. When you are not making any effort to agree or disagree you can put the mind aside. If you are trying to make an effort to agree, how can you put the mind aside? It is the mind which agrees or disagrees.

Understanding is something bigger than the mind. Understanding happens in your total being. It is as much in your head as in your toe. Understanding is something total. The mind is a very tiny part, but very dictatorial, and it goes on pretending that it is the whole.

Second scene:

There was the middle-aged businessman who took his wife to Paris. After traipsing with her from one shop to another, he begged for a day off to rest, and got it. With the wife gone shopping again, he went to a bar and picked up a luscious Parisienne. They got on well until the question of money came up: she wanted fifty American dollars, he offered ten. They couldn't get together on the price, so they didn't get together.

That evening he escorted his wife to one of the nicer restaurants, and there he spotted his gorgeous babe of the afternoon seated at a table near the door.

"See, monsieur," said the babe as they passed her, "Look what you got for your lousy ten bucks."

Your understanding is *your* understanding. Your interpretation is *your* interpretation. You will look from your angle. Whatsoever you hear is your interpretation, always remember. Beware of it! It is not what I have said, it is what you have thought that you have heard – and they are not the same things. You agree with your own echo, you don't agree with me. You agree with your own idea. Then how can you change? The idea is yours; the agreement is yours, so there is no possibility of change.

Please stop agreeing and disagreeing. Just listen to me. Your method of agreement may be a sort of trick to protect yourself, so that you don't get a shock. It functions like a buffer. I say something, you agree immediately

– the shock is avoided. If you were not agreeing with me, it may have shocked you to your very roots, it may have shaken you to your very guts. I say something, you say, "Yes, I agree." With this agreement you cut off. Now there is no need to be shocked, you agree. If you were not agreeing or disagreeing... It is the same thing with disagreement. The moment I say something and there is somebody who says, "I don't agree," he has cut off the energy. Now the energy will not go into his roots and will not shake him.

We have created so many buffers around ourselves, protections. These protections will not allow you to change. To change, you will need to be shocked – shocked tremendously, terribly. It is going to be painful; transformation is going to be painful. Agreement is very comfortable, so is disagreement. I don't make much difference between agreement and disagreement; they are two aspects of the same coin.

The real person who wants to be near me and close to me, who wants to be really in contact with me, will not agree, will not disagree. He will simply listen to me – pure listening, absolutely pure listening, with no interpretation. He will put himself aside. He will give way to me.

The third scene:

The teacher had just finished giving her first-graders the basic facts of life. Little Mary raised her hand from a front-row seat. "Can a six-year-old boy make a baby?"

"No," said the teacher, smiling, "that would be impossible. Any other questions, class?"

Pause. Mary again put her hand up. "Can a six-year-old girl make a baby?"

"No," said the teacher. Whereupon the little boy behind Mary leaned forward and whispered loudly in her ear, "Ya see, I told ya, ya didn't have nothin' to worry about."

All your agreements, all your disagreements, are just finding ways to remain the way you are, not to change. People's whole lives are devoted to one work: how not to change. They go on saying, "I don't want to be miserable," and they go on doing things which make them miserable. They go on saying, "I want to change," but I look deep down in them and they don't want to change. In fact this express desire that they want to change is again a trick not to change, so they can say to the world, "I am trying to change and I am saying loudly and shouting loudly that I want to change, and still if nothing is happening what can I do?"

You cannot change. The last thing I would like to say about this question: *you* cannot change, you can only allow change to happen. Trying to change, you will never change. Who is trying? The old is. Look at the inner logic of it: you are trying to change yourself. It is almost like pulling yourself up by your own shoe-strings. What can happen out of it? Nothing is possible. You cannot change yourself because who is this one who is trying to change? It is your past. It is *you*.

You can allow a change to happen. What can you do to allow it? Please don't agree and disagree with me. Just listen! Just be here. Just let my presence function as a catalytic agent. Just get infected by me. Just catch the disease that I have, the measles that I have. Just allow me, don't try to change yourself. This allowing is what surrender is all about.

A sannyasin is not one who has agreed with me. If he has agreed with me, then he is not a sannyasin, then he is a follower, just as Christians are followers of Christ. They have agreed with Christ, but that has not changed them. Just as Buddhists are followers of Buddha – they have agreed with Buddha, but that has not changed them. Can't you see: the whole world is following somebody or other?

So to follow is a way to avoid change. Please don't follow me. Simply listen to what is happening here, see what is happening here. Just look into me, and give me a way that my energy can start functioning on your energy. It is not a mind thing; it is a total affair – so that you can start vibrating in the same wavelength, even for a few moments. Those moments will bring change; those moments will bring glimpses of the unknown. Those moments will make you aware that there is eternity beyond time. Those moments will give you a feel of what it is to be in meditation. Those moments will allow you a little taste of godliness, of Tao, of Tantra, of Zen. Those moments will bring the possibility of change because those moments will come, not from your past but from your future.

Agreeing, it is your past which agrees with me. Opening, allowing, it is your future which opens, opens with me. Your possibility of transformation is in your future. The past is dead and gone and finished. Bury it! It has no meaning any longer. Don't go on carrying it, it is unnecessary luggage; because of this luggage, you cannot go very high.

What do you mean when you say, "I agree with you"? It means your past agreeing, your past feeling good and nodding and saying, "Yes, that's what I have always been thinking." This is a way to avoid the future. Be aware!

Just being with me – that is *satsang,* that is contact high. Just being with me, in spite of you, a few rays will enter into your being and will start playing. And then you will become aware that whatever life you have lived was not life at all, that you have been in an illusion, you have been dreaming. Those few glimpses of reality will shatter your whole past, and then there is transformation. It comes naturally of its own accord; it follows understanding.

The third question:

Osho,
Sometimes as I watch people playing the same old games over and over, my eyes
feel ancient and jaded and my heart weary and cynical. I guess it's because I'm
seeing more and more my own games and tricks and I hear your maddening voice
between my ears saying, "That's okay – you just have to accept and love yourself,
and there is no problem."
Just...!
I think if you say this word again I will scream. Wasn't I happier when I thought
there was a goal?

The question is from Anando. It is significant. The question can be that of
almost everybody who is present. Listen to it. It simply shows a situation that
every seeker has to pass.

First, Anando says, "Sometimes as I watch people playing the same old
games over and over, my eyes feel ancient and jaded and my heart weary and
cynical." Please don't try to watch others – that is none of your business. If
they have decided to play the old games, if they want to play the old games,
if they are happy in playing their old games, who are you to interfere? Who
are you even to judge? This constant hankering to judge others has to be
dropped. It does not help others; it harms you, it only harms you. Why should
you be bothered? That has nothing to do with you. It is others' joy if they want
to remain the old and they want to move in the same rut, in the same routine.
Good! It is their life and they have every right to live it their own way.

Somehow we cannot allow others to have their own way; in some way or
other we go on judging. Sometimes we say they are sinners, sometimes we say
they are bound to go to hell, sometimes we say they are this and that, criminals.
If all that has changed...now a new evaluation, that they are playing old games
and "I am tired." Why should you be tired of their games? Let them be tired of
their games if they want; or if they don't want, that too is their choice. Please
don't watch others.

Your whole energy has to be focused on yourself. Maybe you are condemning others for their old games just as a trick because you don't want to
condemn yourself. It always happens, it is a psychological trick: we project on
others. A thief thinks everybody is a thief – that is very natural for him, that
is a way to protect his ego. If he feels the whole world is bad he feels good in
comparison. A murderer thinks the whole world is murderous – that makes

him feel good and at ease. It is convenient to think the whole world is murder-ous; then he can murder and there is no need to have any guilt feeling, there is no need to have any prick of conscience.

So we go on projecting on others whatsoever we don't want to see in ourselves. Please stop that! If you are really tired of old games, then this is the old game – the oldest. For many lives you have been playing it: projecting your defects onto others, and then feeling good; and of course you have to exag-gerate, you have to magnify. If you are a thief, you have to magnify others' images, that they are greater thieves than you. Then you feel good in com-parison, you are a far better person.

That's why people go on reading the newspapers. Newspapers help you very much. Early in the morning, before you have even taken your tea, you are ready for the newspaper, and the newspaper brings nothing like news because there is nothing new. It is the same old rotten thing. But you feel good: some-where somebody has been murdered, somewhere there has been a Watergate, and somewhere something else, and somewhere somebody has stolen, and somebody's wife has escaped with somebody else, and so on and so forth. Watching all that, you relax, you feel, "So, I am not so bad – the whole world is going to the dogs. I am a far better person. I have not yet escaped with the wife of the neighbor. I have not killed anybody yet – although I think of it, but thinking is not a crime when people are actually doing things." You feel good, and the moment you feel good, you remain the same.

Please don't watch others. It is not going to help you. Use your energy of observation on yourself. There is something tremendously transforming in obser-vation. If you observe yourself, things will start changing. If you start observing your anger, one day you will suddenly find the anger has no more energy the way it used to have; it is no longer so fiery. Something has gone dead in it.

If you start watching yourself, you will see by and by the negative is dying and the positive is becoming more and more alive, that misery is disappear-ing and bliss is entering into your life, that you smile more, sometimes even for no reason, that a sense of humor is arising in you if you start watching. That old depressed, long face is disappearing; a sense of humor is born. You start taking life more playfully. If you watch, seriousness becomes more and more irrelevant. More and more you become innocent, trusting, less and less doubtful.

I am not saying that your trust will always be respected. No, that is not the point. You may be deceived more, because when you are trusting you can be deceived more. But even when you are deceived, your trust will not be destroyed by it; in fact it may even be enhanced. You may start thinking that even if you are deceived – somebody has taken a little money and deceived you – you will be able to see that you have saved the far more valuable thing, that is trust; and something almost valueless, the money, has gone.

You could have saved the money and the trust would have gone – that would have been a far greater loss, because nobody has ever been found to be happy just because of money. But because of trust, people have lived like gods on earth; because of trust, people have enjoyed life so totally that they could feel grateful to existence. Trust is a benediction. Money at the most can give you a little comfort, but no celebration. Trust may not give you much comfort, but will give you great celebration.

Now to choose comfort against celebration is simply stupid because that comfortable life will be nothing but a comfortable death. Conveniently you can live and conveniently you can die, but the real taste of life is possible only when you are celebrating at the optimum, at the maximum, when your torch is burning from both ends together. Maybe only for a single moment, but the intensity of it, but the totality of it, but the wholeness of it... And this happens only through observation. Observation is one of the greatest forces of transformation.

Start observing yourself. Don't waste your energy with observation of others – that is sheer wastage. Nobody will ever thank you for it; it is a thankless job, and whomsoever you observe will feel offended because nobody likes to be observed, everybody wants to have a private life. Good or bad, stupid or wise, everybody wants to have their own private life. And who are you to interfere? So don't be a peeping tom, don't go to people's keyholes, and don't watch. It is *their* life. If they want and if they love to play the old game, let them play.

So the first thing: please stop watching other people, turn the whole energy on yourself.

Second, you say, "I guess it's because I'm seeing more and more my own games and tricks and I hear your maddening voice between my ears saying, 'That's okay – you just have to accept and love yourself, and there is no prob-lem.'" I have to repeat it: there is no problem. I have never come across a real problem – not up to now, and I must have listened to thousands of people and their thousands of problems. I have not come across a real problem yet, and I don't think that it is ever going to happen because the real problem does not exist. A problem is a created thing. Situations are there, problems are not there. Problems are your interpretations of situations. The same situation may not be a problem to someone and may be a problem to somebody else. So it depends on you whether you create a problem or you don't create a problem, but problems are not there. Problems are not in existence; they are in the psychology of man.

Just look next time you are having a trip and riding a problem. Just watch,

just stand aside and look at the problem. Is it really there or have you created it? Look deeply into it and you will suddenly see it is not increasing, it is
decreasing; it is becoming smaller and smaller. The more you put your energy
into observation, the smaller it becomes. A moment comes when suddenly it
is not there – and you will have a good laugh.

Whenever you are having a problem, just look at it. Problems are fictitious,
they don't exist. Just go around the problem, look from every angle – how can
it be? It is a ghost. You wanted it, that's why it is there. You asked for it, that's
why it is there. You invited it, that's why it is there.

But people don't like it: if you say their problem is not a problem, they
don't like it. They feel very bad. If you listen to their problems they feel very
good. If you say, "Yes, this is a great problem," they are very happy. That's
why psychoanalysis has become one of the most important things of this century. The psychoanalyst helps nobody – maybe he helps himself, but he helps
nobody else. He cannot. But still people go and pay. They enjoy – he accepts
their problems. Whatsoever absurd problem you bring to the psychoanalyst,
he listens to it very sincerely and seriously, as if it is there. He takes it for
granted that you are suffering greatly, and he starts working on it and analyzing
it. And it takes years!

Even after years of psychoanalysis the problem is not solved because in
the first place the problem has never been there – so how can anybody solve
it? But after years of psychoanalysis you get tired, and you get finished with the
old problem; you want some new problem now. So one day you suddenly say,
"Yes, it is no longer there, it has gone," and you thank the psychoanalyst. But
it is simply time that has helped, that has healed. It is not psychoanalysis.
But there are people who do not like to simply wait and watch.

When you bring a mad person to a Zen monastery, they simply put him in
a corner, in a small hut, far away from the monastery; they give him food and
they tell him, "Just be there, quiet." Nobody goes to talk to him; food is sup-
plied, his comforts are looked after, but nobody bothers about him. And what
psychoanalysis does in three years, they do in three weeks. Within three weeks
the person simply comes out and he says, "Yes, the problem is finished."

For three weeks you are left with your problem – how can you avoid
seeing it? And no analysis is given so there is no diversion, you are not distracted. The psychoanalyst distracts you. The problem may have died on its
own within three weeks, but it will not die now because with the support of
the psychoanalyst it will live for three years, or even longer. It depends how
rich you are. If you are rich enough the problem can continue for your whole
life. That means it depends on how much you can afford. Poor people don't
suffer from many problems. Rich people suffer – they can afford to. They can

enjoy the game of having great problems. The poor person cannot afford and cannot enjoy that game.

Next time you are having a problem, look into it, look hard into it; no need for any analysis. Don't analyze it because analysis is a way of diversion. When you start analyzing you don't look at the problem. You start asking why, from where, how did it come? In your childhood, your mother's relationship with you, your father's relationship with you… You have gone astray, now you are not looking into the problem itself. Freudian psychoanalysis is really a mind-game, and played with great expertise.

Don't go into the causes, there is no need because there is no cause. Don't go into the past, there is no need because that will be going away from the present problem. Look into it as a herenow thing, just enter into it, and don't think about causes, reasons. Just watch the problem as it is, and you will be surprised that looking hard into it, it starts dispersing. Go on looking into it and you will find it has gone.

Problems are not there. We create them because we cannot live without problems. That is the only reason we create them. To have a problem is to have an occupation: one feels good; there is something to do. When there is no problem you are left alone, empty – what to do next? All problems finished…

Just think, one day God comes and says, "No problems any longer – finished! All problems gone." What will you do? Just think of that day. People will be stuck. People will start getting very angry about God. They will say, "This is not a blessing! Now what are we supposed to do? No problems?" Suddenly the energy is not moving anywhere; then you will feel stagnant. The problem is a way for you to move, to go on, to carry on, to hope, to desire, to dream. The problem gives so many possibilities to remain occupied.

And to be unoccupied, or to be capable of unoccupation, is what I call meditation. An unoccupied mind that enjoys a moment of unoccupation is a meditative mind.

Start enjoying some unoccupied moments. Even if the problem is there – you feel it is there, I say it is not, but you feel it is there – put the problem aside and tell the problem, "Wait! Life is there, the whole life is there. I will solve you, but right now let me have a little space, unoccupied by any problem." Start having a few moments unoccupied. Once you have enjoyed them you will see the fact that problems are created by you because you were not capable of enjoying the unoccupied moments, so problems fill the gap.

Have you not watched yourself? Sitting in a room, if you have nothing to do you start feeling fidgety, you start feeling uncomfortable, you start feeling restless. You will turn the radio on, or you will turn the TV on, or you will start reading the same newspaper you have read three times since the morning. Or if there is only one way, you will fall asleep so that you can create dreams and again remain occupied. Or you will start smoking. Have you seen it? Whenever you are not having anything to do, it becomes very difficult to be, just to be.

I will say again: there is no problem, Anando. Look into the fact of it, that there is no problem in life. If you want to have it, it is your pleasure – you enjoy with all my blessings. But the truth is, there is no problem.

Life is not a problem at all, it is a mystery to be lived and enjoyed. Problems are created by you because you are afraid to enjoy life, and you are afraid to live life. Problems give you a protection against life, against joy, against love. You can say to yourself, "How can I enjoy? I am having so many problems, how can I enjoy? I am having so many problems, how can I love a man or a woman? I am having so many problems, how can I dance and sing? Impossible!" You can find some reasons not to sing, not to dance. Your problems give you a great opportunity to avoid.

Look into the problems and you will find they are fictitious. Even if you are having a problem and you feel it is real, I say it is okay. Why do I say it is okay? – because the moment you start feeling it is okay, it will disappear. The moment you say to a problem, "It is okay," you have stopped giving energy to it. You have accepted it. The moment you accept a problem, it is no longer a problem. A problem can be a problem only when you go on rejecting it, when you say it should not be so. It is, and it should not be so – the problem is strengthened.

That's why I say it. People come to me with their big problems and I say, "It is okay, it is very good, accept it." And I say, "You just have to accept and love yourself." And I understand that Anando says, "It is very maddening, your voice continuously saying, 'That's okay…and there is no problem.'"

"Just…?" And Anando says, "I think if you say this word again I will scream." You have been screaming your whole life, whether you scream or not is not the point, you have been screaming your whole life. You have not done anything else up to now. Sometimes loudly, sometimes silently, but you have been screaming. That's how I see people – screaming people – their hearts are screaming, their beings are screaming. But that will not help. You can scream, but that will not help.

Try to understand rather than screaming. Try to see what I am telling you. What I am telling you is not a theory; it is a fact. And I am saying it because I have known it that way. If it can happen to me that there is no problem, why can't it happen to you? Take the challenge of it! I am just as ordinary a man as you are; I don't claim any extraordinary miraculous powers. I am very ordinary, just as you are.

The only difference between me and you is that you don't say okay to yourself and I have said an absolute okay to myself – that is the only difference. You are continuously trying to improve yourself and I am not trying to improve myself. I have said: incompletion is the way life is. You are trying to become perfect and I have accepted my imperfections. That is the only difference.

So I don't have any problems. When you accept your imperfection, from where can the problem come? When whatsoever happens you say it is okay, then from where can the problem come? When you accept limitations, then from where can the problem come? The problem arises out of your non-acceptance. You cannot accept the way you are, hence the problem. And you will *never* accept the way you are, so the problem will always be there. Can you imagine yourself some day accepting, totally accepting the way you are? If you can imagine, then why don't you do it right now? Why wait, for whom, for what?

I have accepted the way I am, and that very moment all problems disappeared; that very moment all worries disappeared. Not that I became perfect, but I started enjoying my imperfections. Nobody ever becomes perfect because to become perfect means to become absolutely dead. Perfection is not possible because life is eternal. Perfection is not possible because life goes on and on and on; there is no end to it.

So the only way to get out of these so-called problems is to accept your life as you find it right this moment, and live it, enjoy, delight in it. The next moment will be of more joy because it will come out of this moment; and the next to that will be of even more joy, because by and by you will become more and more joyous. Not that you will become joyous through improvement, but by living the moment.

You will remain imperfect. You will always have limitations, and you will always have situations where if you want to create problems you can immediately create them. If you don't want to create problems, there is no need to create them. You can scream, but that won't help. That's what you have been doing. That has not helped.

Even primal therapy has not proved of much help. It allows people to scream – yes, it feels a little good, it is a tantrum therapy. It allows you to vomit. It feels a little good because you feel a little unloaded, unburdened, but then within a few days that euphoria disappears; again you are the same, again accumulating. Again go to primal therapy – you will feel good for a few days – again the same...

Unless you understand that one has to stop creating problems, you will go on creating problems. You can go into an encounter group, you can do primal therapy, you can do thousands of other groups, and after each group you will feel tremendously beautiful because you dropped something that was on your head – but you have not dropped the mechanism that creates it. You have dropped something which you were having, but you have not dropped the very factory that goes on creating it. Again you will create, so it will not be of much use. It will give you a respite, a rest.

But if you *really* understand that the thing is that you have to stop creating problems... Otherwise you can go from one group to another group, from one psychoanalyst to another psychoanalyst, from one psychiatrist to another psychiatrist, from one therapy to another therapy, and everybody will give you a little respite, a little rest, and again you are doing the same thing.

My whole effort here is to cut the problem from the very roots. Please don't create problems. They are not, they exist not.

And the last thing Anando says: "Wasn't I happier when I thought there was a goal?" Yes, you were happier, and you were more miserable too, because your happiness was in the hope, it was not a true happiness. So I say you were happier and miserable too. You were miserable here in the present, and you were happy in the future – but how can you be in the future? The goal is in the future.

You were unhappy here, you were happy there. There exists not – it is all here. It is always here; everywhere it is here! There exists only in the dictionary. So it is with then – it is always now, then exists not. Yes, you were happier in your dreams of thinking of a goal, of thinking of a beautiful future. But why does a person think about a beautiful future? – because he is miserable in the present.

I don't think about a beautiful future, I cannot conceive how it can be more beautiful. How can it be more beautiful than it is right now, this moment? How is existence going to be more happy and joyous than it is this moment? Have a look – how can it be more happy, more joyful? But that's a trick, again a trick of the mind: to avoid the present we go on thinking about the future so that we need not see the present. And the present is all there is.

So you are right, you were happier – happier in your dreams. Now I have shattered all your dreams. Happier in your hopes – now I am trying in every way to create the state of hopelessness, so there is no hope left. I am trying to bring you to the present. You have been wandering in the future; I am pulling you back to herenow. It is hard work, and to have goals taken away, one feels very angry.

You are sometimes very angry with me. I have taken away your hope, your dreams – or I am trying. You are clinging to them. You are so addicted to your hope that you even start hoping through me. You start hoping through me: "Osho will do this." This man is not going to do anything! You start hoping, "Now I am with Osho so there is no need to be afraid. Sooner or later I am going to become enlightened." Forget all about it. Enlightenment is not a hope. It is not a desire and it is not in the future. If you start living, right this moment you are enlightened. I am trying to make you enlightened every day, and you say, "Tomorrow." Then, as you will, but tomorrow it will never happen. Either it is now or never.

Become enlightened right now! And you can because you are simply deluded, simply thinking that you are not. So don't ask how. The moment you ask how, you start hoping. So don't ask how, and don't say, "Yes, we will become." I am not saying that. I am saying you are.

The goose is out! The goose has never been in. One just has to be alert in the moment. Just a single moment of alertness, a shock, and you are free.

Every day I am trying to make you enlightened because I know you *are* enlightened. But if you want to go on playing the game of samsara, you can go on playing.

Happier certainly you were, and miserable too. I have taken away your happiness so you cannot any longer hope. If you allow me a little more time, I will take your misery too. But first the happiness has to go because misery exists as a shadow to the hope of happiness. So first the hope of happiness has to go, only then will the shadow go.

You can scream if you want to scream, but I will repeat a thousand and one times: Anando, there is no problem. You just have to accept and love yourself. Yes, just!

The fourth question:

Osho,
Isn't Tantra a way of indulgence?

It is not. It is the *only* way to get out of indulgence. It is the only way to get out of sexuality. No other way has ever been helpful to man; all other ways have made man more and more sexual.

Sex has not disappeared. The religions have made it only more poisoned; it is still there, in a poisoned form. Yes, guilt has arisen in man, but sex has not disappeared. It *cannot* disappear because it is a biological reality. It is existential; it cannot simply disappear by repressing it. It can disappear only when you become so alert that you can release the energy capsuled in sexuality. Not by repression is the energy released, but by understanding, and once the energy is released, out of the mud, the lotus... The lotus has to come up out of the mud, it has to go higher – and repression takes it deeper into the mud, it goes on repressing it.

What you have done up to now, the whole humanity, is to repress sex in the mud of the unconscious. Go on repressing it, sit on top of it, don't allow it to move; kill it by fasting, by discipline, by going to a cave in the Himalayas, by moving to a monastery where a woman is not allowed. There are monasteries where a woman has never entered for hundreds of years; there are monasteries where only nuns have lived and a man has never entered. These are ways of repressing, and they create more and more sexuality and more and more dreams of indulgence.

No, Tantra is not a way of indulgence. It is the *only* way of freedom. Tantra says whatsoever is, has to be understood, and through understanding changes occur of their own accord.

So listening to me or listening to Saraha, don't start thinking that Saraha is supporting your indulgence. You will be in bad shape if you accept that. Listen to this story:

An elderly gent named Martin went to a doctor for an examination. He said, "I want you to tell me what's wrong, doctor. I feel some pains here and there, and I can't understand it. I've lived a very clean life – no smoking, drinking or running around. I'm in bed, alone, at nine o'clock every night. Why should I feel this way?"

"How old are you?" asked the doctor.

"I'll be seventy-four on my next birthday," said Martin.

The doctor answered, "After all, you're getting on in years, you've got to expect things like that. But you've lots of time left yet. Just take it easy and don't worry. I suggest you go to Hot Springs."

So Martin went to Hot Springs. There he met another gent who looked so old and decrepit that Martin felt encouraged by the comparison. "Brother," says Martin, "You sure must have taken good care of yourself, living to such a ripe old age. I've lived a quiet, clean life, but not like you, I'll bet. What is your formula for reaching such a ripe old age?"

So this shriveled old guy says, "On the contrary, sir. When I was seventeen my father told me, 'Son, you go and enjoy life. Eat, drink and be merry to your heart's content. Live life to the fullest. Instead of marrying one woman, be a bachelor and have ten. Spend your money for fun, for yourself, instead of on a wife and kids.' Yeah! Wine, women and song, life lived to the full. That's been my policy all my life, brother."

"Sounds like you got something," said Martin. "How old are you?"

The other answered, "Twenty-four."

Indulgence is suicidal, as suicidal as repression. These are the two extremes that Buddha says to avoid. One extreme is repression, the other extreme is indulgence. Just be in the middle: neither be repressive, nor be indulgent. Just be in the middle, watchful, alert, aware. It is your life – it has neither to be repressed, nor to be wasted; it has to be understood.

It is your life – take care of it. Love it! Befriend it! If you can befriend your life it will reveal many mysteries to you, it will take you to the very door of godliness.

Tantra is not indulgence at all. The repressive people have always thought that Tantra is indulgence. Their minds are so much obsessed... For example, a man who goes to a monastery and lives there without ever seeing a woman, how can that man believe that Saraha is not indulging when he lives with a woman? Not only lives, but practices strange things: sitting before the woman naked, the woman is naked and he goes on watching the woman, or even while making love to the woman he goes on watching.

Now you cannot watch his watching; you can watch only that he is making love to a woman, and if you are repressive, your whole repressed sexuality will bubble up. You will start going mad. You will project all that you have repressed in yourself onto Saraha – and Saraha is not doing anything like that. He is moving in a totally different dimension. He is not really interested in the body. He wants to see what this sexuality is, he wants to see what this appeal of orgasm is, he wants to see what exactly orgasm is; he wants to be meditative in that peak moment, so that he can find the clue and the key. Maybe there is the key to open the door of the divine. In fact it *is* there.

Existence has hidden the key in your sexuality. On the one hand, through your sex, life survives; that is only partial use of your sex energy. On another hand, if you move with full awareness in your sex energy, you will find that you have come across a key that can help you to enter into eternal life. One small aspect of sex is that your children will live. The other aspect, a higher aspect, is that you can live in eternity.

Sex energy is life energy.

Ordinarily we don't move further than the porch, we never go into the palace. Saraha is trying to go into the palace. Now the people who came to the king must have been suppressed people, as all people are suppressed.

The politician and the priest have to teach suppression because it is only through suppression that people are driven insane. And you can rule insane people more easily than sane people. When people are insane in their sex energy, they start moving in other directions: they will start moving toward money or power or prestige. They have to show their sex energy somewhere or other; it is boiling there, they have to release it in some way or other. So money-madness or power-addiction becomes their release.

This whole society is sex-obsessed. If sex-obsession disappears from the world, people will not be money-mad – who will bother about money? And people will not be bothered by power. Nobody will want to become a president or a prime minister – for what? Life is so tremendously beautiful in its ordinariness; it is so superb in its ordinariness, why should one want to become somebody? By being nobody it is so delicious, nothing is missing. But if you destroy people's sexuality and make them repressed, so much is missing that they are always hankering: "Somewhere there must be joy – here it is missing."

Sex is one of the activities given by nature and existence, in which you are thrown again and again to the present moment. Ordinarily you are never in the present, except when you are making love, and then too only for a few seconds.

Tantra says one has to understand sex, to decode sex. If sex is so vital that life comes out of it, then there must be something more to it. That something more is the key toward divinity, toward godliness.

The fifth question:

Osho,
What is wrong with me? I understand what you say, I read your books and enjoy them tremendously, but still something very essential is missing.

Meditate on these beautiful words of Wordsworth:

> The world is too much with us; late and soon,
> getting and spending, we lay waste our powers.
> Little we see in Nature that is ours.
> We have given our hearts away – a sordid boon.
> This sea that bares her bosom to the moon,
> the winds that will be howling at all hours
> and are up gathered now like sleeping flowers,
> for this, for everything, we are out of tune.
> It moves us not.

That's what is missing. *It moves us not.* We are out of tune with existence. This *world is too much with us...getting and spending, we lay waste our powers. Little we see in Nature...* How can you find godliness and how can you find bliss if you don't look into nature? Nature is manifested existence. Nature is the body, the form, and temple of existence. *We have given our hearts away.* That's what is missing. *...for this, for everything, we are out of tune. It moves us not.*

So, just reading and listening to me will not help much. Start feeling! Listening, feel too, do not only listen. Listening, listen too through the heart. Let it sink into your feeling aspect. That is the meaning when all the religions say *shraddha:* faith, trust, is needed. Trust means a way of listening from the heart, not through doubt, not through logic, not through reasoning, not through discursive intellect, but through a deep participation through the heart.

As you listen to music, listen to me that way. Don't listen to me as you listen to a philosopher; listen to me as you listen to the birds. Listen to me as you listen to a waterfall. Listen to me as you listen to the wind blowing through the pines. Listen to me, not through the discursive mind, but through the participant heart, and then something that you are continuously feeling is missing, will not be missed.

The head has become too much of an expert; it has gone to the very extreme. It is a good instrument. Yes, as a slave the head is wonderful; as a boss it is very dangerous. It has gone to the very extreme, it has absorbed all your energies; it has become dictatorial. Of course, it works, but because it works you have started depending on it too much. One can always go to the extreme, and the mind tends to go to the extreme.

Young Warren was very ambitious, and when he got a job as an office boy he was determined to learn everything possible so that he could impress the boss and get ahead. One day the boss called for him and said, "Tell the traffic department to book me a passage on the Queen Mary, sailing on the eleventh."

"Excuse me, sir," said the lad, "but that ship doesn't sail until the twelfth."

The boss looked at him, impressed. Then he said, "Have the purchasing department put an immediate order for a six months' supply of aluminium."

"May I suggest," answered Warren, "that the order be placed tomorrow because the price will be reduced. In addition, order only one month's supply because the trend of the market indicates the price will go lower."

"Very good, young man, you're on the ball. Send Miss Kate in to take some dictation."

"Miss Kate is out today," the boy replied.

"What's the matter, is she sick?"

"No, sir, not until the ninth."

Now, this is knowing too much, this is going too far. That's what has happened to the human mind: it has gone too far; it has crossed its limit and has absorbed all the energy, so nothing is left for the heart. You have completely bypassed your heart. You don't go through the heart, you don't move that way anymore. The heart is almost a dead thing, a dead weight – that's what is missing.

You can listen to me through the head, and of course you will understand whatsoever I am saying – and still you will not understand anything, not a single word because this is an understanding of a totally different kind. This is an understanding which is more akin to love than to knowledge.

If you are in love with me, only then... If you have started feeling for me, only then... If an affection is growing between me and you, if it is a love affair, only then...

And the last question:

Osho,
How do you define a good speech?

Difficult to say, I have never delivered a single speech in my life. You are asking the wrong person. But I have heard a definition that I liked and I would like you to know it.

A good beginning and a good ending make a good speech, if they come really close together – the beginning and the end. Of course the best speech has no middle at all, and the very best is never delivered.

And I have always been delivering the very best, the undelivered one. I have never delivered a single speech in my life because I deal in silence, not in words. Even when you hear words, that is not the purpose. Even when I use words, the words are used only as necessary evils – because they have to be used, because you cannot understand silence yet.

I am not talking to you. I have nothing to say because that which I have cannot be said, it cannot be discoursed about. But you don't understand anything else but words, so I have to suffer, I have to use words which are meaningless. I have to say things which should not be said, in the hope that by and by you will start looking more directly into me – by and by you will not listen to the words but to the message.

Remember: the medium is not the message. The words are not my message. The message is wordless.

I am trying to hand you the undelivered speech. It is a transfer beyond words, so only those who are joined with me through their hearts will be able to receive it.

Enough for today.

spontaneity with awareness

As a cloud that rises from the sea
absorbing rain, the earth embraces.
So, like the sky, the sea remains,
without increasing or decreasing.

So, from spontaneity that's unique,
replete with the Buddha's perfections,
are all sentient beings born,
and in it come to rest.
But it is neither concrete nor abstract.

They walk other paths and so forsake true bliss,
seeking the delights that stimulants produce.
The honey in their mouths and to them so near,
will vanish if at once they do not drink it.

Beasts do not understand the world to be a sorry place.
Not so the wise who the heavenly nectar drink,
while beasts hunger for the sensual.

Everything changes. Heraclitus is right: you cannot step in the same river twice. The river is changing, and you are changing too. It is all movement, it is all flux; everything is impermanent, momentary. Only for a moment is it there, and then gone, and you will never find it again. There is no way to find it again. Once gone, it is gone forever.

And nothing changes – that too is true. Nothing ever changes. All is always the same. Parmeneides is also right: he says there is nothing new under the sun. How can there be? The sun is old, so is everything. If you ask Parmeneides, he will say you can step in any river you want, but you will always be stepping in the same river. Whether it is the Ganges or the Thames does not make any difference, the water is the same, it is all H_2O. Whether you step in the river today or tomorrow or after millions of years, it will be the same river.

And how can you be different? You were a child, you remember it. Then you were a young man, you remember that too. Then you became old, that too you remember. Who is this one who goes on remembering? There must be a non-changing element in you: unchanging, permanent, absolutely permanent. Childhood comes and goes; so comes youth and is gone, so old age – but something remains eternally the same.

Now let me say to you: Heraclitus and Parmeneides are both right, in fact they are both right together. If Heraclitus is right, it is only half the truth; if Parmeneides is right, that too is only half the truth, and half the truth is not the true thing. They are stating half-truths. The wheel moves and the hub does not move. Parmeneides talks about the hub, Heraclitus talks about the wheel – but the wheel cannot exist without the hub. What use is a hub without the wheel? So those two contradictory-looking half-truths are not contradictory but complementary. Heraclitus and Parmeneides are not enemies but friends. The other can stand only if the complementary truth is there, otherwise not.

Meditate on the silent center of a cyclone...

But the moment you state something, it can at the most only be half the truth. No statement can cover the whole truth. If any statement wants to cover the whole truth, then the statement will have to be, of necessity, self-contradictory, then it will have to be, of necessity, illogical. Then the statement will look crazy.

Mahavira did that; he is the craziest man because he tried to state the whole truth and nothing but the whole truth. He drives you crazy because each statement is immediately followed by its contradiction. He developed a sevenfold way of making statements. One is followed by its contradiction; that is followed by its contradiction, and so on and so forth. He goes on contradicting seven times, and only when he has said seven different things contradictory to each other seven times, then he says, "Now the truth is told perfectly" – but then you don't know what he has said.

If you ask him, "God is?" he will say, "Yes," and he will say, "No," and he will say, "Both," and he will say, "Both not," and so on and so forth he goes. Finally you don't come to any conclusion. You cannot conclude. He does not give you any chance to conclude; he leaves you hanging in the air. This is one possibility, if you are insistent on saying the truth.

The other possibility is that of Buddha. He keeps silent, knowing that whatsoever you say will be only half, and half is dangerous. He does not say anything about ultimate truths. He will not say the world is a flux, and he will not say that the world is permanent. He will not say that you are, and he will not say that you are not. The moment you ask anything about the absolute truth, he prohibits. He says, "Please don't ask, because by your question you will put me into trouble. Either I have to be contradictory, which is going crazy, or I have to utter a half-truth, which is not truth and dangerous, or I have to keep quiet." These are the three possibilities. Buddha had chosen to keep silent.

This is the first thing to be understood about today's sutras; then with this context it will be easy to understand what Saraha is saying.

The first sutra:

> As a cloud that rises from the sea
> absorbing rain, the earth embraces.
> So, like the sky, the sea remains,
> without increasing or decreasing.

He is saying to the king: look at the sky. There are two phenomena, the sky and the cloud. The cloud comes and goes. The sky never comes and never goes. The cloud is sometimes there, and sometimes it is not there; it is a time phenomenon, it is momentary. The sky is always there; it is a timeless phenomenon, it is eternity. The clouds cannot corrupt it, not even the black clouds can corrupt it. There is no possibility of corrupting it; its purity is absolute, its purity is untouchable. Its purity is always virgin, you cannot violate it. Clouds can come and go, and they have been coming and going, but the sky is as pure as ever; not even a trace is left behind.

So there are two things in existence: something is like the sky and something is like the cloud. Your actions are like the cloud, they come and go. You – you are like the sky: you never come and you never go. Your birth and your death are like the clouds, they happen. You – you never happen; you are always there. Things happen in you, you never happen.

Things happen just like clouds happen in the sky. You are a silent watcher of the whole play of clouds. Sometimes they are white and beautiful and sometimes they are dark and dismal and very ugly. Sometimes they are full of rain and sometimes they are just empty. Sometimes they do great benefit to the earth, sometimes great harm. Sometimes they bring floods and destruction, and sometimes they bring life, more greenery, more crops. But the sky remains the same all the time: good or bad, divine or devilish, the clouds don't corrupt it.

Actions are clouds, doings are clouds; being is like the sky.

Saraha is saying, "Look at my sky; don't look at my actions." It needs a shift of awareness, nothing else, just a shift of awareness. It needs a change of gestalt. You are looking at the cloud, you are focused on the cloud; you have forgotten the sky. Then suddenly you remember the sky. You unfocus on the cloud, you focus on the sky; then the cloud is irrelevant, then you are in a totally different dimension.

Just the shift of focusing, and the world is different. When you watch a person's behavior, you are focusing on the cloud. When you watch the innermost purity of his being, you are watching his sky. If you watch the innermost purity, then you will never see anybody evil, then the whole existence is holy. If you see the actions, then you cannot see anybody holy. Even the holiest person is prone to commit many faults as far as actions are concerned. If you watch the actions you can find wrong actions in Jesus, in Buddha, in Mahavira, in Krishna, in Rama. Then even the greatest saint will look like a sinner.

There are many books written about Jesus, he is the object of thousands of studies. Many are written in favor of him, which prove that he is the only begotten son of God. Of course they can prove it. Then many are written to prove that he is just a neurotic and nothing else – and they can also prove it. And they are talking about the same person. What is happening? How do they manage? They manage well. One party goes on choosing the white clouds, another party goes on choosing the black clouds – and both are there because no action can be just white or just black. To be, it has to be both.

Whatsoever you do will bring some good into the world and will bring some bad into the world – *whatsoever* you do. Just the very choice that you did something – many things will be good and many things will be wrong after that. Think of any action: you go and you give some money to a beggar – you are doing good, but the beggar goes and purchases some poison and commits suicide. Now your intention was good but the total result is bad. You help a man – he is ill, you serve him, you take him to the hospital – and then he is healthy, well, and he commits murder. Now without your help there would have been one murder less in the world. Your intention was good, but the total result is bad.

So, whether to judge by the intention or to judge by the result? And who knows about your intention? Intention is internal – maybe deep down you were hoping that when he got healthy he would commit a murder. Sometimes it happens your intention is bad and the result is good. You throw a rock at a person, and he was suffering from migraine for many years, and the rock hit his head and since then the migraine has disappeared – now what to do? What to say about your act: moral, immoral? You wanted to kill the man; you could only kill the migraine.

That's how acupuncture was born – such a great science, so beneficial, one of the greatest boons to humanity, but it was born in this way. A man was suffering from headaches for many years, and somebody, his enemy, wanted to kill him. Hiding behind a tree, the enemy shot an arrow; the arrow hit the man's leg, he fell down, but his headache disappeared. The people who were looking after him, the doctor of the town, were very much puzzled as to how it happened. They started studying. By chance, by coincidence, the man had hit one acupuncture point just on the leg; some point was touched on the leg by the arrow, was hit by the arrow, and the inner electric flow of the man's body energy changed. And because the inner flow of the electricity changed, his headache disappeared.

That's why when you go to the acupuncturist and you say, "I have a headache," he may not touch your head at all. He may start pressing your feet or your hand, or he may needle your hand or your back. You will be surprised: "What are you doing? My head is wrong, not my back!" But he knows better. The whole body is an interconnected electric phenomenon, there are seven hundred points, and he knows from where to push the energy to change the flow. Everything is interconnected – this is how acupuncture was born.

Now the man who shot the arrow at his enemy, was he a great saint or was he a sinner? Difficult to say, very difficult to say, if you watch the actions, then it is up to you. You can choose the good ones or you can choose the bad ones. In the total reality, each act brings something good and something bad. In fact, this is my understanding, meditate on it; whatsoever you do, the goodness of it and the badness of it are always in the same proportion. Let me repeat, it is always in the same proportion because good and bad are two aspects of the same coin. You may do good, but something bad is bound to happen because where will the other aspect go? You may do bad, but good is bound to happen because where will the other aspect go? The coin exists with both aspects together, and a single aspect cannot exist alone.

So sinners are sometimes beneficial and saints are sometimes very harmful. Saints and sinners are both in the same boat. Once you understand this then a change is possible; then you don't look at the actions. If the proportion is the same whether you do good or bad, then what is the point of judging a man by his actions? Then change the whole emphasis, move to another gestalt: the sky.

That's what Saraha is saying to the king. He is saying: "You are right. People have told you and they are not wrong. I run like a mad dog. Yes, if you just watch the action you will be misguided, you will not be able to understand me. Watch my inner sky. Watch my inner priority, watch my inner core – that's the only way to see the truth. Yes, I live with this woman – and ordinarily living with a woman means what it means." Now Saraha says, "Watch! This is no ordinary living. There is no man-woman relationship at all. It has nothing to do with sexuality. We live together as two spaces, we live together as two freedoms; we live together as two empty boats. But you have to look into the sky, not into the clouds."

As a cloud that rises from the sea absorbing rain, the earth embraces. So, like the sky, the sea remains, without increasing or decreasing. Another thing he reminds him of: watch the sea. Millions of clouds rise out of the sea, so much water evaporates, but the sea does not decrease because of that. And then the clouds will rain on the earth, and rivulets will become great rivers, and many rivers will be flooded, and the water will rush back toward the ocean, toward the sea. All the rivers of the earth will pour down their water into the sea, but that does not make the sea increase, the sea remains the same. Whether something is taken out of it or something is poured into it makes no difference; its perfection is such that you cannot take anything out of it and you cannot add anything to it.

He is saying: "Look, the inner being is so perfect that your actions may be those of a sinner, but nothing is taken away. Your actions may be those of a saint, but nothing is added unto you. You remain the same."

It is a tremendously revolutionary saying, it is a great statement. He says that nothing can be added to man and nothing can be deleted from man, his inner perfection is such. You cannot make man more beautiful and you cannot make man ugly. You cannot make him richer, you cannot make him poor. He is like the sea.

In one of the Buddhist sutras, *Vaipulya Sutra*, there is a statement that there are two very costly jewels in the ocean: one prevents it from becoming less when water is drawn from it, and the other from becoming too large when water flows into it. Two great jewels are there in the ocean, and those two great jewels prevent it; it never becomes less and it never becomes more, it just remains the same. It is so vast, it does not matter how many clouds arise out of it and how much water evaporates. It is so vast, it does not matter how many rivers fall into it and bring great amounts of water. It just remains the same.

So is the inner core of man. So is the inner core of existence. Increase and decrease is on the periphery, not at the center. You can become a man of great knowledge or you can remain ignorant; that is only on the periphery. No knowledge can make you more knowing than you already are. Nothing can be added to you. Your purity is infinite; there is no way to improve upon it.

This is the Tantra vision. This is the very core of the Tantra attitude: that man is as he is, there is no hankering for improvement. Not that man has to become good, not that man has to change this and that; man has to accept all, and remember his sky, and remember his sea. By and by an understanding arises when you know what is a cloud and what is the sky, what is a river and what is the sea. Once you are in tune with your sea, all anxiety disappears, all guilt disappears. You become innocent like a child.

The king had known Saraha. He was a great man of knowledge and now he is behaving like an ignorant man. He has stopped reciting his Vedas, he no longer does the rituals that his religion prescribes; he no longer even meditates. He does nothing that is ordinarily thought to be religious. What is he doing here living on a cremation ground, dancing like a madman, singing like a madman, and doing many untraditional things? Where has his knowledge gone?

Saraha says: "You can take all my knowledge away; it does not make any difference because I am not lessened by it. Or you can bring all the scriptures of the world and pour them into me; that doesn't make any difference, I don't become more because of that." He was a very respectable man, the whole kingdom had respected him; now suddenly he has become one of the most unrespectable men.

And Saraha is saying: "You can give me all the honors that are possible, and nothing is added unto me. You can take away all the honors, and you can insult me, and you can do whatsoever you want to destroy my respect – nothing is happening. All the time, I remain the same. I am that which never increases and never decreases. Now I know that I am not the cloud, I am the sky.

"So I am not much worried whether people think the cloud is black or white, because I am not the cloud. I am not the small river, the tiny river, or a tiny pool of water. I am not a cup of tea. Storms come in the cup of tea very easily, it is so tiny. Just take one spoonful out of it and something is lost, pour in one more spoonful and it is too much and there is a flood."

He says: "I am the vast sea. Now take whatsoever you want to take, or give whatsoever you want to give – either way it does not matter."

Just look at the beauty of it. The moment nothing matters, you have come home. If something still matters, you are far away from home. If you are still watching and being cunning and clever about your actions – you have to do this and you have not to do that, and there are still shoulds and should-nots – then you are far away from home. You still think of yourself in terms of the momentary and not in terms of the eternal. You have not yet tasted godliness.

Like the sky and like the sea, are you.

The second sutra:

So from spontaneity that's unique,
replete with the Buddha's perfections,
are all sentient beings born
and in it come to rest.
But it is neither concrete nor abstract.

So from spontaneity that's unique... First, in Tantra spontaneity is the greatest value. To be just natural, to allow nature to happen, not to obstruct it, not to hinder it, not to distract it, not to take it in some other direction where it was not going on its own, to surrender to nature, to flow with it, not pushing the river, but going with it *all* the way, wherever it leads – this trust is Tantra. Spontaneity is its mantra, its greatest foundation.

Spontaneity means you don't interfere, you are in a let-go. Whatsoever happens, you watch, you are a witness to it. You know it is happening but you don't jump into it, and you don't try to change its course. Spontaneity means you don't have any direction. Spontaneity means you don't have any goal to attain. If you have some goal to attain you cannot be spontaneous. How can you be spontaneous if suddenly your nature is going one way and your goal is not there? How can you be spontaneous? You will drag yourself towards the goal. That's what millions of people are doing – dragging themselves towards some imaginary goal, and because they are dragging themselves towards some imaginary goal, they are missing the natural destiny, which is the *only* goal. That's why there is so much frustration and so much misery and so much hell, because whatsoever you do will never satisfy your nature.

That's why people are dull and dead. They live, and yet they live not. They are moving like prisoners, chained. Their movement is not that of freedom, their movement is not that of dance; it cannot be – because they are fighting, they are continuously in a fight with themselves. There is a conflict each moment: you want to eat this, and your religion does not prescribe it; you want to move with this woman, but that will not be respectable. You want to live this way, but the society prohibits it. You want to be one way, you feel that that is how you can flower, but everybody else is against it.

So do you listen to your being or do you listen to everybody else's advice? If you listen to everybody's advice, your life will be an empty life of nothing but frustration. You will finish without ever being alive; you will die without ever knowing what life is.

Society has created such conditioning in you that it is not only outside, but it is sitting inside you. That's what conscience is all about. Whatsoever you want to do, your conscience says, "Don't do it!" The conscience is your parental voice, the priest and the politician speak through it. It is a great trick. They have made a conscience in you. From the very childhood when you were not at all aware of what was being done to you, they have put a conscience in you. So whenever you go against the conscience, you feel guilty. Guilt means you have done something which others don't want you to do. So whenever you are natural you are guilty, and whenever you are not guilty you are unnatural. This is the dilemma, this is the dichotomy, this is the problem.

If you listen to your own naturalness, you feel guilty, then there is misery. You start feeling you have done something wrong, you start hiding, you start defending yourself; you start continuously pretending that you have not done it, and you are afraid – somebody is bound to catch you sooner or later. You will be caught, and anxiety, and guilt, and fear... And you lose all love of life.

Whenever you do something against others you feel guilty. Whenever you do something that others say to, you never feel happy doing it because it has never been your own thing to do. Between these two, man is caught.

I was just reading one anecdote...

"What's this double jeopardy that the constitution is supposed to guarantee one against?" asked Roland of his lawyer friend Milt.

Said the other, "It is like this, Rollie: if you are out driving your car and both your wife and her mother are sitting in the backseat telling you how to drive, well that's double jeopardy. You have a constitutional right to turn around and say, 'Now, who in hell's driving this car, dear, you or your mother?'"

You may be at the wheel, but you are not driving the car. There are many people sitting in the back seat: your parents, your parents' parents, your priest, your politician, the leader, the mahatma, the saint; they are all sitting in the back seat. And they all are trying to advise you: "Do this! Don't do that! Go this way! Don't go that way!" They are driving you mad, and you have been taught to follow them. If you don't follow them that too creates such fear in you that something is wrong: how can you be right when so many people are advising? And they are always advising for your own good. How can you alone be right when the whole world is saying: "Do this!" Of course, they are in the majority and they must be right.

But remember, it is not a question of being right or wrong, the question basically is of being spontaneous or not. Spontaneity is right. Otherwise you will become an imitator, and imitators are never fulfilled beings.

You wanted to be a painter, but your parents said, "No, because painting is not going to give you enough money, and painting is not going to give you any respect in society. You will become a hobo and you will be a beggar. So don't bother about painting. Become a magistrate!" So you have become a magistrate. Now you don't feel any happiness. It is a plastic thing, this being a magistrate. Deep down you still want to paint.

While sitting in the court you are still, deep down, painting. Maybe you are listening to the criminal, but you are thinking about his face, what a beautiful face he has got, and what a beautiful portrait would have been possible. You are looking at his eyes and the blueness of his eyes, and you are thinking of colors – and you are a magistrate. So you are constantly at unease, a tension follows you. By and by you will also start feeling you are a respectable man and this and that. You are just an imitation, you are artificial.

I have heard...

One woman gave up smoking when her pet parrot developed a persistent cough. She was worried, naturally she thought it must have been the smoke, that she went on smoking continuously in the house and that it didn't suit the parrot. So she took the parrot to a vet. The vet gave the bird a thorough checkup and found that it didn't have pneumonia or psittacosis.

The final diagnosis was that it had been imitating the cough of its cigarette-smoking owner. It was not smoke, it was just imitating: the woman was coughing and the parrot had learned coughing.

Watch! Your life may be just like a parrot. If it is like a parrot then you are missing something tremendously valuable, you are missing your life. Whatsoever you gain will not prove of much value because there is nothing more valuable than your life.

So Tantra makes spontaneity the first virtue, the most fundamental virtue. That is unique. Now one more thing Tantra says, and that has to be understood very, very minutely. The spontaneity can be of two types. It can be only of impulsiveness, but then it is not very unique; if it is of awareness, then it has that quality of being unique, the Buddha quality.

Many times listening to me you think you are becoming spontaneous, while you are simply becoming impulsive. What is the difference between being impulsive and being spontaneous? You have two things in you, the body and the mind. The mind is controlled by society and the body is controlled by your biology. The mind is controlled by your society because the society can put thoughts into your mind; and your body is controlled by millions of years of biological growth.

The body is unconscious, so is mind unconscious; you are a watcher beyond both. So if you stop listening to the mind and to the society, there is every possibility you will start listening to the biology. So sometimes you feel like murdering somebody, and you say, "I am going to be spontaneous – Osho has said, 'Be spontaneous!' so I have to do it, I have to be spontaneous." You have misunderstood – that is not going to make your life beautiful, blissful. You will be continuously in conflict again, now with outside people.

By spontaneity Tantra means a spontaneity full of awareness. So the first thing: to be spontaneous is to be fully aware. The moment you are aware, you are neither in the trap of the mind nor in the trap of the body. Then real spontaneity flows from your very soul, from the sky and from the sea, your spontaneity flows. Otherwise you can change your masters: from the body you can change to the mind, or from the mind you can change to the body.

The body is fast asleep; following the body will be following a blind man and spontaneity will just take you into a ditch. It is not going to help you. Impulsiveness is not spontaneity. Yes, impulse has a certain spontaneity, more spontaneity than the mind, but it has not that quality which Tantra would like you to imbibe.

That's why Saraha says: *So from spontaneity that's unique...* He adds the word *unique* – unique means not of impulsion but of awareness, of consciousness.

We live unconsciously. Whether we live in the mind or in the body does not make much difference – we live unconsciously.

"Why did you tear out the back part of that new book?" asked the long-suffering wife of an absent-minded doctor.

"Excuse me, dear," said the famous surgeon, "The part you speak of was labeled *Appendix* and I took it out without thinking."

His whole life taking out the appendix from everybody's body... It must have become an unconscious habit. Seeing *Appendix* he must have taken it out. That's how we are existing and working. It is an unconscious life. An unconscious spontaneity is not much of a spontaneity.

A drunk staggered from a tavern and started walking with one foot in the street and one on the sidewalk. After a block or two a policeman spotted him. "Hey," said the cop, "you're drunk!"

The drunk sighed with relief. "Gosh!" he said, "Is that what's wrong? I thought I was lame."

When you are under the influence of the body, you are under the influence of chemistry. You are out of one trap but you are again in another trap. You are out of one ditch, you have fallen in another ditch.

When you *really* want to be out of all ditches and in freedom, you will have to become a witness of body and mind both. When you are witnessing, and you are spontaneous out of your witnessing, then there is unique spontaneity.

So, from spontaneity that's unique, replete with the Buddha's perfections... And Saraha says the real spontaneity is *...replete with Buddha's perfections.* What are Buddha's perfections? Two: *pragyan* and *karuna* – wisdom and compassion. These are Buddha's two perfections. If these two are there, reflecting in your spontaneity, then it is unique. Wisdom does not mean knowledge. Wisdom means awareness, meditativeness, silence, watchfulness, attentiveness. Out of that attentiveness, out of that silence, flows compassion for beings.

The whole world is suffering. The day you start enjoying your bliss you will start feeling for others too. They can also enjoy; they are just standing at the door of the shrine and are not entering in, but are rushing outward. They have the treasure, the same treasure that you have attained; they are carrying it, but they are not using it because they are not aware of it.

When one person becomes enlightened, his whole being becomes full of compassion towards all beings. The whole existence is filled by his compassion. Rivers of compassion start flowing from him and start reaching to everybody else – to men, to women, to animals, to birds, to trees, to rivers, to mountains, to stars. The whole existence starts sharing his compassion.

These two are the qualities of Buddha: that he understands, and that he feels and cares.

When your spontaneity is really of awareness, you cannot do anything against compassion, you cannot murder. People come to me and they ask, "Osho, you say to be spontaneous, but sometimes I want to murder my wife – then what?" You cannot murder. How can you murder? Yes, you cannot even murder your wife.

When your spontaneity is alert, when it is luminous, how can you even think of murder? You will know that there is no possibility; nobody is ever murdered. The being is the sky; you can only disperse the cloud, but you cannot murder. What is the point? And how can you murder if you are so alert and so spontaneous? Compassion will flow side by side in the same proportion. As you become aware, in the same proportion there is compassion.

Buddha has said: If there is compassion without awareness, it is dangerous. That's what is in the people we call do-gooders. They have compassion, but no awareness. They go on doing good, and yet that good has not even happened to their own beings. They go on helping others, and they themselves need much help. They themselves are ill, and they go on helping other people – it is not possible. Physician, heal thyself first!

Buddha says if you have compassion without awareness, your compassion will be harmful. Do-gooders are the most mischievous people in the world. They don't know what they are doing, but they are always doing something or other to help people.

Once a man came to me. He had devoted his whole life, forty, fifty years – he is seventy. When he was twenty, he came under the influence of Mahatma Gandhi and become a do-gooder. Gandhi created the greatest lot of do-gooders in India; India is still suffering from those do-gooders and it seems difficult to get rid of them. This man, under Mahatma Gandhi's influence, went to a primitive tribe in Bastar and started teaching the primitive people – forty years' effort, fifty years' effort. He had opened many schools, high schools, and now he was opening a college.

He came to me, he wanted my support for the college. I said, "Just tell me one thing. Fifty years you have been with them; can you say certainly that this education has been good, that they are better than they were when they were uneducated? Can you be certain that your fifty years' work has made them more beautiful human beings?"

He was a little puzzled. He started perspiring. He said, "I never thought that way, but maybe you have something. No, they are not better. In fact with education they have become cunning, they have become just as other people are. When I reached them fifty years ago, they were tremendously beautiful people. Yes, uneducated, but they had a dignity. Fifty years ago there was not a single murder, and if sometimes it used to happen, then the murderer would go to the court and report it. There was no stealing; and if sometimes somebody did steal, he would come to the chief of the tribe and confess that, 'I have stolen because I was hungry, but punish me.' There were no locks fifty years ago in those villages. They had always lived in a very silent, peaceful way."

So I asked him, "If your education has not helped them, then think again. You started doing good to others without knowing what you were doing. You just thought education has to be good."

D. H. Lawrence has said that if man has to be saved, then for one hundred years all universities should be closed – completely closed. For one hundred years nobody should be given any education. For one hundred years all schools, colleges, universities, gone: a gap of one hundred years. That is the only way to save man, because education has made people very cunning – cunning to exploit more, cunning to use others more as means, cunning to be immoral. If you don't know what you are doing, you can think that you are doing good, but good cannot happen.

Buddha says compassion is good when it follows awareness; otherwise it is not good. Compassion without awareness is dangerous, and awareness without compassion is selfish. So Buddha says a perfect buddha will have both awareness and compassion. If you become aware and you forget about others and you say, "Why should I bother now I am happy?" You close your eyes, you don't help others, you don't help others to become aware; then you are selfish, then a deep ego still exists.

Awareness kills half the ego, and the other half is killed by compassion. Between these two the ego is utterly destroyed, and when a man has become a no-self, he has become a buddha.

Saraha says: *So, from spontaneity that's unique, replete with the Buddha's perfections, are all sentient beings born, and in it come to rest. But it is neither concrete nor abstract.* He says from such unique spontaneity we are born, out of such godliness we are born, and again we go back to this godliness to rest. In the meantime, in the middle of these two, we become much too attached to the clouds. So all that is needed is not to be attached to the clouds. That is the whole of Tantra in one word: not to be attached to the clouds because clouds are there only for the moment. We come out of that source, that innocent source, and we will go back to rest in that innocent source. In the middle of these two there will be many clouds – don't get attached to them. Just watch! Remember that you are not the clouds.

...are all sentient beings born, and in it come to rest. We are out of God. We are gods, and again we go back to God. In the meantime we start dreaming a thousand and one dreams of being this and that.

God is the most ordinary reality. God is your source. God is your goal. God is right now here! In your very presence, God is – it is God's presence. When you look at me, it is God looking at me; it is nobody else. A shift, a change of focus from the cloud to the sky, and suddenly you will fall silent, and suddenly you will feel full of bliss, and suddenly you will feel benediction surrounding you.

But it is neither concrete nor abstract. It is neither mind nor body, this godliness. Mind is abstract, body is concrete; body is gross, mind is subtle. Body is matter, mind is thought. This inner godliness is neither. This inner godliness is transcendence.

Tantra is transcendence.

So if you think you are a body, you are clouded, then you are identified with a cloud. If you think you are a mind, again you are clouded. If you think in any way that makes you identified with body or mind, then you are missing the mark.

If you become awake, and suddenly you see yourself only as a witness who sees the body, sees the mind, you have become a Saraha: the arrow is shot. In that change of consciousness – it is just a small change of gear – the arrow is shot, you have arrived. In fact you had never left.

The third sutra:

> *They walk other paths and so forsake true bliss,*
> *seeking the delights that stimulants produce.*
> *The honey in their mouths, and to them so near,*
> *will vanish if at once they do not drink it.*

If you are not becoming one with the sky with which you are really one, then you are walking other paths. There are millions of other paths; the true path is one. In fact the true path is not a path: the sky never goes anywhere. Clouds go sometimes west and sometimes east and south and this way and that, and they are great wanderers. They go, they find paths, they carry maps, but the sky is simply there. It has no path, it cannot go anywhere. It has nowhere to go. It is all in all.

So those who remember their sky being are at home, at rest. Except for these few beings, few buddhas, the others walk so many paths *...and so forsake true bliss...* Try to understand this. It is a very profound statement. The moment you are walking on any path you are going astray from your true bliss, because your true bliss is your nature. It has not to be produced, it has not to be achieved, it has not to be attained.

We follow paths to reach somewhere; it is not a goal, it is already there. It is already the case. So the moment you start moving, you are moving away. *All* movement is movement away. *All* going is going astray. Non-going is arriving. Not going is the true path. Seek and you will miss; don't seek, and find.

They walk other paths and so forsake true bliss, seeking the delights that stimulants produce. There are two types of bliss. One is conditional; it happens only in certain conditions. You see your woman, you are happy. Or you are a lover of money and you have found a bag full of hundred rupee notes by the side of the road, and there is happiness. Or you are an egoist and a Nobel Prize is awarded to you, and you dance, there is happiness. These are conditional; you have to arrange for them. And they are momentary.

How long can you be happy with conditional happiness? How long can the happiness remain? It comes only like a glimpse, for a moment, and then it is gone. Yes, when you find a bag full of hundred rupee notes you are happy, but for how long will you be happy? Not too long. In fact for a moment there will be a surge of energy and you will feel happy and the next moment you will become afraid – are you going to be caught? Whose money is this? Has somebody seen?

And the conscience will say, "This is not right. It is a sort of stealing. You should go to the court, you should go to the police and you should surrender the money to the police. What are you doing? You are a moral man..." And anxiety and guilt... But you have brought it home, now you are hiding it. Now you are afraid: maybe the wife will discover it, maybe somebody has really seen, somebody may have looked – who knows? Somebody may have reported to the police. Now the anxiety...

Even if nobody has reported and nobody has seen, what are you going to do with this money? Whatsoever you are going to do will again and again give you a moment of happiness. You purchase a car, and the car is in your porch, and for a moment you are happy. Then...? Then the car is old; next day it is the same car. After a few days you don't look at it at all.

A momentary happiness comes and goes; it is like a cloud and it is like a river, a very tiny river. A little rain and it is flooded – rain stopped and the flood has gone to the sea, again the tiny river is tiny. It floods for one moment and then is empty the next. It is not like the sea which is never more, never less.

There is another kind of bliss that Saraha calls the true bliss. It is unconditional. You don't need certain conditions. It is there! You just have to look into yourself and it is there. You don't need a woman, you don't need a man; you don't need a big house, you don't need a big car; you don't need to have much prestige and power and pull – nothing. If you close your eyes and just go inward, it is there.

Only this bliss can be always and always. Only this bliss can be eternally yours. Seeking, you will find momentary things. Without seeking, you will find this eternal one.

They walk other paths and so forsake true bliss, seeking the delights that stimulants produce. The honey in their mouths, and to them so near, will vanish if at once they do not drink it. The honey is in your mouth, and you are going to seek it in the Himalayas, in some mountains? You have heard stories: there is much honey available in the Himalayas, and you are going to seek it. The honey is in your mouth.

In India the mystics have always talked about the musk deer. There is a certain kind of deer, which has musk in a gland. When the musk starts increasing – it happens only when the deer is really in sexual heat... The musk is a natural trick, a biological trick. When the musk starts releasing its fragrance, the female deer become attracted to the male deer. They come through the musk, through the smell.

Smell is one of the most sexual senses – that's why man has destroyed his nose. It is a dangerous sense. You don't smell really. In fact the word itself has become very much condemned. If somebody has good, beautiful eyes, you say he sees well; if somebody has perfect ears for music, you say he hears well, but you don't say he smells well. Why? In fact to say that he smells means something just the opposite; it means that he stinks, not that he has the capacity to smell. That capacity has been lost.

Man does not smell. We try to hide our sexual smells by perfuming, by cleansing, by this and that we hide. We are afraid of the smell because smell is the closest sense to sex. Animals fall in love through smell. The animals smell each other, and when they feel that their smell suits, only then do they make love; then there is a harmony in their being.

This musk is born in the deer only when he is in sexual heat and he needs a female. The female will come to find him. But he is in trouble, because he starts smelling the musk and he cannot understand that it is coming from his own body. So he runs mad, tries to find out from where this smell is coming – naturally so. How can he think? Even man cannot think from where bliss comes, from where beauty comes, from where joy comes. The deer can be forgiven, poor deer. He goes on rushing here and there in search of the musk, and the more he rushes, the more the fragrance is spread all over the forest; wherever he goes, there is the smell. It is said that sometimes he becomes almost mad, not knowing that the musk is within him.

And so is the case with man. Man goes mad seeking and searching: sometimes for money, sometimes respect, this and that. But the musk is within you, the honey is in your mouth. Look at what Saraha is saying: *The honey in their mouths, and to them so near, will vanish if at once they do not drink it.* Then he says, "Drink it at once! Don't lose a single moment, otherwise it will vanish. Now or never, at once! Time must not be lost." This can be done immediately because there is no need for any preparation. It is your innermost core; this honey is yours, this musk is hidden in your body. You have brought it from your birth, and you have been searching and seeking in the world.

The fourth sutra:

> *Beasts do not understand the world to be a sorry place.*
> *Not so the wise who the heavenly nectar drink,*
> *while beasts hunger for the sensual.*

The word *beast* is a translation of a Hindi or Sanskrit word, *pashu*. That word has a significance of its own. Literally *pashu* means the animal, the beast, but it is a metaphor. It comes from the word *pash* – *pash* means bondage. *Pashu* means one who is in bondage.

The beast is one who is in bondage – the bondage of the body, instincts, unconsciousness; the bondage of society, mind, thought. The beast is one who is in bondage.

Beasts do not understand the world... How can they understand? Their eyes are not free to see, their minds are not free to think, their bodies are not free to feel. They don't hear, they don't see, they don't smell, they don't touch – they are in bondage. All senses are crippled, chained. *Beasts do not understand the world...* How can they understand the world? The world can be understood only in freedom. When no scripture is a bondage to you, and no philosophy is a chain on your hands, and when no theology is a prison for you, when you are out of all bondages, then you can understand. Understanding happens only in freedom. Understanding happens only in an uncluttered mind.

Beasts do not understand the world to be a sorry place. And they cannot understand that the world is a sorry place. The so-called world created by the mind and by the body is a mirage. It appears so, it appears very beautiful, but it only appears – it is not really so. It is a rainbow, so beautiful, so colorful – you come closer and it disappears. If you want to grasp the rainbow your hand will be empty, there will be nothing. It is a mirage, but because of unconsciousness we cannot see that.

Only with awareness does the vision arise; then we can see where it is only a mirage and where it is truth. Any happiness that happens by any outer coincidence is a mirage, and you will suffer through it. It is a deception; it is a hallucination. You feel that you are very happy with a woman or with a man? You are going to suffer. Sooner or later you will find that all happiness has disappeared. Sooner or later you will find out that maybe you were just imagining it, it had never been there. Maybe it was just a dream, you were fantasizing it. When the reality of the woman and the man is revealed, you find two ugly beasts trying to dominate each other.

I have heard...

The best man was doing his utmost to make the groom brace up. "Where is your nerve, old man?" he asked. "You are shaking like a leaf."

"I know I am," said the groom, "but this is a nerve-wracking time for me. I've got some excuse for being frightened, haven't I? I've never been married before."

"Of course you haven't," said the best man. "If you had, you would be much more scared than you are."

As you look into life, as you watch life, as you learn more about it, by and by you will feel disillusioned. There is nothing – just mirages calling you. Many times you have been befooled. Many times you rushed, you traveled long, to find just nothing.

If you are alert, your experience will make you free of the world. And by the world, remember, I don't mean and neither does Saraha mean, the world of the trees and the stars and the rivers and the mountains. By the world he means the world that you project through your mind, through your desire. That world is maya, that world is illusory, that is created by desire, that is created by thought.

When thought and desire disappear and there is just awareness, alertness, when there is consciousness without any content, when there is no thought-cloud, just consciousness, the sky, then you see the real world. That real world is what religions call God, or Buddha calls nirvana.

Beasts do not understand the world to be a sorry place. Not so the wise who the heavenly nectar drink, while beasts hunger for the sensual. But when you are defeated in your hope, when you are defeated in your dream, you think maybe this dream was wrong, and you start dreaming another dream. When you are not fulfilled in your desire, you think you didn't make as much effort as was needed. Again you are deceived.

A woman sitting in a streetcar noticed that the man next to her kept shaking his head from side to side like a metronome. The woman's curiosity got the best of her and she asked why he was doing it.

"So I can tell the time," replied the fellow.

"Well, what time is it?" asked the woman.

"Four-thirty," he said, still shaking his head.

"You're wrong, it's a quarter to five."

"Oh! Then I must be slow," the man answered as he speeded up.

That's how it goes on: if you don't achieve something, you think maybe you have not been making as much effort as was needed, or your speed was slow, your competitive spirit was not enough to compete with others, you were not aggressive enough, you were not violent enough; that you were lethargic and lazy, that next time you have to pull yourself up, that you have to pull yourself together; next time you have to prove your mettle.

It has nothing to do with your mettle. You have failed because success is not possible. You have not failed for reason of your effort, speed, aggression, no. You have not failed because you were defective. You have failed because failure is the only possibility in the world. Nobody succeeds – nobody can succeed! Success is not possible. Desires cannot be fulfilled. Projections never allow you to see the reality, and you remain in bondage.

You also experience the same failure again and again, as I have experienced. You also experience the same failure again and again as Buddha or Saraha has experienced. Then what is the difference? You experience the failure, but you don't learn anything from it. That is the only difference. The moment you start learning from it you will be a buddha.

One experience, another experience, another experience... But you don't put all the experiences together, you don't conclude. You say, "This woman proved horrible, okay, but there are millions of women. I will find another." This woman proves a failure again, you again start hoping, dreaming you will find another. It does not mean that all women have failed if one woman has failed. It does not mean that one man has failed so all men have failed. You go on hoping, you go on hoping, the hope goes on winning over your experience and you never learn.

One relationship becomes bondage; you feel that something has gone wrong, next time you will make every effort not to make it into bondage. But you are not going to succeed because success is not in the very nature of things here. Failure is the only possibility. Success is impossible. The day you recognize that failure is the only possibility, that all rainbows are false and all happiness that glitters and shines from far away and attracts you like a magnet, is just empty dreams, desires – you are deluding yourself; the day you recognize the fact, a turning, a conversion, a new being is born.

With a banging of doors and an angry swish of skirts, the hefty female entered the registrar's office.

"Did you or did you not issue this license for me to marry John Henry?" she snapped, slamming a document on the table.

The registrar inspected it closely through his glasses. "Yes, madam," he said cautiously, "I believe I did. Why?"

"Well, what are you going to do about it?" she screamed. "He's escaped!"

All relationships are just beautiful on the surface; deep down they are a sort of bondage. I am not saying don't relate to people; I am saying relate, but never think that any relationship is going to give you happiness. Relate! Of course you will have to relate, you are in the world. You have to relate to people, but no relationship is going to give you happiness because happiness never comes from the outside. It always glows from the inside; it always flows from the inside.

And Saraha says the man who believes that it comes from the outside is a beast; he is a *pashu,* he is in bondage. The man who recognizes the fact that it never comes from the outside, whenever it comes it comes from the inside, is free. He is a man, he is *really* a man; he is no longer a beast. With that freedom man is born.

Beasts do not understand the world to be a sorry place. Not so the wise who the heavenly nectar drink... What is this heavenly nectar? It is symbolic of the honey that you have already in your mouth, and have not tasted. You don't have any time to taste it. The whole world is too much, and you are rushing from one place to another. You don't have any time to taste the honey that is already there.

That is the heavenly nectar; if you taste it, you are in heaven. If you taste it, then there is no death – that's why it is called "heavenly nectar" – you become an immortal. You *are* an immortal. You have not seen it, but you are an immortal. There is no death, you are deathless. The sky is deathless; only clouds are born and die. Rivers are born and die, the sea is deathless. So are you.

Saraha speaks these sutras to the king. Saraha is not trying to convince him logically. In fact he is simply making his being available to him. He is giving him a new gestalt to look at Saraha. Tantra is a new gestalt with which to look at life, and I have never come across anything more profound than Tantra.

Enough for today.

CHAPTER 4

stop becoming and be!

The first question:

Osho,
You are everything that I have ever wanted or could ever want. So why is there so
much resistance in me toward you?

That's why. If you have deep love for me, there will be deep resistance
also. They balance each other. Wherever love is, there is resistance too.
Wherever you are tremendously attracted to, you would also like to escape
from that place, from that space, because to be immensely attracted means you
will fall into the abyss, you will no longer be yourself.

Love is dangerous. Love is a death. It is more deathly than death itself,
because you survive after death, but after love you don't survive. Yes, somebody else is born, but you have gone; hence the fear.

Those who are not in love with me can come very close and there will be
no fear. Those who love me will be afraid of taking each step; reluctantly they
will take those steps, it is going to be very hard for them, because the closer
they come to me the less will be their ego. That's what I mean by death. The
moment they have come *really* close to me, they are not – just as I am not.
Coming closer to me is coming closer to a state of nothingness. Even in ordinary love there is resistance; this love is extraordinary, this love is unique.

The question is from Anupam. I have been watching her, she is resisting.

The question is not just intellectual, it is existential. She has been fighting hard, but she cannot win. She is blessed because she cannot win. Her defeat is certain, it is absolutely certain. I have seen that love in her eyes; that love is so strong that it will destroy all resistance, it will win over all efforts of the ego to survive. When love is strong the ego can try, but it is already a losing battle for the ego. That's why so many people live without love. They talk about love, but they live without love. They fantasize about love, but they never actualize love because to actualize love means you will have to destroy yourself utterly.

When you come to a master, it is either utter destruction or nothing. Either you have to dissolve into me and you have to allow me to dissolve into you, or you can be here but nothing will happen. If the ego remains, then there is a China Wall between me and you. A Wall of China can be broken easily, but the ego is a more subtle energy.

But once love has arisen, then the ego is impotent – and I have seen this love in Anupam's eyes. It is there. It is going to be a great struggle, but good, because those who come very easily don't come; those who take a long time, those who fight inch by inch, only they come.

But nothing to be worried about... The journey is going to be a long journey; Anupam will take time, maybe years, but nothing to be worried about, she is on the right track. She has crossed the point from where she could have gone back, she has crossed the point of no return. So it is only a question of time. She is available to me. I never force anybody because there is no need. It is good to give them time and enough rope, so they come on their own. When surrender is out of freedom it has beauty.

But you can trust it is coming, it is on the way. In the deepest core of your being it has already happened; now it is just a question of time, so that the deepest core informs your superficial mind. In your heart you have already come to me; only in the mind is there a struggle. At the center you have already come closer to me; only on the periphery is there fighting going on. The headquarters have really surrendered already.

You must have heard about a Japanese soldier who was still fighting. The Second World War was over, so many years had passed, and twenty years after the Second World War he was still fighting; he had not heard that Japan had surrendered. He was somewhere in the deepest forests of Indonesia, and still thinking that he belonged to the emperor of Japan and the fight was on. He must have been mad; he was hiding and escaping and killing people, alone.

When just a few years ago he went back to Japan, he was given a hero's reception. He is a hero in a way. He was unaware... But he must be a man of great will. It was not that he had not heard that Japan had surrendered, the war had finished – how could you avoid it for twenty years? He had heard from others but he insisted: "Unless I receive an order from my commander, I will not surrender." Now the commander was dead, so there was no way to receive an order from the commander, and he was going to fight his whole life. It was very difficult to catch hold of him, he was very dangerous, but he *was* caught.

Exactly that is the case with Anupam. The headquarters have already surrendered; the commander is dead. Just on the periphery, somewhere in the forests of Indonesia you are fighting, Anupam. But sooner or later, however mad you are, you will receive the news.

The second question:

Osho,
I would like to become true, but what is it and how is it? I feel in a devil-circle, in a prison. I would like to come out, but how?

The first thing: you are not in a prison. Nobody is, nobody ever has been. The prison is make-believe. You are unconscious, certainly, but you are not in a prison. The prison is a dream, a nightmare that you have managed to see in your sleep. So the basic question is not how to come out of the prison, the basic question is how to come out of the sleep. There is a great difference in how you articulate the question. If you start thinking, "How to come out of the prison?" then you will start fighting with the prison, which is not there; then you will be moving in a wrong direction.

That's what many people have been doing down the centuries. They think they are in a prison, so they fight with the prison, they fight with the guards, they fight with the jailer; they fight with the system. They fight with the walls; they go on filing the bars of the windows. They want to escape from the prison, they try to unlock the prison, but it cannot be done – because the prison does not exist. The jailer and the guard and the bars and the locks are all imagination.

You are in a deep sleep and you are seeing a nightmare. The basic question is how to come out of sleep.

I have heard...

No durance vile could be more pathetic than that suffered by the drunk who was found wandering agonizedly around and around on the sidewalk outside the fence which encloses a public park, beating upon the bars and screaming: "Let me out!"

That is your situation. You are not locked up, you are not imprisoned; you are simply drunk. You think that you are imprisoned. This is just a thought. I know why that thought arises in your mind: because you feel yourself so limited from everywhere, out of the limitation the idea of prison arises. Wherever you move there is a limitation, you can go only so far and then you cannot go any further; then there must be a wall which is hindering you. So you infer that there is a wall all around – maybe not visible, maybe it is a glass wall made of very transparent glass: you can see through it, but whenever you move in any direction you stumble again and again and you cannot go beyond a certain point. This gives you the idea of a prison, that you are imprisoned. But this limitation is also because of sleep. In sleep you become identified with the body, so the limitations of the body become your limitations. In sleep you become identified with the mind, so the limitations of the mind become your limitations.

You are unlimited. You are unbounded. As you are in your pure being, no limitation exists; you are a god. But to know that godhood, don't start fighting with the prison; otherwise you will never be a winner. More and more you will be defeated, and more and more you will feel frustrated, and more and more you will lose self-confidence; more and more you will feel that it seems impossible to get out of it.

Start by becoming more aware. Start by becoming more alert, more attentive. That is the only thing that has to be done. Being aware, you will start feeling that the walls that were too close are no longer so close; they are widening. Your prison is becoming bigger and bigger. The more your consciousness expands, the more you will see that your prison is no longer that small, it is becoming bigger and bigger. More expansive consciousness and bigger space is available to you to move, to be, to live, to love. Then you know the basic mechanism: less conscious, and the walls come closer; unconscious, and the walls are just touching you from everywhere; you are in a small cell, even a slight movement is not possible.

Remember this phrase: expansion of consciousness. With that expansion, *you* expand. One day, when your consciousness is absolute and there is not a lingering shadow of darkness inside, when there is no unconscious in you, all has become conscious, when the light is burning bright, when you are luminous from the inner awareness, then suddenly you see that even the sky is not your limit. There is no limitation to you.

This is the whole experience of the mystics of all the ages. When Jesus says, "I and my father in heaven are one," this is what he means. He is saying, "I have no limitations." It is a way of saying the same thing, a metaphorical way, a symbolic way: "I and my father in heaven are not two but one – I, staying in this small body and he, spread all over existence, are not two but one." My source and I are one. I am as big as existence itself. That is the meaning when the mystic of the Upanishad declares: "*Aham Brahmasmi:* I am the absolute; I am God!" This is uttered in a state of awareness where no unconsciousness exists. This is the meaning when the Sufi, Mansoor declares: "*Ana'l Haq:* I am the truth!"

These great utterances are very significant. They simply say that you are as big as your consciousness, never more, never less. That's why there is so much appeal in drugs, because they chemically force your consciousness to become a little wider than it is. LSD or marijuana or mescaline gives you a sudden expansion of consciousness. Of course it is forced and violent and should not be done. It is chemical; it has nothing to do with your spirituality. You don't grow through it. Growth comes through voluntary effort. Growth is not cheap, not so cheap that just a small quantity of LSD, a *very* small quantity of LSD, can give you spiritual growth.

Aldous Huxley was very wrong when he started thinking that he had attained, through LSD, the same experience as Kabir, or as Eckhart, or as Basho. No, it is not the same experience. Yes, something is similar; that similarity is in the expansion of consciousness. But it is very dissimilar too; it is a forced thing, it is violence on your biology and on your chemistry. And you remain the same; you don't grow through it. Once the influence of the drug wears off, you are the same man again, the same small man.

Kabir will never be the same again because that expansion of consciousness is not just a forced thing; he has grown to it. Now there is no going back. It has become part of him, it has become his being; he has absorbed it.

But the appeal can be understood. The appeal has always been there, it has nothing to do with the modern generation. It has always been there – since the Vedas. Man has always felt tremendously attracted toward drugs. It is a false coin, it gives you a little glimpse of the real in a very unnatural way. But man is always seeking expansion; man wants to become great. Sometimes through money he wants to become great – yes, money also gives you a feeling of expansion; it is a drug. When you have much money, you feel your boundaries are not so close to you, they are far away. You can have as many cars as you want; you are not limited. If suddenly you want to have a Rolls Royce, you can have it, you feel free. When the money is not there, a Rolls Royce passes by, the desire arises, but the limitation... Your pocket is empty, you don't have any bank balance; you feel hurt – the wall, you cannot go beyond it. The car is there, you see the car, you can have it right now, but there is a wall between you and the car: the wall of poverty.

Money gives you a feeling of expansion, a feeling of freedom. But that too is a false freedom. You can have many more things, but that doesn't help you grow. You don't become more, you have more, but your being remains the same. So is power – if you are a prime minister or a president of a country you feel powerful, the army, the police, the court, the whole paraphernalia of the state is yours. The boundaries of the country are your boundaries; you feel tremendously powerful. But that too is a drug.

Let me say to you: politics and money are as much drugs as LSD and marijuana, and far more dangerous. If one has to choose between LSD and money, LSD is far better. If one has to choose between politics and LSD, then LSD is far better and far more religious. Why do I say so? – because through LSD you will only be destroying yourself, but through money you destroy others too. Through LSD you will be simply destroying your chemistry, your biology, but through politics you will destroy millions of people. Just think, if Adolf Hitler had been a drug addict, the world would have been far better; if he had been on LSD or with a syringe in his hand we would have felt blessed, we would have thanked God: "It is very good that he remains in his house and goes on taking shots and is stoned. The world can go on easily without him."

Money and politics are far more dangerous drugs. Now this is very ironical; politicians are always against drugs, people who have money are always against drugs, and they are not aware that they themselves are drug addicts. And they are on a far more dangerous trip because their trip implies others' lives too. A man is free to do whatsoever he wants to do. LSD can at the most be a suicidal thing, but it is never murder, it is suicide. And one is free to commit suicide – at least one has to be free to commit suicide because it is your life – if you don't want to live, it is okay. But money is murder, so is power politics murder; it kills others.

I am not saying to choose drugs. I am saying *all* drugs are bad: money, politics, LSD, marijuana. You choose these things because you have a false idea that they will expand your consciousness. The consciousness can be expanded very simply, very easily, because in fact it is already expanded. You are just living in a false notion; your false notion is your barrier, is your prison.

You ask, "I would like to become true..." You cannot like or dislike. It is not a question of your choice. Truth is! Whether you like it or do not like it is irrelevant. You can choose lies but you cannot choose truth. Truth is there. That's why Krishnamurti insists so much on choiceless awareness. You cannot choose truth. Truth is already there. It has nothing to do with your choice, liking, disliking. The moment you drop your choice, truth is there. It is because of your choice that you cannot see the truth. Your choice functions like a screen over your eyes. Your liking and disliking is the problem: because you like something, you cannot see that which is, and because you dislike something you cannot see that which is. Through like and dislike you have colored glasses on your eyes and you don't see the real color of existence as it is.

You say: "I would like to become true…"

That's how you remain untrue. You *are* true – drop likes and dislikes! How can you be untrue? Being is true, to be is true. You are here, alive, breathing – how can you be untrue? Your choice! By choice you have become a Christian or a Hindu or a Mohammedan; by truth you are not Hindu, Mohammedan, Christian. By choice you have become identified with India, with China, with Germany, but by truth the whole belongs to you and you belong to the whole. You are universal. The total lives through you, you are not just a part. The total lives through you as totality. Choose like, dislike, and you go astray.

Now you say, "I would like to become true…" – then in the name of truth you will also become untrue. That's how a person becomes a Christian, because he thinks Christianity is true and, "I would like to become true," so he becomes a Christian. Please don't become a Christian, don't become a Hindu. You are a christ. Why become a Christian? Christhood is your nature. Christhood has nothing to do with Jesus; it is as much yours as Jesus'. Christhood is a state of choiceless awareness.

So please don't start thinking in terms of desire: "I would like to become true." Now this is the way to become untrue. Drop this desire, just be, don't try to become. Becoming is becoming untrue; being is truth. See the difference: becoming is in the future, it has a goal, being is herenow; it is not a goal, it is already the case. So whosoever you are, just be that, don't try to become anything else. You have been taught ideals, goals – become! Always you have been forced to become something.

My whole teaching is: whatsoever, whosoever you are, that's beautiful. It is more than enough, just be that. Stop becoming and be!

Now naturally when you ask, "I would like to become true, but what is it and how is it?"… Once you start thinking in terms of becoming, then certainly you want to know what the goal is. "What is it, what is this truth that I want to become?" And then naturally, when *goal* comes there, *how* also comes: how to attain it? Then the whole technology, methodology…

I am saying you *are* that. The mystic in the Upanishad says: "*Tat-tvam-asi:* Thou art that." Already you are that, it is not a question of becoming. God is not somewhere in the future; God is just now, this very moment, within you, without you, everywhere, because only God is, nothing else exists. All that exists is divine.

So be! Don't try to become. Then one thing leads to another. If you want to become, then naturally the idea arises: what ideal, what am I to become? Then you have to imagine an ideal that you have to be like this: Christ-like, Buddha-like, Krishna-like. Then you will have to choose an image, and you will become a carbon copy.

Krishna has never been repeated. Can't you see a simple truth? Krishna has never been again. Can't you see a very simple truth, that Buddha is unrepeatable? Each being is unique, utterly unique – so are you. If you try to become somebody, you will be a false entity, a pseudo-existence; you will be a carbon copy. Be the original! So, you can only be yourself; there is nowhere to go, nothing to become.

But the ego wants some goal. The ego exists between the present moment and the goal. See the mechanism of the ego: the bigger the goal you have, the bigger the ego. If you want to become a Christ, if you are a Christian, then you have a big ego – maybe even pious, but it doesn't make any difference. The pious ego is as much an ego as any other ego, sometimes even more dangerous than ordinary egos. If you are a Christian, then you are on an ego trip. Ego means the distance between you and the goal. People come to me and they ask how to drop the ego. You cannot drop the ego unless you drop becoming. You cannot drop the ego unless you drop the idea, the ideal, the hope, the future.

The ego exists between the present moment and the future ideal. The bigger the ideal, the farther away the ideal, the more space the ego has to exist, the more possibilities. That's why a religious person is more of an egoist than a materialist. The materialist cannot have as much space as the religious person has. The religious person wants to become God. Now this is the greatest possibility. What more can you have as an ideal? The religious person wants to go to *moksha,* to heaven, to paradise. Now what farther shore can you imagine? The religious person wants to be absolutely perfect. Now ego will exist in the shadow of this idea of perfection.

Listen to me. I don't say you have to *become* gods, I declare you *are* gods. Then there is no question of any ego arising, there is no space left. You have not to go to heaven; you are already there. Just have a good look around; you are already there. It is a now-ness, paradise is a now-ness; it is a function of the present moment.

The ego thrives when you have goals and ideals. There are a thousand and one problems with the ego. On the one hand it feels very good to have great ideals; on the other hand it makes you feel guilty. You continuously feel guilty because you are always falling short. Those ideals are impossible, you cannot attain them. There is no way to attain them, so you are always falling short. So on one hand the ego thrives; on another hand guilt… Guilt is the shadow of the ego.

Have you watched this strange phenomenon? An egoistic person feels very guilty about small things. You smoke a cigarette; if you are an egoist you will feel guilty. Now smoking is an innocent, stupid thing – very innocent and very stupid, nothing worth feeling guilty about. But a religious person will feel guilty because he has an ego ideal that he should not smoke. Now that ideal that he should not smoke and the reality that he smokes create two things. The ideal gives him a good feeling: "I am a religious person. I know that one should not smoke; I even try, I try my best." But he will also feel that again and again he falls. He cannot reach the ideal so he feels guilty, and the person who feels guilty will start making everybody feel guilty. It is natural, how can you just feel guilty alone? It will be too hard, it will be too burdensome.

So a guilty person creates guilt all around. He makes everybody feel guilty for small things, for irrelevant things. If you have long hair, he will make you feel guilty. There is nothing much in it; it is one's own life, if one wants to have long hair – good. If you are doing things in your own way he will make you feel guilty. Whatsoever you are doing he will find faults. He has to find faults; he is suffering from guilt. How can he suffer alone? When everybody is feeling guilty he feels at ease, at least one consolation: "I am not alone in this boat, everybody is in the same boat."

The trick to make others feel guilty is to give them ideals. This is a very subtle trick. The parents give an ideal to the child: "Be like this!" *They* have never been like this, *nobody* has ever been. Now they give an ideal to the child – this is a very subtle and cunning way to make the child feel guilty. Now again and again the child will feel: "I am not coming closer to the ideal; in fact I am going farther away from it." So it hurts; it keeps him down, depressed. Hence you see so much misery in the world. It is not *actual* misery; ninety percent is because of the ideals that have been imposed upon you. They don't allow you to laugh, they don't allow you to enjoy. A man who has no ideals will never make anybody else feel guilty.

Just the other night, a young man came and he said, "I feel very, very guilty about my homosexuality. It is unnatural." Now if he had gone to Mahatma Gandhi or to the Vatican pope or to Puri's Shankaracharya, what would have happened? They would have *really* made him feel guilty, and he is ready to fall into the hands of any torturer. He is ready; he himself is inviting. He is calling the mahatmas to come and make him feel guilty. He cannot do that job very well alone, so he is asking the experts.

But he has come to the wrong person. I told him, "So what! Why do you say it is unnatural?"

He said, "It is not unnatural?" He was surprised and shocked: "It is not unnatural?"

I said, "How can it be unnatural? My definition of nature is: that which happens is natural. How can the unnatural happen in the first place?"

Immediately I could see he was coming out of the ditch; his face started smiling. So he said, "It is not unnatural? It is not a perversion? It is not some sort of abnormality?"

And I told him, "It is not!"

"But," he said, "Animals don't become homosexual."

I said, "They don't have that much intelligence. They live a fixed life, whatsoever biology allows, they live that way. You can go and see a buffalo eating grass, she only eats a certain grass, nothing else. You can put the choicest food… She will not bother, she will go on eating her grass. She has no alternatives; consciousness is very narrow, almost nil. Man has intelligence; he tries to find new ways to relate, to live. Man is the only animal who finds new ways.

"Now to live in a house is unnatural, because no animal lives that way, so is it a perversion? Or to wear clothes is abnormal, because no animal wears clothes – is it a perversion? To cook food is unnatural, no animal has ever done it. Is it wrong to eat cooked food? To invite people to your house for a drink or for lunch is unnatural because no animal ever invites any other animal, because animals in fact always go in privacy when they want to eat. You give something to a dog, he will immediately go into a corner and will keep everybody at the back, and will be in a hurry to eat. He will never invite, he will not call his friends: "Come on!" That is natural to a dog, but you are not dogs; you are far superior. You have more intelligence, you have more possibilities. Man makes everything in his own way – that is *his* nature."

He was relieved. I could see a great burden, a mountain that was on his head, had gone. But I am not certain how long he will remain free and unburdened. Some mahatma may catch hold of him and again put the same idea that it is unnatural. Mahatmas are either sadists or masochists – avoid! Whenever you see a mahatma, run as fast as you can before he puts some guilt in your mind.

Whatsoever you can be you are. There is no goal, and we are not going anywhere. We are simply celebrating here. Existence is not a journey, it is a celebration. Think of it as a celebration, as a delight, as a joy. Don't turn it into suffering, don't turn it into duty, work. Let it be play.

This is what I mean by becoming religious: no guilt, no ego, no trip of any kind, just being herenow. Being with the trees and the birds and the rivers and the mountains and the stars. You are not in a prison. You are in God's house, you are in God's temple. Please don't call it a prison, it is not. You have misunderstood, you have interpreted it wrongly. Listening to me you can also interpret many things wrongly; you go on interpreting.

Two scenes. One…

The nurseryman who spoke at the garden club meeting placed emphasis on the advantage to be gained by the use of old horse manure for fertilizing spring gardens. During the question and answer period, a city lady who had been taking notes raised her hand. The speaker nodded to her and she earnestly inquired, "You said old horse manure was the best fertilizer. Would you mind telling me how old the horse should be?"

The second...

A hillbilly-type woman brought her little boy to the county school. When questioned about her husband she confided, "I never knew much about this boy's father. He came through here, courted me and we got married. Soon afterward I found out he was a hobosexual."

"You mean homosexual," came the correction.

"No, sir, I mean hobosexual. He was just a no-good, passionate bum."

Each one has his own interpretation of words. So when I am saying something, I don't know what you are going to understand by it. Each one has a private dictionary hidden in the unconscious. That private dictionary goes on filtering, changing, coloring.

I have been telling you to become free; you have misunderstood me, you thought you were in a prison. Yes, I say become free – immediately you interpret it as if you are in a prison, the whole emphasis has changed. My emphasis was on *you*: be free! Your emphasis has gone onto the prison. Now you say, "I am in a prison; unless I get out of the prison, how can I be free?" My emphasis was: be free, and if you are free there is no prison. The prison is created by your habit of being unfree.

Look! The emphasis has changed, and it seems that it almost means the same. When I say, "Be free!" what difference is there if somebody says, "Yes, I am in a prison?" A lot of difference, a great difference – the whole thing has changed. It is a totally different thing when you say, "I am in prison." Then the guard and the prison, they become responsible. Then unless they allow you, how can you get out of it? You have thrown the responsibility on somebody else.

When I was saying, "Be free!" I was saying, "You are responsible." It is your thing to be free or not to be free. If you have chosen not to be free then there will be a prison, then there will be guards and the prisoner. If you have chosen to be free, the guards and the prison and everything disappear. Just drop the habit of being unfree.

How can you drop it? Freedom and consciousness go hand in hand: more conscious, more free; less conscious, less free. The animals are less free because they are less conscious. The rock is even less free because the rock has no consciousness, almost nil. Man is the most highly evolved being, at least on this earth. Man has a little freedom; a buddha has absolute freedom. His consciousness... So it is only a question of the degrees of consciousness. Your prison consists of the layers of your unconsciousness; start becoming conscious and there is no other prison.

And remember the mind is very cunning, it can always find ways to befool you; it has learned very many tricks to befool. The mind can just use another word and you may not even see the difference. The difference may be so subtle that it is almost synonymous – and the mind has played a trick.

So when I am saying something, please don't interpret it. Just listen to it as attentively as possible; don't change a single word, not even a single comma. Just listen to what I am saying. Don't bring your mind into it; otherwise you will hear something else. Always be alert about the cunningness of the mind – and you have cultivated that cunningness. You have not cultivated it for yourself, but you have cultivated it for others. We try to befool everybody; by and by the mind becomes expert in befooling, then it starts befooling you.

I have heard...

A journalist died. Naturally... He was a journalist and even in the president's house and the prime minister's house he had been immediately welcomed and taken in. No appointment was ever needed; he was a great journalist. So he rushed toward heaven – why should he go to hell? However, he was prevented by Saint Peter, and Saint Peter said, "Wait, no more journalists are needed here. We already have the full quota; we only need one dozen. In fact they are also useless because there is no newspaper being printed in heaven."

In fact there is no news. Nothing happens there – ever. Things are going so smoothly; how can news happen? And what news can you think about saints' lives; they are sitting under their trees, *bodhi* trees, meditating. So the newspaper is not much of a newspaper, but just to have it published, just as a formality, the newspaper is published – and every day ditto is written: the same as before.

"We don't need any journalists, go to hell. There are always more and more journalists needed there because there is much news, and newspapers and newspapers – and new newspapers are being planned, I have just heard. Go there and you will have a great job and great joy."

But the journalist wanted to be in heaven, so he said. "Do one thing; I know journalists, if I can manage to get some journalist to go to hell, will his place be given to me?"

Saint Peter took pity on him, he said, "Okay, how much time do you need to convert a journalist to go to hell?"

He said, "Twenty-four hours, just twenty-four hours."

So he was allowed into heaven for twenty-four hours. He immediately started circulating a rumor that one of the greatest newspapers is being planned, and the chief editor is needed, assistant editors are needed, subeditors are needed, and great are the possibilities – but you will have to go to hell.

For twenty-four hours he went round and round. He met all the journalists, and after twenty-four hours, when he went to Saint Peter to see whether anybody had left, Saint Peter simply closed the door and told him, "Don't go outside, because they have all left."

But the journalist said, "No, then I will have to go – maybe there is something in it; please don't prevent me, I will have to go."

He himself has spread the rumor, but when twelve persons have believed, then one starts believing it oneself. That's how mind has become so cunning. You have been deceiving and deceiving; it has become such an expert in deception that it deceives you too.

The plaintiff in an accident-injury case, appearing in court in a wheelchair, won a huge settlement. Enraged, the lawyer for the defense advanced on the winner in his wheelchair. "You're faking and I know you're faking," he shouted. "So help me God, I'm going to follow you around for the rest of your life until I get proof."

The lawyer knew perfectly well that the man was a fake, the wheelchair was a show; he was perfectly okay, there was nothing wrong in his body. So he said, "So help me God, I'm going to follow you around for the rest of your life, until I get proof."

"Be my guest," responded the man in the wheelchair with a smile. "Let me tell you my plans. First I'm going to London for some clothes, then to the Riviera for the sun, and after that, to Lourdes for the miracle."

Mind is so cunning that it can find a way out – always. It can go to Lourdes… But once you are playing these tricks on others, sooner or later you will be the victim yourself. Beware of your own mind; don't trust it, doubt it. If you start doubting your mind, that is a great moment. The moment the doubt about mind arises, you start trusting the self. If you trust the mind, you doubt the self. If you mistrust the mind, you start trusting the self.

That is the whole meaning of trusting a master. When you come to me, it is simply a technique to help you to doubt your own mind. You start trusting me, you say, "I will listen to you, I won't listen to my mind. I have listened to my mind long enough; it leads nowhere, it goes round and round. It again and again takes to the same trip; it is a repetition, it is monotonous." You say, "I will listen to you."

A master is just an excuse to get rid of the mind. Once you have got rid of the mind there is no need to trust the master because you will have come upon your own master. The master is simply a passage to your own master. Via the master it becomes easy; otherwise the mind will go on deceiving, and you will not know what to do with the mind.

Listening to the master, trusting the master, by and by the mind is neglected. Many times you have to drop the mind, because the master is saying something which goes against it – it *always* goes against it. Neglected, mind starts dying. Not trusted, mind starts dying. It comes to its right size. Right now it is pretending, right now it pretends as if it is your whole life. It is just a small, tiny mechanism: good to use, very dangerous to make your master.

The mind says, "Become!" The master says, "Be!" The mind says, "Desire!" The master says, "Delight!" The mind says, "You have to go a long way," the master says, "You have arrived. You are Saraha – you have shot the target already."

The third question:

Osho,
What do you think about civilization? Are you absolutely against it?

There is no civilization anywhere, so how can I be against it? It exists not. It is just a pretension. Yes, man has lost his primitive, primordial innocence, but man has not become civilized – because that is no way to become civilized. The only way to become civilized is to be based in your innocence, to be based in your primitive innocence – to grow from there.

That's why Jesus says: "Unless you are reborn, unless you become a child again, you will never know what truth is."

This so-called civilization is a fake; it is a pseudo coin. If I am against it I am not against civilization, because this is not civilization. I am against it because this is not civilization at all; it is a fake.

I have heard...

Someone once asked the former Prince of Wales, "What is your idea of civilization?"

"It is a good idea," he replied. "Somebody ought to start it."

I love the answer. Yes, somebody ought to start it; it has not yet been started. Man is not civilized, man only pretends.

I am against pretensions. I am against hypocrisies. Man only *shows* that he is civilized; scratch him a little and you will find an uncivilized man. Scratch him a little and all that is good is just superficial, and all that is bad is very deep-rooted. It is a skin-deep civilization. Everything goes well, you are smiling and everything – and somebody just throws a word at you, an insult, and you are mad, you are a maniac and you want to kill. Just a moment before you were smiling; and just a moment afterward you are ready to kill, your murderous possibilities have surfaced. What kind of civilization is this?

A man can be civilized only when he has become really meditative. Only meditation can bring real civilization to the world. Only buddhas are civilized. And this is the paradox: buddhas are not against the primitive; they use the primitive as the base, they use the childhood innocence as the base, and on that base a great temple is erected. This civilization destroys the innocence of child-hood, and then it gives you just false coins. First it destroys your primal inno-cence. Once primal innocence is destroyed you have become cunning, clever, calculating; then you are trapped, then this society goes on civilizing you.

First it makes you alienated from your own self. Once you are alienated, then it gives you false coins; you have to depend on it. Real civilization will not be against your nature, will not be against your childhood; it will be a growing upon it. It will not have any antagonism toward primitive innocence; it will be a flowering of it. It will go higher and higher, but it will be rooted in the primal innocence.

This civilization is nothing but a maddening affair. Can't you see the whole earth has become a big madhouse? People have lost their souls, people are no longer people; they have lost their self, they have lost their individuality. They have lost all. They are just pretenders, they have masks, they have lost their original faces. I am all for civilization – but this is not civilization, that's why I am against it. I would like a man really civilized, really cultured. But that culture can only grow; it cannot be forced from the outside, it can come only from the within. It can spread toward the periphery, but it should rise, it has to rise, at the center.

This civilization is doing just the opposite; it forces things from the outside. There is a nonviolent preaching all over the world: Mahavira, Buddha, Jesus, all teach nonviolence. They teach nonviolence because they have enjoyed non-violence. But followers have never enjoyed any moment of nonviolence. They know only violence. But they are followers so they pretend to be nonviolent, they force nonviolence upon themselves, they create a character. That char-acter is just around them. It is armor. Deep down they are boiling like volcanoes ready to erupt, and on the surface they smile a false smile, a plastic smile.

This is not civilization. This is a very ugly phenomenon. Yes, I would like the nonviolence to come from within, not to be cultivated from the outside, but helped. That is the root meaning of the word *education*. It is almost like drawing water from a well: *education* means to draw out, that is the root meaning of the word *education*. But what has education been doing? It never draws anything out, it forces in. It goes on forcing things into the head of the child; it is not worried about the child at all, it does not think about the child. The child is just used as a mechanism into which more and more information has to be fed. This is not education.

The child's soul has to be brought out. That which is hidden in the child has to be brought out. The child has not to be patterned; his freedom should be left intact and his consciousness has to be helped to grow. More information is not more education. More awareness is education, more love is education. And education creates civilization.

This civilization is false, its education is false; that's why I am against it. I am against it because it is not really a civilization.

The fourth question:

Osho,
I laugh so much at your jokes. I would like to ask one question: Why does a joke create so much laughter?

One thing: you have never been allowed to laugh; your laughter is repressed. It is like a repressed spring – any excuse is enough and it comes out. You have been taught to be sad – long faces. You have been taught to be serious.

If you are serious nobody thinks that you are doing something wrong; it is accepted, it is the way things have to be. But if you are laughing, laughing too much, then people will start feeling embarrassed by you. They will start thinking something is weird: "Why is this man laughing?" And if you are laughing without any reason, then you *are* mad; then they will take you to the psychiatrist, then they will hospitalize you. They will say, "He laughs without any reason, only mad people laugh without any reason."

In a better world, in a more civilized world, in a *really* civilized world, laughter will be accepted as natural. Only when a person is sad will we hospitalize him. Sadness is illness, laughter is health. So because you have not been allowed to laugh, any small excuse... Jokes are excuses to laugh, you can laugh without being called mad. You can say, "Because of the joke..." And a joke has a mechanism; it helps you uncoil. The whole mechanism of a joke is very complex; in a way simple-looking, deep down very complex. A joke is not a joke; it is a difficult phenomenon. In a few words, in a few lines, it can create such a change in the whole climate.

What happens? When a joke is told, first you start expecting that there is going to be some laughter. You are ready for it, you autohypnotize yourself; you become alert. You may have been dozing and sleeping, but now there is a joke you become alert. Your backbone is straight, you listen attentively, you become more aware. Then the story goes on in such a way that it creates more and more tension in you. You want to know the conclusion. The joke goes on one plane and there seems to be nothing much like a joke in it, and then there is a sudden turn. That sudden turn releases your spring. You become tense and more tense because you are waiting and waiting and waiting, and you see that there seems to be nothing much in it. Then suddenly it is there, and it is there so suddenly, so out of the blue, that you forget your seriousness, you forget who you are; you become a child again in that suddenness and you laugh. Your repressed laughter is released.

Jokes simply show that the society has forgotten how to laugh. In a better world, where people will be laughing more, we will miss one thing: the joke. There will be no need; people will be laughing and people will be happy. Why? Each moment will be a moment of laughter. And if you can see life, it is all a joke. But you are not allowed to see. Blinkers have been put on your eyes; you are only allowed to see so much. You are not allowed to see the ridiculousness of it. It *is* ridiculous!

Children can see it more easily, that's why children laugh more easily and more loudly. And they create embarrassment in parents, because they can see the whole nonsense of it. The blinkers are not yet fixed. The father goes on saying to the child, "Be true, always be true!" And then a man knocks on the door, and the father says, "Go and tell him that father is not at home." Now the child... The father cannot see what is happening, but the child laughs. He cannot believe what is happening, it is so ridiculous. The child goes to the stranger knocking on the door and he says, "Father says he is not at home." He takes the whole juice out of it; he enjoys every bit of it.

We live with blinkers. We are cultivated in such a way that we don't see the ridiculousness of life; otherwise it is ridiculous. That's why sometimes even without a joke, in some small thing, for example: President Ford slipped and fell on the ground. Why did people who were standing there have a good laugh? They may not have shown it, but they had a good laugh.

Just think, if a beggar slips on a banana peel, nobody will bother. But a president of a country slips on a banana peel, the whole world will laugh. Why? – because the banana peel brought things right. That banana peel showed to the president that he is as much a human being as a beggar is. The banana peel makes no difference at all: come beggar, come president, come prime minister, makes no difference; a banana peel is a banana peel, it does not bother. If an ordinary man falls, you will have a little laughter but not much, because he is an ordinary man; he never tried to prove that he is more than life-size, so there is not much laughter. But if a president slips on a banana peel, suddenly the ridiculousness of it, the reality of it, that this man was thinking that he is at the top of the world… Whom were you trying to befool? Even a banana peel is not befooled, and you laugh.

Watch! Whenever you laugh, the ridiculousness of life has entered through your blinkers; you are a child again. A joke brings you back your childhoodness, your innocence. For a moment it helps the blinkers to slip from the eyes.

Listen to a few jokes…

One of the local men was found dead under unusual circumstances, therefore a coroner's jury was impaneled and the foreman called in the woman on whose bed the man had died, to testify. The foreman assured her that all present knew each other, and that she should just tell in her own words what had happened.

The woman related that she and the man, now deceased, had met in the local pub, and when time was called, had gone on to her place to have another drink. One thing led to another and they ended up in bed together. Suddenly she noticed a strange look in his eyes which she described to the coroner's jury in these words: "Coming, I thought; but going he was."

And the second…

An old deacon having occasion to spend a night at a hotel was assigned a room containing three single beds, two of which already had occupants. Soon after the light was extinguished, one of these began to snore so loudly as to prevent the deacon from getting to sleep. The tumult increased as the night wore on, until it became absolutely fearful. Some two or three hours after midnight the snorer turned in bed, gave a hideous groan and became silent.

The deacon had supposed the third gentleman to be asleep, but at this juncture he heard him exclaim, "He is dead! Thank God, he is dead."

And the last is a very precious one – meditate over it…

One day when Jesus was walking through a village, he came upon an angry mob who had backed a woman up against a wall and were getting ready to stone her. Raising his hand Jesus quieted the mob, and then said solemnly, "Now let the one who is without sin cast the first stone." Immediately a little old lady picked up a big rock and hurled it at the woman.

"Mother," said Jesus between gritted teeth, "you exasperate me."

And the last question:

Osho,
It is obvious that you are in love with orange, but then why don't you yourself
wear orange?

I, and in love with orange? God forbid! I hate it. That's why I force you to
wear it – it is a sort of punishment for not being enlightened yet.
Enough for today.

CHAPTER 5

we are one energy

To a fly that likes the smell of putrid meat,
the fragrance of sandalwood is foul.
Beings who discard nirvana
covet coarse samsara's realm.

An ox's footprints filled with water
will soon dry up;
so with a mind that's firm,
but full of qualities that are not perfect,
these imperfections will in time dry up.

Like salt sea water that turns sweet
when drunk up by the clouds,
so a firm mind that works for others,
turns the poison of sense-objects
into nectar.

If ineffable, never is one unsatisfied.
If unimaginable, it must be bliss itself.
Though from a cloud one fears the thunderclap,
the crops ripen when from it pours the rain.

Man is a myth, and the most dangerous myth, because if you believe that man exists then you don't try to evolve the man at all, there is no need. If you believe that you are already a man, then all growth stops. You are not already a man, you are just a potentiality to be. You can be, you may not be, you may miss. Remember, it can be missed. Man is not born; it is not a given fact, you cannot take it for granted. It is just a possibility. Man exists as a seed, not as a tree – not yet. Man is not yet actual, and the difference between the potential and the actual is great.

Man as he exists is just a machine, yet he works, yet he succeeds in the world, yet he lives a so-called life and dies. But remember, he exists not. His function is that of a mechanism, he is a robot. Man is a machine. Yes, this machine can grow something in it which can go beyond a mechanism. This machine is no ordinary machine; it has tremendous potentiality to go beyond itself. It can produce something transcendental to its own structure. Sometimes it has produced a Buddha, a Christ, a Gurdjieff, sometimes it *has* produced a man. But don't you believe that you are already a man. If you believe, your belief will be suicidal – because once we believe that something is already there, then we stop looking for it, then we stop creating it, then we stop discovering it, then we stop evolving it.

Just think: an ill person, a seriously ill person, thinks he is healthy. Why should he go to the doctor? Why should he take any medicine? Why should he go under treatment? Why should he be willing to go to the hospital? He believes he is healthy, he's in perfect health – and he is dying. His belief will kill him. That's why I say this myth is very dangerous, the most dangerous myth ever evolved by the priests and the politicians: that man is already on the earth. These millions of people on the earth are just possibilities, and unfortunately, the majority of them are never going to become actual; unfortunately, many of them will die as machines.

What do I mean when I say man is a machine? I mean that man lives out of the past. Man lives out of a dead structure, man lives out of habit, man lives a life of routine. Man goes on moving in the same circle, in the same rut, again and again and again. Can't you see the vicious circle in your life? You have been doing the same things every day: hoping, being angry, desiring, being ambitious, being sensual, sexual, being frustrated, again hoping, again the whole circle moves. Each hope leads to a frustration, never is it otherwise; and after each frustration, a new hope, and the circle starts moving again.

In the East we call it the wheel of samsara. It is a wheel; the spokes are the same. You are deluded by it again and again; you again start hoping, and you know you have hoped before, you have hoped millions of times, and nothing happens out of that hope. Just the wheel goes on moving, and goes on killing you, goes on destroying your life. Time is running out of your hands. Each moment that is lost is lost forever, and you go on repeating the old.

This is what I mean when I say man is a machine. I agree with George Gurdjieff absolutely; he used to say that you don't yet have a soul. He was the first man to say it so drastically, that you don't yet have a soul. Yes, the soul can be born in you, but you will have to give birth to it; you will have to become capable of giving birth to it.

Down the centuries the priests have told you that you already have that soul, that you already are that man. That is not so, you are only potentially so. You can become actually too, but the myth has to be destroyed. See the fact of it: you are not a conscious being; and if you are not a conscious being, how can you be a man?

What is the difference between a rock and you? What is the difference between an animal and you? What is the difference between a tree and you? The difference is that of consciousness. But how much consciousness do you have? Just a flicker here and there, just sometimes, in rare moments, you become conscious, and that is only for seconds and again you fall back into unconsciousness. Yes, sometimes it happens because it is your potentiality.

Sometimes it happens in spite of you. One day the sun is rising and you fall in tune with existence, and suddenly it is there, the beauty of it, the benediction of it, the fragrance of it, the light of it. Suddenly it is there and you have a taste of what it would be, what it can be, what it is. But the moment you become alert that it is there, it has already gone. Only a memory is left. Only for rare moments: sometimes in love, sometimes watching a full moon, sometimes a rising sun, sometimes sitting in a silent mountain cave, sometimes looking at a child playing, giggling; yes, sometimes in music, but these moments are rare.

If an ordinary man, the so-called man achieves seven moments of awareness in his whole life that will be too much. Rarely, very rarely, just a ray enters, and then it has gone, and you are back to your trivial life, dull and dead. This is not so only with ordinary people, it is so with your so-called extraordinary people.

Just the other day I was reading about Carl Jung, one of the greatest psychologists of this age – but sometimes one wonders whether to call these people psychologists or not. He was a very restless man, absolutely restless. He could not sit silently for a single moment; he would toss and turn, he would do something or other. If there was nothing to do, he would smoke his pipe, and he was a chain-smoker. Then he had a heart attack and the doctors said to stop smoking, an absolute stop. Now it was very difficult. He started feeling his restlessness too much, he started feeling crazy. He would walk up and down in the room, he would go outside, for no reason; he would sit in this chair and the other. Then he recognized the fact that the pipe had been very, very helpful. It was a release, a sort of release of his restlessness. So he asked the doctors, "Can I put the empty pipe in my mouth? Is it allowed?" An empty pipe! "That will help me."

He was allowed to, and for years he used to put the empty pipe in his mouth, just pretending that he was smoking. Then he would look at the pipe, would keep the pipe in the hand, would play with the pipe. This is about a great psychologist of this age. What unconsciousness! So much in the grip of the habit, so much in the grip of the unconscious – it looks very childish. And we go on finding rationalizations; we go on pretending to ourselves, we go on protecting and defending ourselves as to why we are doing this.

At the age of forty-five Carl Jung fell in love with a woman. He was a married man with a very loving wife. Nothing was wrong, but it must have been the restlessness. It almost always happens that nearabout the age of forty-five one starts feeling that their whole life has gone. Death is coming closer, and because of death coming closer, either you become spiritual or you become more sexual.

These are the only two defenses: either you turn in search of truth, of the eternal which will have no death, or you start drowning yourself in more erotic fantasies. And particularly intellectuals – those who have lived their whole lives through the head – are greater victims at the age of forty-five. Then sexuality takes revenge. It has been denied; now death is coming closer and then one never knows whether you will be here again or not, whether life will be there or not. Death is coming here and you have lived a life of the head. Sexuality erupts with a vengeance.

Carl Gustav Jung fell in love with a young woman. Now it was very much against his prestige. The wife was disturbed, and the wife had loved him tremendously and trusted him. He rationalized it beautifully. Look at his rationalization – that's how unconscious man goes on living. He will do something unconsciously, then will try to rationalize it and will try to prove that it is not unconscious: "I am doing it very consciously – in fact, it *has* to be done."

What did he do? He suddenly developed a theory that there are two types of women in the world: one, the mother type, the caring type, the wife type; and the other, the mistress type, the beloved, who becomes an inspiration. Man needs both – and a man like Carl Gustav Jung certainly needs both. He needs inspiration too. He needs a caring woman, that his wife is fulfilling – she is loving, a mother type. But that doesn't fulfill his need, he needs inspiration too, he needs a romantic woman too, a mistress who can take him into deep dreams; that is a must for him. Jung developed this theory – this is a rationalization.

Now he never developed the other part of it, that men are two types. That's where you find that it is a rationalization. If it was a real insight then the other part, that men are two types, the father type and the lover type – then Jung's wife needs two. If Jung thinks that he is a lover type, then she needs the father type; if Jung thinks he is a father type, then she needs a lover type. But that he never developed. That's how you can see it is not an insight; it is just a tricky mind, a rationalization. We go on rationalizing. We do things unconsciously, we do them without knowing why we are doing them. But we cannot accept the fact, it is very humiliating to accept that: I have been doing something of which I am not aware and I don't know why. Beware of rationalizations.

How can such people be beneficial to others? It is a well-known fact that many of Carl Jung's patients committed suicide. Why? They had come to be helped, why did they commit suicide? Something must have been basically wrong. His analysis was just lousy. He was a very arrogant man, very egoistic, continuously ready to fight. Maybe his whole psychoanalysis developed only as his arrogance against Sigmund Freud. Maybe it was again just a rationalization, because he himself seemed to be suffering from the same problems he was thinking to help others with.

Jung was always afraid of ghosts, even in his old age he was afraid of ghosts. He did not publish his most important book while he was alive because he was afraid that people would come to know the facts. So his memoirs were published, but he made certain that they should be published only when he was dead. Now what type of truth and authenticity is this? He was so afraid of being found wrong, or in the wrong, that he never allowed any fact to be disclosed about his life while he was alive.

I was reading one anecdote...

A man came to a psychiatrist and proceeded to unfold his life story before the doctor, covering his childhood experiences, his emotional life, his eating habits, his vocational problems, and everything else he could think of. "Well," said the doctor, "it doesn't seem to me as though there is anything wrong with you. You seem as sane as I am."

"But, doctor," protested the patient, a note of horror creeping into his voice, "it's these butterflies. I can't stand them. They're all over me."

"For heaven's sake," cried the doctor, recoiling, "Don't brush them off on me!"

The patients and the doctors are all in the same boat. The psychoanalyst and the analyzed are not very far apart. It is a game. Maybe the psychoanalyst is cleverer, but it is not that he knows the reality, because to know the reality you will have to become tremendously conscious; there is no other way. It is not a question of intellectual thinking, it has nothing to do with your philosophizing. To know reality one has to grow into awareness.

Gurdjieff used to talk about a future psychology. He used to say that psychology still does not exist, because how can it exist? Even man exists not! When man is not there, how can there be a science about man? First the man has to exist; then the science about the man can exist. Right now whatsoever exists is not psychology. Maybe it is something about the machine that is man.

Psychology can exist only around a buddha. A buddha lives with consciousness. You can find what his psyche is, what his soul is. Ordinary man lives without a soul. Yes, you can find something wrong in his mechanism, and that wrong can be put right. What we know as psychology today is nothing but behaviorism. In that sense, Pavlov and Skinner are far truer than Freud and Jung because they think man is a machine. They are true about the man that exists, although they are not absolutely true because they think this is the end, man cannot be otherwise. That is their limitation: they think man can only be a machine. They are true as far as the present-day man is concerned – man *is* a machine – but they think that man cannot be otherwise. There they are wrong. But Freud and Jung and Adler are more wrong because they think man is already on the earth; all that you need is to study man and you will know. But man is not there. It is a very unconscious phenomenon.

Man is a myth. Let that be one of the most basic insights. It will help you to come out of the lie, out of the deception.

Tantra is an effort to make you more conscious. The very word *Tantra* means expansion of awareness. It comes from a Sanskrit root *tan: tan* means expansion. Tantra means expansion of consciousness – and the basic fact and the most fundamental fact to be understood is that you are fast asleep. You have to be awakened.

Tantra believes in school methods – that has to be understood also. In that sense Gurdjieff is one of the greatest Tantrikas of this age. For example, if one is asleep, there is very little possibility that one can become awake alone. Look at it in this way: on New Year's day you think as you have always thought – and many New Year days have passed – and you have always taken a vow that never again will you smoke; and again the New Year has come and you start thinking this time it is going to happen. You take a vow that you will never smoke, but you don't go and tell it to others, you are afraid to. To say it to others is dangerous because you know yourself, many times you have broken your vows; then it is very humiliating, so you keep it to yourself. Now there is only one possibility out of a hundred that the vow will be kept; ninety-nine possibilities are that it will be broken sooner or later.

You are an unconscious being; your vow does not mean much. But if you go and you tell everybody in the town – friends, colleagues, children, wife, you go and tell everybody, "I have taken a vow that I am not going to smoke," there is more possibility, at least ten percent that you will not smoke. First there was only one possibility, now there are ten. The possibility that you will smoke is ninety per cent, but non-smoking has gained ground, has more solidity; from one percent it has gone to ten percent. But if you join a group of non-smokers, if you join a society of non-smokers, then the possibility is even greater: ninety-nine percent is the possibility that you will not smoke.

What happens? When you are alone you don't have any support from outside – you are alone, you can easily fall asleep. And nobody knows, so you are not worried either. When all know, their knowing will function to keep you more alert. Now your ego is at stake, your respect and honor are at stake. But if you join a society of non-smokers, then the possibility is even greater because you live through habits. Somebody takes his cigarette box out of his pocket, and suddenly you start looking in your pocket. You are just mechanical: somebody is smoking and you start thinking how beautiful it was to smoke. Nobody smokes, and you are in a society of non-smokers, then nobody will remind you and the habit by and by will disappear out of disuse. If a habit is not used, by and by it disappears; it tends to become dead, it loses its grip on you.

Tantra says that man can become awake only through group methods, through schools. That's why I insist so much for sannyas. Alone, you don't stand a chance. Together, there is much more possibility. It is as if ten persons are lost in a desert and it is very dangerous in the night: the enemies can kill them, the wild animals can kill them, the robbers can come, the murderers can come – it is very difficult. Now they decide on a group method, they say, "Each one will be awake for one hour." To think that each one will be capable of remaining awake for eight hours in the night is to ask too much from an unconscious man, but each one will remain awake for one hour. Before he starts falling asleep he should wake somebody else, then there is more possibility that at least one of the group will be awake the whole night.

Or, as Gurdjieff used to say, you are in a prison and you want to get out of the prison. Alone there is not much chance; but if all the prisoners become a group, then there is much more chance – they can overthrow the guard, they can kill the guard, they can break down the wall. If all the prisoners are together, then there is much more chance that they can get out into freedom.

But the chances will increase even more if they are in contact with a few people who are outside the prison, who are already free. That is the whole meaning of finding a master: finding somebody who is already outside the prison. He can be of tremendous help, for many reasons. He can supply necessary things,

things which will be needed for you to come out of the prison; he can send instruments, files, so that you can break out of the prison. He can watch from the outside and he can inform you when the guards change; in that interval there is a possibility to get out. He can inform you when the guards fall asleep in the night. He can make arrangements so that the guards are drunk on one particular night, he can invite the jailer to his house for a party; he can do a thousand and one things which you cannot do from the inside. He can find support for you from the outside. He can create an atmosphere so that when you are released from the jail you will be accepted by the people, you will be sheltered, taken into houses. If the society outside is not ready to accept you, you may get out of the jail but the society will deliver you back to the prison authorities.

To be in contact with someone who is already awake is a must. To be together with those people who are all thinking to become awake is also a must. This is the meaning of a school method, a group method. Tantra is a group method. It says: be together, find out all the possibilities. So many people can be together and they can pool their energies. Somebody is very intelligent and somebody is very loving – both are half, but together they become more of a unity, more wholeness.

Man is half, woman is half. Except for Tantra, all the seekers have tried to do without the other. Man has tried alone, women have tried alone. Tantra says why not be together, join hands together? The woman is half, the man is half – together they are a greater energy, a more whole energy, a healthier energy. Join together, let yin and yang function together – there will be more possibility of getting out of it.

Other methods use fight and conflict. Man starts fighting with women, starts escaping from women; rather than using the possibility of the help he starts thinking of the woman as the enemy. Tantra says this is sheer foolishness, you are wasting your energy unnecessarily fighting with the woman because there are greater things to be fought about. It is better to keep company with the woman; let her help you, and you help her. Go together as one unit and you have more chances to stand against the unconscious nature.

Use all the possibilities; only then is there a chance that you can evolve into a conscious being, you can become a buddha.

Now the sutras, these are very significant sutras.

First sutra:

> *To a fly that likes the smell of putrid meat*
> *the fragrance of sandalwood is foul.*
> *Beings who discard nirvana*
> *covet coarse samsara's realm.*

First thing: just as I said, man is a machine. Man lives out of habit, out of the past, out of memories; man lives out of knowledge that he has known, acquired before. So he goes on missing the new; and the truth is always the new. He is like a fly that likes the smell of putrid meat, the foul and fetid odor; the fragrance of sandalwood is foul to that fly. She has a certain cast of memory, a certain past; she has always thought that the putrid smell of meat is fragrance. That is her knowledge, that is her habit, that is her routine – that is her dead past. Now suddenly she comes across sandalwood; the fragrance of sandalwood will look to the fly as if it is a very foul and fetid odor.

Don't be surprised – that's what is happening to you. If you have lived too much in the body then even coming closer to a man who lives in his soul, you will feel something is wrong. Coming to a buddha you will not feel the fragrance; you may even start sensing a bad smell. Your interpretation... Otherwise why did people murder Jesus? Jesus was sandalwood, and people simply killed him. Why did people poison Socrates? Socrates was sandalwood. But the flies understand their own past, they interpret according to their past.

One day I was reading...

A prostitute, the most famous prostitute of Athens, once came to Socrates. A few people were sitting there, just a few people, just as here a few people are sitting, and Socrates was talking to them. The prostitute looked around and said to Socrates, "Why – such a great man like you, and only so few people listening to you? I had thought the whole of Athens would be here. I don't see the most respectable, the most honored – the politicians, the priests, the intellectuals – I don't see them here. What is the matter? Come some day to my house, Socrates; you will find them standing in a queue."

Socrates said, "You are right, because you cater to a universal demand. I don't. I attract only a few, a chosen few. Others cannot feel my fragrance, they avoid. Even if they come across me, they escape, they are afraid. It is a totally different fragrance," said Socrates.

The prostitute must have been of tremendous intelligence. She looked into the eyes of Socrates, bowed down, and said, "Socrates, accept me as one of your friends," and never left, became part of that small school.

Must have been a woman of great awareness – so sudden a change, she understood it so, immediately. But Athens killed Socrates; they did not like the man. The man looked very dangerous. Against him there were many charges. One was that he destroys people's beliefs, he destroys young people's minds, that he is anarchic; that if he is allowed to live any longer the society will be uprooted. He is a dangerous enemy.

What was he doing? He was doing something totally different, he was try-ing to create a state of no-mind. But the people thought, "He destroys people's minds." They, the flies, are also right. Yes, young people were tremendously attracted to Socrates, because only young people can be attracted to such things. Only youth has that courage. Even if old people come to me or to Socrates, they are young people only; that's why they come, otherwise they cannot come. An old, rotten mind cannot come to me. Maybe the body is old, but if an old man comes to me or an old woman, she comes only because she still has the youth of her soul, she is still young somewhere; she is still able to understand the new, to learn the new. They say you cannot teach an old dog new tricks; it is very difficult, the old dog knows old tricks and he goes on repeating them. It is very difficult to teach anything to an old mind.

And these things are so radically different, so diametrically opposite to all that has been taught to you, that unless a man is really young he cannot even listen. So young people were attracted. That was a sign that something of the eternal, something of the eternal youngness of the universe was pouring through Socrates. When Jesus was alive you would find young people fol-lowing him. You will not find young people going to see the pope; old people, dead people, long, long ago dead, they go to see the pope. When the original Shankaracharya was alive you would find young people all around him. But only dead bodies, corpses listen to the Shankaracharya of Puri. Alive persons – you cannot find them.

You can go and look into any temple and you will find old women and old men; youth is not there. In fact whenever a religion is really there, youth is attracted; when truth is there, youth is attracted. When there are only lies left – doctrines, dogmas, creeds – then old people come. When youth is attracted, that means truth is young and youth is attracted. When truth is old, almost dead, then dead people are attracted. Old people are attracted only because of the fear of death. In old age even atheists become theists – afraid. When a young man is attracted toward something, it is not because of the fear of death because he does not know any death yet; it is because of tremendous love for life, and that is the difference between real religion and unreal religion. Unreal religion is fear-oriented. Real religion is love-oriented.

You must have heard... In all the languages of the world the ugly words exist: *God fearing.* That must have been coined by dead, dull, old people. God fear-ing? How can one fear God? And if you fear God, how can you love him? Out of fear, only hatred can arise, never love. Out of fear you can be against God, because he will be your enemy; how can you love him? And if you love him, how can you be afraid? Have you ever been afraid of the person you love? Have you ever been afraid of your mother if you love her? Have you ever been afraid of your woman if you love her? If you love, there is no fear; love casteth out all fear. God loving, romantically in love with God, ecstatically in love with God…

But that is possible only for the young mind. Whether the young mind is in a young body or in an old body is irrelevant, but it is possible only for the young mind. Now Socrates was punished because he attracted young people. Buddha was punished because he attracted young people. But always remember, whenever a religion is born, young people rush from all corners of the world. They should be the symbol that something has happened. When old people are rushing somewhere, you can be certain nothing is happening there, that is not where the action is. Where young people are going, that is the place where action is. But: *To a fly that likes the smell of putrid meat, the fragrance of sandalwood is foul. Beings who discard nirvana covet coarse samsara's realm.* Truth is the unknown, the mysterious. You cannot approach it through your past habit. You can approach it only when you are naked of all habits.

The Christian priest's robe is called the habit – it is a beautiful use of the word *habit.* Yes, I say, when you are nude of all habits, naked of all habits, all dresses are dropped; you function not through memory but through awareness. These are two different functions. You function through memory, then you don't see that which is; you go on seeing that which you have seen before. You go on interpreting the present in terms of the past, you go on imposing something which is not there; you go on seeing things which are not, and you go on not seeing things which are. Memory has to be put aside. Memory is good, use it, but truth has never been known through memory. How can you know truth through memory? You have never known truth in the past.

Truth is not known. Truth is a stranger. You will have to put all memory aside; you will have to say to your mind, "Keep quiet, let me see without you. Let me look only with clarity, not with clouded eyes: no thoughts, no beliefs, no scriptures, no philosophies, no religions. Let me look directly, immediately. Let me look herenow, let me look into that which is confronting me." Only then are you in tune with the mystery of truth.

Remember, truth never becomes a memory. Even when you have known it, it never becomes a memory. Truth is so vast it cannot be contained by the memory. Whenever it is there again, you will know it; it will again be new. It is never old, it is always new, it is always fresh. That is one of its qualities, that it never becomes old. It is always young.

So if you want to know the truth… Saraha says to the king, "Sir, if you really want to know the truth of what has happened to me, put aside your mind. I know you are just like a fly; you have lived a life of body and mind, you don't know anything beyond them. I am standing here; I am beyond both. There is no way to explain it to you according to your mind; no, it cannot be explained. If you really want to experience it, you can experience it, but it cannot be explained."

Godliness cannot be defined; godliness cannot be explained. Please remember: never explain it, because if you explain it you will be explaining it away. Godliness cannot be contained by any thought. But godliness can be lived; godliness can be loved. You can *become* gods. That is possible, but the mind cannot contain godliness. The mind is a very small container, it is like a teaspoon – and you want to have the Pacific Ocean in the teaspoon? Yes, you can have a little salty water in your teaspoon, but that won't give the idea of the Pacific, of the vastness. Storms won't happen in your teaspoon, great waves will not arise. Yes, it will taste like it, but it will not be an ocean.

Saraha says: "If you want to see me, sir, you will have to put your mind aside." You have a fly's mind. You have certain habits of thinking, of feeling; you have certain habits of living. You have lived a life of body and mind, and at the most, whatsoever you have known up to now was just heard by you. You have read scriptures. Saraha himself was reading scriptures to the king before, he knows it well. He knows what the king knows, his knowledge is just information. Saraha says: "It has happened to me, but to see it you will need a different quality of seeing."

The mind never meets the truth, never encounters the truth. The ways of the mind and the ways of the truth are absolutely separate. It is a separate reality, hence the insistence of all the mystics of the world to attain to a state of no-mind. That's what meditation is all about: a state of no-mind, a state of nonthinking – yet fully aware, luminous with awareness. When there is not a single thought, your sky is clean of all clouds, and then the sun shines bright.

Ordinarily we are clouded with so many thoughts, desires, ambitions, dreams that the sun cannot shine. It hides behind those dark clouds. Desire is a cloud, thought is a cloud, imagination is a cloud, and one needs to be unclouded to know that which is.

Saraha says: *Beings who discard nirvana covet coarse samsara's realm.* Samsara means to live as body, as mind, as ego. Samsara means to live outwards, samsara means to live with things. Samsara means to live with the idea that all is matter and nothing else. Samsara means three poisons: power, prestige, pull – to live in the world with the idea of having more power, more prestige, more money, more pull, this and that, to live in things and for things. That is the meaning of the word *samsara:* the world.

Just watch yourself, have you ever lived with persons or do you live only with things? Is your wife a person or a thing? Is your husband a person or a thing? Do you treat your husband as a person, as a superbly, intrinsically valuable person, or just as a utility, that he is the provider of bread and butter, or that she is the housekeeper, looks after the children? Is your wife an end unto herself, or is she just a utility, a commodity to be used? Sometimes you use her sexually, sometimes you use her in other ways – but using the person means the person is a thing to you, not a person.

A person cannot be used; only things can be used. A person cannot be purchased; only things can be purchased. A person has such tremendous value, such divinity, such dignity – how can you use a person? Yes, he can give out of her or his love, but you cannot use. And you have to be thankful. Have you ever been thankful to your wife? Have you ever been thankful to your father, to your mother? Have you ever been thankful to your friends? Sometimes you are thankful to a stranger but never to your own people because you take them for granted.

To live with things is to live in samsara. To live with persons is to live in nirvana.

And once you start living with persons, things start disappearing. Ordinarily even persons are reduced to things, and when a person starts becoming meditative even things start becoming persons; even a tree becomes a person, a rock becomes a person. Everything by and by starts having a personality, because godliness is spread all over existence.

Saraha says: "Sir, you have lived in samsara and you cannot understand the way of nirvana. If you really want to understand it you will have to live it, there is no other way. To know, you will have to taste something of it. I am here, standing before you, and you are asking for explanations? Nirvana is standing in front of you, and you are asking for theories – not only that, you must be utterly blind, you have come to persuade me to come back to your samsara. A fly is persuading me to leave the forest of sandalwood and its fragrance for the putrid smell of meat."

"Have you gone mad?" said Saraha to the king. "Let me persuade you to come to my world rather than you persuading me to come to your world. I have known your world and I have known this new reality too; I can compare. You have known only your world; you don't know my reality, you can't compare."

When a buddha says this world is illusory, meditate over it, because he has known this world too. When some atheist, materialist, some Communist says that the world of nirvana is just illusory, there is no need to bother about it at all, because he has not known it. He knows only this world; you cannot trust his assertions about the other world. He has never meditated, he has never entered into it.

Look at it: of all those who have meditated, not a single one has denied the inner reality. Not a single one! Without exception, all the meditators have become mystics. Those who have not meditated know only the world of the fly, and the world of the foul and fetid odor of putrid meat. They live in the rotten world of things, but they know only that, and certainly their statements cannot be trusted. A Buddha can be trusted, a Christ can be trusted, a Mahavira can be trusted; they have known both. They have known the lower and the higher, and by knowing the higher they say something about the lower which has to be meditated upon. Don't reject it outright.

For example: Marx, Engels, Lenin, Stalin, Mao have never meditated, and they say there is no God. Now it is almost as if a man has never gone to the lab of the scientist and says something about science. A man who has never gone into the lab and says that the theory of relativity is just mumbo-jumbo, it cannot be relied upon. You have to go to the lab, you have to go into higher mathematics, you have to prove it. Just because you cannot understand it you cannot be allowed to deny it.

There are very few people who understand the theory of relativity. It was said when Einstein was alive that there were only twelve persons alive who understood his theory – all over the world. There are a few people who think that is an exaggeration, that twelve is not right; there are not even twelve persons who understood his theory correctly. But because of that you cannot say it is not right; you cannot take a vote on it, you cannot defeat it in an election. You will have to go through the same processes as they did.

Now Marx saying there is no God is simply making a stupid statement. Never meditated, never contemplated, never prayed – his statement is irrelevant. Those who have meditated, those who have dug a little deeper into their being have come to the same truths.

Beings who discard nirvana covet coarse samsara's realm. Saraha is saying: "You discard nirvana and you go on rushing after illusions. You have come to persuade me, sir? Look at me, how ecstatic I am. Look at me; I am not the same person who had left your court, I am a totally different person."

He was trying to bring the king's awareness to the present moment, and he succeeded. He must have been a man of great presence. He pulled the king out of the world of the flies, out of the world of putrid meat. He pulled him to the world of sandalwood and its fragrance.

The second sutra:

> *An ox's footprints filled with water*
> *will soon dry up;*
> *so with a mind that's firm,*
> *but full of qualities that are not perfect,*
> *these imperfections will in time dry up.*

He says: "Look! An ox has walked, and there is a footprint on the land, and the footprint is filled with water, rainwater." How long will it be there? Sooner or later it will evaporate, and the ox's footprint filled with water will not be there any longer. But the ocean is always there. Although the water in the ox's footprint is also from the ocean, still something is different. The ocean always remains, never increasing, never decreasing. Great clouds arise out of it, it never decreases. Great rivers pour their waters into it, it never increases. It remains always the same. But this small footprint of an ox is full of water right now; within hours or days it will be gone, it will dry up. So is the skull of the human mind; it is just an ox's footprint, such a small thing. Just a little water is there – don't trust it too much, it is already drying up, it will disappear. The skull is a very small thing; don't think that you can contain the universe in the skull. It can only be temporary; it can never be the eternal.

An ox's footprints filled with water will soon dry up; so with a mind that's firm, but full of qualities that are not perfect, these imperfections will in time dry up. What are you keeping in your small skull? What are the contents? Desires, dreams, ambitions, thoughts, imagination, will, emotions – these are the things that you are keeping as content. They will all dry up, all contents will dry up; so change the emphasis from the contents to the container: that is the whole secret of Tantra. Look at the container and don't look at the content. The sky is full of clouds; don't look at the clouds, look at the sky. Don't look at what is there in your head, what is there in your mind; just look at your consciousness. Emotion is there, anger is there, love is there, greed is there, fear is there, jealousy is there – these are contents. Just behind them is the infinite sky of consciousness.

A man who lives through the contents lives the life of a machine. The man who starts changing his emphasis from the contents to the container starts living the life of awareness, of buddhahood.

And says Saraha: "Sir, these contents that you are having in your mind will soon dry up. Look at that ox's footprint, your head is not bigger than that, the skull is not bigger than that. But your consciousness is infinite."

Now this has to be understood: emotions are in your head, but consciousness is not in your head. In fact your head is in your consciousness. Consciousness is vast, infinite. Emotions, desires, ambitions, are in your head; they will dry up. But even when your head has completely dropped and disappeared into the earth, your consciousness will not disappear. You don't contain the consciousness in you; the consciousness contains you, it is bigger than you.

There are people who ask, sometimes somebody comes to me and asks, "Where is the soul in the human body – in the heart, in the navel, in the head? Where is the soul?" They think they are asking a very pertinent question. It is nowhere in the body; your body is in the soul. The soul is a bigger phenomenon than your body, the soul surrounds you.

And your soul and my soul are not different. We live in existence, we live in one soul's ocean. One soul surrounds us, within and without; it is all one energy. I don't have a different soul and you don't have a different soul. We have different bodies. It is almost like the electricity running into the bulb and running into the radio and running into the TV and moving the fan, and doing a thousand and one things. The fan is different from the bulb, but the electricity that runs them is the same.

We are one energy. Our expressions are different, but our reality is one. If you look at the content, if I look at the content, then my dreams are different from yours, certainly. We cannot share our dreams. I have my ambitions, you have your ambitions, and it is not only that we cannot share our dreams; our dreams are in conflict. My ambition is against your ambition; your ambition is against my ambition. But if we forget the contents and just look at consciousness, pure consciousness, cloudless sky, then where are "you" and where am "I"? We are one.

In that moment there is unity. And in that moment there is universal consciousness.

All consciousness is universal. Unconsciousness is private, consciousness is universal. The day you become really a man, you are a universal man. That is the meaning of *christ*: universal man, son of existence. That is the meaning of *buddha*: universal man come to total and absolute awareness.

Man as a machine is different, this has to be understood. If you are having kidney trouble, I am not having; if I am having a headache, you are not having the headache; even if you love me you cannot share the headache. Even if I love you I cannot have your pain. But if we two are sitting together and meditating and a moment comes when I have no content in my mind and you also don't have any content in your mind, we will not be two. Meditators begin as separate, but end as one.

If you are all sitting in meditation here, listening to me, then you are not many, then you are one. Then you are not only one, the speaker and the listener is not separate; we are bridged together. Twenty meditators in a room meditating, when they come to real meditation, are no longer twenty, there is only one meditative quality in the room.

There is a story...

A few people came to see Buddha. Ananda was sitting on guard outside the room, but those people took such a long time that Ananda became worried. Many times he looked in, but they continued and continued and continued...

Then he came inside the room to see what was happening, and he found nobody there, just Buddha sitting. So he asked Buddha, "Where have those fellows gone? There is no other door, and I am sitting at the only door, so where have they gone?"

And Buddha said, "They are meditating."

It is a beautiful story. They all fell into meditation, and Ananda could not see them because he was still not a meditator. He could not see this new phenomenon, this total shift of energy. They were not there because they were not as their bodies there, they were not as their minds there. Those egos dissolved. Ananda could see only what *he* could see. A new reality had happened.

A great king once came to see Buddha. His prime minister persuaded him to come, but he was a very suspicious man, as politicians and kings usually are, very suspicious. He didn't want to come in the first place. Just for political reasons he came to see him, because in the capital the rumor was spreading that he was against Buddha; and all the people were for Buddha, so he became afraid, it was not diplomatic. So he went there to see, with his prime minister.

When he reached closer to the grove where Buddha was sitting with his ten thousand monks, he became very much afraid. He pulled his sword out and he said to the prime minister, "What is the matter? – because you said ten thousand people are staying there, and we have come so close and there is no noise. Is there some conspiracy?"

The prime minister laughed and said, "You don't know Buddha's people. Just put your sword back. Come on – there is no conspiracy or anything. You need not be afraid, they are not going to kill you. You don't know Buddha's men."

But very suspicious, holding his hand on the sword, the king went into the grove. He was surprised. He could not believe there were ten thousand people sitting under the trees silently, as if there was no one. He said to Buddha, "This is a miracle, ten thousand people – even ten people together create so much noise. What are these people doing? What has happened to these people, has something gone wrong? Are they still alive? They look like statues. What are they doing sitting here? They should do something."

And Buddha said, "They *are* doing something, but it has nothing to do with the outside. They are doing something in their inner world. They are not in their bodies; they are in their beings, at the very core, and these are not ten thousand people right now, they are all part of one consciousness."

The third sutra:

Like salt sea water that turns sweet
when drunk up by the clouds,
so a firm mind that works for others,
turns the poison of sense-objects
into nectar.

The basic Tantra attitude is: the sensual can be transformed into the sublime, matter can be transformed into mind, the unconscious can be transformed into consciousness.

Modern physics says matter can be transformed into energy, energy can be transformed into matter. In fact they are not two but the same energy functioning as two forms. Tantra says sex can be transformed into *samadhi* – the same approach, very basic and fundamental. The lower can be transformed into the higher because lower and higher are joined together; it is a ladder. They are never separate, nowhere separate, there is no gap between them. You can move from the lower to the higher, you can move from the higher to the lower.

And that ladder is what man is. He can exist on the lowest rung; that is his decision. He can move upward, he can exist on the highest rung. He can exist as a beast or he can exist as a buddha – both are his rungs, the lowest and the highest. Man is a ladder; he can fall into deep unconsciousness and become a rock, and he can rise to absolute consciousness and can become a god. But they are not separate, that is the beauty of Tantra.

Tantra is non-divisive; Tantra is the only religion which is not schizophrenic. Tantra is the only religion which is really sane, the sanest religion, because it doesn't divide. If you divide you create a split. If you tell people that the body is bad, that the body is the enemy, that the body has to be condemned, that the body is in the service of the Devil; then you are creating a split in man, then the man becomes afraid of the body. And by and by an unbridgeable gulf is created and he is torn into two parts, he is pulled in two opposite directions. The body pulls the body in two, the mind tries to pull the mind in two; there is conflict and confusion.

Tantra says you are one – there is no need to have any confusion. You can be fused into one reality. There is no need to have any conflict, there is no need to be torn apart, there is no need to go insane. You can love all that is available, and you can evolve it – with deep love, care, creativity, it can be evolved. The body is not the enemy of your soul; the body is just the sheath of your sword. The body is just the temple, it is your abode; it is not the enemy, it is your friend.

Tantra drops all sorts of violence, not only violence to others but violence to oneself. Tantra says: love reality in its totality. Yes, much can be evolved, but all evolution is through love; there is no need to fight.

Like salt seawater that turns sweet when drunk up by the clouds... You cannot drink the salt seawater; it is so salty, it is all salt. You will die if you drink the salty seawater. But when a cloud comes and draws the water from the sea, it turns sweet, and then you can drink it.

Saraha says *samadhi* is like a cloud, meditative energy is like a cloud which turns your sexuality into higher realms, which turns your physical existence into non-physical existence, which turns the salty, bitter experiences of the world into sweet, nectarlike experiences of nirvana. Samsara itself becomes nirvana, if you can create the cloud that transforms it. That cloud Buddha has actually called *dharmamegha samadhi,* the *samadhi* of the cloud of the fundamental law: *dharmamegha samadhi.*

You can create that cloud. That cloud is created by meditation. You go on intensely meditating, dropping thoughts, dropping desires, ambitions, by and by your consciousness is a burning fire: that cloud is there. Now you can transform anything through that fire; that fire transmutes, that fire is alchemical. Through meditation the lower becomes higher, the baser metal is turned into gold.

Like salt sea water that turns sweet when drunk up by the clouds, so a firm mind that works for others, turns the poison of sense-objects into nectar. Two things: first, one has to create a cloud of meditation in one's being; and the second thing is compassion – one who works for others. Buddha insists on two things: meditation and compassion, *pragyan* and *karuna.* He says that sometimes it happens that a meditator can become too selfish; then too something goes sour. Meditate, delight, but share the delight, go on sharing it. Don't hoard it, because once you start hoarding, ego starts arising. Never hoard anything. The moment you get it, give it, and you will be getting more and more and more. The more you give, the more you get. Then everything becomes nectar. Everything *is* nectar; we just have to know how to turn it, we have to know the alchemy.

The last sutra:

If ineffable, never is one unsatisfied.
If unimaginable, it must be bliss itself.
Though from a cloud one fears the thunderclap,
the crops ripen when from it pours the rain.

The ineffable... Saraha says: "Don't ask me what it is – it is ineffable, it cannot be said. It cannot be expressed, no language exists which can express it. But it can be experienced. Look at my contentment. Look how satisfied I have become. You knew me before too, how restless I was, how unsatisfied with everything. All was available; I was your favorite, all was available to me, yet I was not satisfied. Now look! I am standing in a cemetery ground, not even a roof over my head, and I don't live with kings and queens; I am living with this arrowsmith woman. But look into my eyes, how contented I am. Can't you see something ineffable has happened? Can't you feel my vibe? Are you so dull and dead that you need explanations?"

If ineffable, never is one unsatisfied. That is the only criterion: whether a man has attained to truth or not. He will never be unsatisfied; his contentment is absolute. You cannot drag him out of his contentment, you cannot make him discontented; whatsoever happens, he remains the same, contented. Success or failure, life or death, friends or no friends, lovers or no lovers, it makes no difference, his tranquility, his stillness is utterly absolute. He is centered: *If ineffable, never is one unsatisfied.*

If that which cannot be said has happened, then there is only one way to know it, and that way is to see the contentment.

If unimaginable, it must be bliss itself. "And I know." he says, "You cannot imagine what has happened to me." How can you imagine? You have never known it. Imagination is always repeating the same that you have known. You can imagine happiness; you have known bits and pieces of it. You can imagine unhappiness; you have known it, a lot of it. You can imagine happiness even if you don't know happiness; you can imagine it as the contrary of unhappiness. But how can you imagine bliss? You have not known it. And there is nothing as contrary to it, it is not a duality. It is impossible to imagine.

So Saraha says, "I can understand that you cannot imagine it, but I am not saying to imagine it. Look! It is present herenow. If you cannot imagine it, that also is one of the criteria of truth: truth cannot be imagined. It can be seen, but not imagined. You can have a vision of it, but you cannot dream about it. That is the difference between a dream and a vision."

A dream is yours. A vision is not yours.

Christ saw God, and the scriptures say he saw the vision. Now the psychoanalyst will say it was just a dream; he does not know the difference between a dream and a vision. A dream is yours: you were imagining, you created it, it was your fantasy. A vision is something out of the blue that you have never thought about, not even a part of it has ever been thought by you. It is so utterly new – then it is a vision. A vision is from existence, a dream is from your mind. *If unimaginable, it must be bliss itself.*

Look at me – you cannot imagine what has happened. Can't you see it?

You have eyes to see – look, watch, hold my hand! Come closer to me, just be vulnerable to me, so my vibration can vibrate your being, and the unimaginable and the ineffable can be experienced.

Though from a cloud one fears the thunderclap... And Saraha says, "I know." He must have seen the king a little afraid. I see it every day. People come to me and I see them trembling, afraid, fearful, and they say, "We are afraid, Osho." I know. Saraha must have seen the king was trembling deep inside, maybe not on the outside. He was a great king, he must have been a very disciplined man, he must have been standing erect – but deep down he must have been afraid.

It always happens when you are close by a Saraha-like man, or a Buddha-like man, you are bound to be afraid. Just the other night a young man came and he said, "But why am I afraid of you? You have not done anything wrong to me – why am I afraid of you? Certainly I love you, but why am I afraid of you?"

It is natural. When you come close to an abyss, what do you expect? You will be afraid. There is every possibility you may fall into it and will not be able to recover yourself again; it is going to be irrevocable, irrecoverable. You will be completely, utterly gone in it. You will not be able to recapitulate. Fear is natural.

Saraha says: *Though from a cloud one fears the thunderclap...* He says, "I am like a cloud and you are afraid because of the thunderclap, of the lightning. But remember...*the crops ripen when from it pours the rain.* If you allow me to rain on you, the seeds will sprout, sir, and the man that is still hidden behind you, still not yet born, will be born. You will be able to ripen, to mature; you will be able to blossom. I invite you," says Saraha, "for a great harvest: the harvest of consciousness, the harvest of awareness."

Enough for today.

CHAPTER 6

no problem is serious

The first question:

Osho,
I have taken lately to daydreaming about enlightenment – even more delicious than love and fame.
Have you any comment to make about daydreaming?

he question is from Pankaja. Daydreaming is perfectly okay as far as love and fame are concerned. They are part of a dream world, you can dream as much as you like. Love is a dream, so is fame; they are not against dreaming. In fact, when dreaming stops they disappear. They exist in the same dimension, the dimension of dream.

But you cannot dream about enlightenment. Enlightenment is possible only when dreaming disappears. Enlightenment is absence of dreaming – day or night doesn't matter. Enlightenment means that now your consciousness is fully aware; in an aware consciousness dreaming cannot exist. Dreaming is like darkness, it exists when the light is not there. When the light is there, darkness simply cannot exist.

Dreaming exists because life is dark, dim, dismal. Dreaming exists as a substitute because we don't have real joy; hence we dream because we don't really have anything in life, hence we dream. Otherwise how will we be able to tolerate the emptiness that we are, how will we be able to tolerate our existence? It will be absolutely unbearable. Dreams make it bearable, dreams help us. They say to us, "Wait, today things are not going right? Don't be worried, tomorrow everything will be put right. Everything has to be right. We will try – maybe we have not tried enough yet. Maybe we have not worked in the right direction. Maybe fate was not with us, God was against us, but it cannot be forever…" And God is compassionate, kind; all the religions of the world say God is very kind, very compassionate – it is a hope.

Mohammedans continually repeat: "God is *rahim*, *rahman*: compassion- ate, kind." Why, for what do they repeat this again and again? Each time they utter the word *God* they will repeat *the compassionate, the kind*. Why? If he is not kind, then where will our hope and dreaming exist? He *has* to be kind for our dreams to exist because our hope exists there: in his kindness, in his com- passion – tomorrow things will be okay, tomorrow they are going to be okay.

Daydreaming is good as far as love and fame are concerned, as far as outgoing energies are concerned, because outgoing we are going in a dream. The world is a dream phenomenon; that is what Hindus mean when they call it *maya*: illusion. It is made of the same stuff dreams are made of. It is a day- dream seen with open eyes.

But enlightenment is on a totally different plane of being. Dreams don't exist there. If you continue to dream, enlightenment will not be possible.

I was reading, just the other day, a beautiful anecdote…

A parson had a parrot, but despite all efforts to try and teach it to speak the bird remained dumb. The parson mentioned this one day to an elderly lady parishioner who visited him. She was interested and said, "I also have a parrot which does not speak. It might be a good idea to put the two birds together and see what happens."

Well this they did, the parrots being put in a large cage while the parson and his lady parishioner withdrew out of sight but not out of hearing. At first all was quiet, then came some fluttering and the old lady's parrot was heard to exclaim, "What about a spot of love, deary?"

To which the parson's parrot replied, "That's what I have been silently pray- ing and waiting for, for years. Today my dream is fulfilled, today I can speak."

If you are waiting and praying and dreaming for love and fame, it will hap- pen one day. It is not a difficult phenomenon. One just needs stubbornness and it happens. One just needs to go on and on and on. It is bound to happen, because it is *your* dream. You will find some place or other where you can project it and you can see it, almost as if it has become a reality.

When you fall in love with a woman or a man, what are you doing exactly? You were carrying a dream inside you; now suddenly the woman functions as a screen, you project your dream onto her. You start feeling: "My dream is fulfilled." The woman projects her dream on you; you function as a screen, and she feels her dream is fulfilled. If you go on dreaming some day or other you will find a screen, somebody will become a screen, and your dream will be fulfilled.

But enlightenment is not a dream; it is a dropping of all dreams. So please don't dream about enlightenment. Love is possible through dreaming; in fact it is possible *only* through dreaming. Fame is possible through dreaming; in fact it is only possible through dreaming, it happens only to dreamers. But enlightenment is not possible through dreaming; the very existence of dreaming will make it impossible.

Dream for it and you will miss. Wait for it and you will miss. Hope for it and you will miss. Then what are you supposed to do? What you are supposed to do is to understand the mechanism of dreaming. You can leave enlightenment aside – it is none of your business. Just look deep into the faculty of dreaming, understand how dreaming functions; that very understanding will bring clarity. In that clarity dreaming stops, disappears.

When dreaming is not, enlightenment is.

Forget about enlightenment. You are not to even think about it. How can you think about it? And whatsoever you think is going to be wrong. How can you hope for it? All hopes about it are going to be wrong. How can you desire it? It cannot be desired. Then what are we supposed to do?

Try to understand desiring. Try to understand hoping. Try to understand dreaming. That's what is needed. Simply try to understand how your mind has been functioning up to now. Seeing into the functioning of the mind, mind disappears. Just a good look into the inner mechanism of the mind, and suddenly it comes to a halt. In that halt there is enlightenment. In that halt there is a taste of a totally new dimension of existence.

Dreaming is one dimension; existence is another dimension. Existence is. Dreaming is simply a belief.

The second question:

Osho,
You spoke in several recent discourses on the no-problem, the nonexistence of our problems.
Having been brought up in a repressive Catholic family, and having spent twenty-one years in an equally crazy educational system, are you saying that all the coats of armor, all the conditionings and all the repressions do not exist, can be dropped immediately – *now*? What about all the imprints left on the brain, on the musculature of the body?

This is a very significant question. It is from Jayananda. The question is significant because it shows two different approaches concerning the inner reality of man. The Western approach is to think about the problem, to find the causes of the problem, to go into the history of the problem, into the past of the problem, to uproot the problem from the very beginning, to uncondition the mind, or to recondition the mind, to recondition the body, to take out all those imprints that have been left on the brain – this is the Western approach. Psychoanalysis goes into the memory – it works there. It goes into your child-hood, into your past, it moves backward, it finds out from where the problem has arisen. Maybe fifty years before, when you were a child, the problem arose in your relationship with your mother. Then psychoanalysis will go back...

Fifty years of history; it is a very long, dragging affair, and even then it doesn't help much because there are millions of problems, it is not only a question of one problem. You can go into one problem's history; you can look into your autobiography and find out the causes. Maybe you can eliminate one problem, but there are millions of problems. If you start going into each prob-lem, to solve one life's problems you will need millions of lives. Let me repeat it: to solve *one* life's problems you will have to be born again and again, millions of times. This is most impractical; this cannot be done. All those millions of lives when you will be solving the problems of this life, those lives will create their own problems, and so on and so forth. You will be dragged more and more into the problems; this is absurd.

Now the same psychoanalytical approach has gone into the body: Rolfing, bio-energetics and other methods, which try to eliminate imprints on the body, in the musculature. Again you have to go into the history of the body. But one thing is certain about both approaches, which are of the same logical pattern: that the problem comes from the past, so somehow it has to be tackled in the past.

Man's mind has always been trying to do two impossible things. One is to reform the past – which cannot be done. The past has happened, you cannot really go into the past. When you think of going into the past, at the most you go into the memory of it; it is not the real past, it is just the memory. The past is no longer there, so you cannot reform it. This is one of the impossible goals of humanity; man has suffered very much because of it: you want to undo the past. How can you undo it? The past is absolute. The past means: all potential-ity of it is finished; it has become actual. Now there is no longer any potential to reform it, to undo it, to redo it. You cannot do anything with the past.

And the second impossible idea that has always dominated the human mind is: to establish the future, which again cannot be done. The future means that which is not yet, you cannot establish it; the future remains un-established, the future remains open. The future is pure potentiality. Unless it happens, you cannot be certain about it. The past is pure actuality, it has happened. Now nothing can be done about it.

Between these two, man stands in the present, always thinking of impossibles. He wants to make everything certain about the future, about tomorrow – which cannot be done. Let it sink as deeply in your heart as possible: it cannot be done. Don't waste your present moment for making the future certain; the future is uncertainty – that is the very quality of the future. And don't waste your time looking back; the past has happened, it is a dead phenomenon, nothing can be done about it. What at the most you *can* do is you can reinterpret it, that's all. That's what psychoanalysis is doing: reinterpreting it. Reinterpretation can be done, but the past remains the same.

Psychoanalysis and astrology… Astrology tries somehow to make the future certain, and psychoanalysis tries to re-do the past. Neither is a science. Both are not sciences; both things are impossible, but both have millions of followers because man likes it that way. He wants to be certain about the future, so he goes to the astrologer, he consults the I Ching, he goes to a Tarot reader, there are a thousand and one ways to fool oneself, to deceive oneself. Then there are people who say they can change the past – he consults them also.

Once these two things are dropped, you become free of all sorts of foolishnesses; then you don't go to the psychoanalyst and you don't go to the astrologer. Then you know the past is finished. You also be finished with it. The future has not happened, whenever it happens we will see; nothing can be done about it right now. You can only destroy the present moment, which is the only moment available, real.

The West has been continually looking into problems: how to solve them. The West takes problems very seriously. When you are using a certain logic, given the premises, that logic looks perfect.

I was just reading an anecdote…

A great philosopher and world-renowned mathematician is aboard an airplane. He is sitting in his seat and thinking great mathematical problems when suddenly an announcement comes from the captain: "I am sorry, there will be a slight delay. Engine number one has cut out and we are now flying on three engines."

About ten minutes later another announcement: "I am afraid there will be further delay – engines two and three have cut out and there is only number four left."

So the philosopher turns to the fellow sitting next to him and says, "Good golly! If the other one cuts out, we will be up here all night."

When you are thinking along a certain line, the very direction of it makes certain things possible, absurd things also possible. Once you have taken human problems very seriously, once you start thinking about man as a problem, you have accepted a premise; you have taken the first step wrongly. Now you can go in that direction, and you can go on and on. Now such great literature has come up in this century about mind phenomena, psychoanalysis – millions of papers, treatises and books are written. Once Freud opened the doors of that certain logic, it dominated the whole century.

The East has a totally different outlook. First, it says no problem is serious. The moment you say no problem is serious, the problem is almost ninety-nine percent dead. Your whole vision about it changes. The second thing the East says is: the problem is there because you are identified with it. It has nothing to do with the past, nothing to do with its history. You are identified with it – that is the *real* thing, and that is the key to solve all problems.

For example, you are an angry person. If you go to the psychoanalyst, he will say, "Go into the past, how did this anger arise? In what situations did it become more and more conditioned and imprinted on your mind? We will have to wash out all those imprints; we will have to wipe them off. We will have to clean your past completely."

If you go to an Eastern mystic, he will say, "You think that you are anger, you feel identified with the anger – that is where things are going wrong. Next time anger happens just be a watcher; just be a witness. Don't get identified with the anger. Don't say, 'I am anger.' Don't say, 'I am angry.' Just see it happening as if it is happening on a TV screen. Look at yourself as if you are looking at somebody else."

You are pure consciousness. When the cloud of anger comes around you, just watch it and remain alert so that you don't get identified. The whole thing is how not to become identified with the problem. Once you have learned it… And then there is no question of "so many problems," because the key, the same key, will open all the locks. It is so with anger, it is so with greed, it is so with sex; it is so with everything else that the mind is capable of.

The East says just remain unidentified. Remember – that's what Gurdjieff means when he says *self-remembering* – remember that you are a witness. Be mindful! That's what Buddha says. "Be alert that a cloud is passing by." Maybe the cloud comes from the past, but that is meaningless. It must have a certain past, it cannot come just out of the blue; it must be coming from a certain sequence of events – but that is irrelevant. Why be bothered about it? Right now, this very moment, you can become detached from it, you can cut yourself away from it. The bridge can be broken right now – and it can be broken *only* in the now.

Going into the past won't help. Thirty years before, the anger arose and you got identified with it that day. Now you cannot get unidentified from that past, it is no longer there. But you can get unidentified this moment, this very moment, then the whole series of angers of your past is no longer part of you.

The question is relevant. Jayananda has asked, "You spoke in several recent discourses on the no-problem, the nonexistence of our problems. Having been brought up in a repressive Catholic family…" You can right now become a non-Catholic. *Now*, I say! You will not have to go back and undo whatsoever your parents and your society and the priest and the church have done. That will be a sheer wastage of precious present time. In the first place it has destroyed many years; now it will again be destroying your present moments. You can simply drop out of it, just as a snake slips out of the old skin.

"Having been brought up in a repressive Catholic family, and having spent twenty-one years in an equally crazy educational system, are you saying that all the coats of armor, all the conditionings and all the repressions do not exist?" No, they exist. But they exist either in the body or in the brain; they don't exist in your consciousness, because the consciousness cannot be conditioned. Consciousness remains free. Freedom is its innermost quality; freedom is its nature. In fact even asking it, you are showing that freedom.

When you say, "twenty-one years in a crazy educational system," when you say, "having been brought up in a repressive Catholic family," in this moment you are not identified. You can look – so many years of Catholic repression, so many years of a certain education. In this moment, when you are looking at it, this consciousness is no longer Catholic – otherwise who will be aware? If you had really become Catholic, then who would be aware? Then there would be no possibility of becoming aware.

If you can say, "twenty-one years in an equally crazy educational system," one thing is certain: you are not yet crazy. The system has failed; it didn't work. Jayananda, you are not crazy, hence you can see the whole system as crazy. A madman cannot see that he is mad, only a sane person can see that this is madness. To see madness as madness, sanity is needed. Those twenty-one years of a crazy system have failed, all that repressive conditioning has failed. It cannot really succeed. It succeeds only in the proportion that you get identified with it; any moment you can stand aloof. It is there – I am not saying it is not there – but it is no longer part of your consciousness.

This is the beauty of consciousness: consciousness can slip out of any-thing; there is no barrier to it, no boundary to it. Just a moment before you were an Englishman. Understanding the nonsense of nationalism a second later, you are no longer an Englishman.

I am not saying that your white skin will change, it will remain white; but you are no longer identified with the whiteness, you are no longer against the black. You see the stupidity of it. I am not saying that just by seeing that you are no longer an Englishman, you will forget the English language, no. It will still be there in your memory, but your consciousness has slipped out, your consciousness is standing on a hillock, looking at the valley. Now the Englishman is dead in the valley, and you are standing on the hills, far away, unattached, untouched.

The whole Eastern methodology can be reduced to one word: *witnessing*, and the whole Western methodology can be reduced to one thing: analyzing. Analyzing, you go round and round. Witnessing, you simply get out of the circle.

Analysis is a vicious circle. If you *really* go into analysis, you will be simply puzzled – how is it possible? If, for example, you try to go into the past, where will you end? Where exactly? If you go into the past, where did your sexuality start? When you were fourteen years of age? But then it came out of the blue? It must have been getting ready in the body. So when? When you were born? But then, when you were in the mother's womb, wasn't it getting ready? Then when? The moment you were conceived? But before that half of your sexuality was maturing in your mother's egg and half of the sexuality was maturing in your father's sperm. Now go on – where will you end? You will have to go to Adam and Eve. Even then it does not end, you will have to go to Father God himself: why in the first place did he create Adam?

Analysis will always remain half, so analysis never really helps anybody, it cannot. It makes you a little more adjusted to your reality, that's all. It is a sort of adjustment, it helps you to attain a little bit of understanding about your problems, their genesis, how they have arisen. And that little intellectual understanding helps you to adjust to the society better, but you remain the same person. There is no transformation through it, there is no radical change through it.

Witnessing is a revolution. It is a radical change from the very roots. It brings a totally new man into existence, because it takes your consciousness out of all the conditionings. Conditionings are there in the body and in the mind, but consciousness remains unconditioned. It is pure, always pure; it is virgin. Its virginity cannot be violated.

The Eastern approach is to make you mindful of this virgin consciousness, of this purity, of this innocence. That's what Saraha is saying to the king again and again. Our emphasis is on the sky and the Western emphasis is on the clouds. Clouds have a genesis: if you want to find out from where they come, you will have to go to the ocean, then to the sunrays and the evaporation of the water and the clouds forming, and you can go on, but it will be moving in a circle. The clouds form, then again they come, fall in love with the trees, start pouring again into the earth, become rivers, go to the ocean, start evaporating, rising again on sunrays, become clouds, again fall on the earth; it goes on and on, round and round and round. It is a wheel. From where will you get out? One thing will lead to another and you will always be on the wheel.

The sky has no genesis, the sky is uncreated; it is not produced by anything. In fact for anything to be, a sky is needed as a must, a priori: it has to exist before anything else can exist. You can ask the Christian theologian – he says God created the world – ask him whether before he created the world there was any sky or not. If there was no sky, where did God used to exist? He must have needed space – if there was no space, where did he create the world? Where did he put the world? Space is a must – even for God to exist. You cannot say, "God created space," that would be absurd, because then he would not have had any space to exist. Space must precede God.

The sky has always been there. The Eastern approach is to become mindful of the sky. The Western approach makes you more and more alert to the clouds and helps you a little, but it doesn't make you aware of your innermost core. Circumference yes; you become a little more aware of the circumference but not aware of the center. The circumference is a cyclone; you have to find the center of the cyclone, and that happens only through witnessing.

Witnessing will not change your conditioning, witnessing will not change your body musculature. But witnessing will simply give you an experience that you are beyond all musculature, all conditioning. In that moment of beyondness, in that moment of transcendence, no problem exists, not for you.

And now it is up to you – the body will still carry the musculature and the mind will still carry the conditioning, now it is up to you. If sometimes you are hankering for the problem, you can get into the mind-body and have the problem and enjoy it. If you don't want to have it, you can remain outside. The problem will remain as an imprint in the body-mind phenomenon, but you will be aloof and away from it.

That's how a buddha functions. You use memory; a buddha also uses memory, but he is not identified with it. He uses memory as a mechanism. For example, I am using language; when I have to use language I use the mind and all the imprints, but I am continuously not the mind – that awareness is there. So I remain the boss, the mind remains a servant. When the mind is called, it comes; its use is there, but it cannot dominate.

So your question is right: problems will exist, but they will exist only in the seed form in the body and the mind. How can you change your past? You have been a Catholic in the past; if for forty years you have been a Catholic, how can you change those forty years and not be a Catholic? No, those forty years will remain as a period of being Catholic. But you can slip out of it; now you know that was just identification. Those forty years cannot be destroyed, and there is no need to destroy them. If you are the master of the house, there is no need. You can use even those forty years in a certain way, in a creative way. Even that crazy education can be used in a creative way.

"What about all the imprints left on the brain, on the musculature of the body?" They will be there but as a seed, potentially there. If you feel too lonely and you want problems, you can have them. If you feel too miserable without miseries, you can have them; they will remain always available. But there is no need to have them, there is no necessity to have them; it will be your choice.

Future humanity will have to decide whether it is to go on the path of analysis or it is to change to the path of witnessing. I use both methods. I use analysis, particularly for seekers who come from the West; I put them in the groups. Those groups are analytical, those groups are by-products of psychoanalysis. They have grown. Freud will not be able to recognize encounter if he comes, or primal therapy. It will be difficult for him to recognize. "What is happening? Have all these people gone mad?" But they are offshoots of his work; he was the pioneer, without him there would be no primal therapy. He started the whole game.

When Western people come to me, I put them into the groups. That is good for them; they should start with what is easier for them. Then by and by slowly I change it. First they go into cathartic groups like encounter, primal therapy, and then I start putting them into Enlightenment Intensive, then *vipassana*. *Vipassana* is witnessing. From encounter to *vipassana* there is a great synthesis. When you move from encounter to *vipassana*, you are moving from West to East.

The third question:

Osho,
Do your actions also bring the same proportion of good and bad in the world?

What actions? Can you detect any actions in me – except talking? And in that too I take every care to contradict everything I say. So in the end, just emptiness... That is the use of contradiction. If I say plus one, immediately I say minus one, and the total result is zero.

I am not a doer; I don't do anything. All that you can call action is my talking to you, and that is so contradictory that it cannot bring either good or bad. I go on negating myself. If you understand this state of no-action, you will have understood the highest possibility of consciousness.

The highest consciousness is not a doer; it is a being. If something like action appears there, it is just playful. My talking is just a play. The whole effort is that you don't become dogmatic about me. You cannot, I don't allow that possibility. I contradict so much, how can you create a dogma? If you try to create a dogma, you will find I have immediately contradicted it.

A Christian missionary used to come to see me, and he said, "You have spoken so much. Now what is needed is a small book which introduces your philosophy, something like a Christian catechism in short."

I said, "That will be difficult. If somebody is going to put me 'in short,' he will go mad. And he will not find any way to choose and what to choose."

Once I am gone many people are going to become insane working on their PhD theses on me, because I have said all that can be said, and I have denied all that can be denied.

The fourth question:

Osho,
A question in bad faith: Why do you talk so much against the ego? Isn't the ego also a manifestation of existence, a game played by existence?

If you understand that, then there is no problem about the ego. That is the whole purpose of why I go on talking against the ego, so that you are not and existence is. If you have come to such a deep understanding, that the ego is also a play of existence, then it is perfectly good! Then there is no problem, there is no need to drop because you have nothing to drop. If you understand that ego is also a play of existence, then you are not in it. Everything is of existence – that's what egolessness means – even ego.

But beware! You may be just playing a trick upon yourself, and mind is very cunning. In the name of existence you may be trying to save your ego. It is up to you, but be watchful. If you have *really* understood that all is existence, then you are not. So where is the ego? What does ego mean? It means I have a private life, I am not part of the universal flux. I am not part of the river, I am swimming, I am going upstream; I have my own private goals. I don't care where existence is going; I have my own private goals and I am trying to find them and achieve them. Ego means having a private goal. Ego is idiotic.

The word *idiot* is very beautiful. It means having a private idiom, it means having a private goal, a private style. Ego is idiotic. It simply says, "I am not part of the universal; I am private, I am separate. I am an island, I don't belong to the continent." This not belonging to the whole is what ego is, this idea of being separate.

That's why all the mystics have been saying, "Drop the ego!" What are they saying? They are saying, "Don't be separate." Dropping the ego does not mean anything else: don't be separate, be together with existence. And don't flow against the river – that is foolish; you will simply be tired and defeated. Go with the river, all the way. Go with the river; you are part of the river. Then there will be relaxation and rest and joy. With the river there is joy, against the river there is strain, anxiety. Ego creates anxiety and strain.

Now you ask, "Why do you talk so much against the ego? Isn't the ego also a manifestation of God, a game played by existence?" If you have come to understand that, then to you at least I am not saying to drop the ego; then you don't have any ego to drop. But be very careful and cautious, mind is so cunning.

I have heard this small anecdote...

A monkey and a hyena were walking through the jungle together when the hyena said, "Every time I go through those bushes over there, a big lion jumps out and keeps on hitting me and hitting me, and I don't know why!"

"Well I will come with you this time," said the monkey, "and I will stick up for you."

So they walked along together, and just as they got to the bushes a lion jumped out on them and started hitting the hyena. The monkey just climbed up in a tree and watched. So when the lion had gone the half-dead hyena asked the monkey, "Why didn't you come down and help me?"

And the monkey said, "You were laughing so much I thought you were winning."

Beware of the ego! It can find ways and means to protect itself. It can rationalize well; the ego is a great rationalist, and rationalization is its whole foundation.

The fifth question:

Osho,
Please say this to me, so I can stop worrying about it: "Arup, everything is going absolutely beautifully with you. No matter how much your mind is trying, now it is too late. I have got you safely under my wing and there is no way back. And you are going to be more and more blissful from now on."
Thank you Osho. I hope it is so, but sometimes I waver.

The question is from Arup. Now the first thing: you say that I have to say to you, "Everything is going absolutely beautifully with you."

Just by my saying it, it will not become beautiful. It may give you a consolation, but I am not here to give you any consolation. Either take the real thing or don't bother at all. Consolation is a false thing. It is a toy to play with, it is just to pass time, and passing time is wasting time.

And another thing, you say, "Everything is going absolutely beautifully" – difficult, "absolutely beautifully" – difficult. Nothing is absolute here on the earth, except witnessing. Ugly is not absolute, beautiful is not absolute, happiness is not absolute, unhappiness is not absolute – only witnessing. When you witness, you feel neither ugly nor beautiful, neither happy nor unhappy; you simply feel a witness.

My whole work is to make you a witness. You would like to have everything beautiful, you don't want to be a witness. You want to have more pleasurable experiences; that's why you constantly seek consolation. People come to me not really to be helped but to be consoled, just to be patted on the back. If I say everything is going well, they feel good, but for how long is this feeling going to help? It will wear off sooner or later. Again they have to come, and again they wait for me to pat them on the head. This will create a dependence on me, and I am not to make you dependent on me. It is not going to help you; you need a transformation. You have to be independent, you have to be your own self; you have to be on your own.

"No matter how much your mind is trying, now it is too late." It is never too late. You can go back any time, because the mind is always there. You can slip into the old skin again, you can become identified with it again. And when it is *really* too late, you will not ask this question. Then you will know that now there is no possibility of going back. This will be a certainty in you, this will be your own knowing; you will not need my certificate for it. Just because you need a certificate, it shows it has not happened; you are wavering.

I have heard...

Mulla Nasruddin was standing in the court. "This crime was the work of a master criminal," said the prosecutor, "and was carried out in a skillful, clever manner."

Blushing, Mulla Nasruddin, the defendant, rose to his feet and said, "Sir, flattery will get you nowhere; I ain't gonna confess."

But he *has* confessed. Arup has confessed. This is not a question; this is a confession that she feels worried. It is natural. It is inhuman to expect no worry, at this stage at least. Sometimes she feels she is wavering, that is human, natural; it is good to accept it rather than deny it, rather than create a screen and hide it: "Please say this to me so that I can stop worrying about it."

How will you stop worrying about it just by my saying it? If it were so easy, I would have said it to everybody. It is not so easy. Whatsoever I say, you will interpret it in your own way, and you will find new worries. Whatsoever I say, you will have to interpret it – you cannot accept it totally, you cannot trust it totally. And I am not saying that you have to trust it totally, I am saying this is simply natural.

I don't ask any unnatural thing from you. I don't ask any absurd things from you. It is natural: sometimes you waver, sometimes you are against me; sometimes you are very negative, sometimes you feel just to drop everything and go away back to your old world. I don't say that you are doing something criminal, no; it is just human, it is very natural. If you are not doing such things, then something is wrong, then something is amiss.

Whatsoever I say will again be interpreted by the same worrying mind. Even if I say exactly, "Yes, Arup, everything is going absolutely beautifully with you," you will think, "Was Osho joking? Does he really mean it?" The worrying mind will jump upon it; your interpretations are bound to be there.

Listen to this small story…

A priest was returning home late at night from a meeting. As he drove along, he suddenly remembered that he had not said evensong. He pulled up at the side of a quiet country lane, got out of his car and using the light of his car headlamps began to say the office.

Not long after he had begun, and much to his surprise, a lorry came along. The driver of the lorry, thinking that something was wrong, stopped, let down his window, and asked, "Having a spot of trouble, mate?"

"No, everything is all right, thank you," replied the priest.

The driver put his lorry in gear and, not to be outdone as he pulled away, cried out, "All I can say is, that must be a helluva good book you are reading there!"

Now just think of somebody reading a book on a lonely lane by the headlights of the car – what will you think? Can you imagine somebody reading the Bible? What is the hurry to read the Bible? Can somebody be so interested in reading the Bible, can't he wait and go home and read it there? The lorry driver must have interpreted according to his mind – he said, "All I can say is, that must be a helluva good book you are reading there."

You continually interpret, and you interpret naturally according to your mind. What I say will not be heard, you will hear it in your own way. If you are worrying, you will worry about it. If you are doubting, you will doubt about it. If you are negative, you will be negative about it. If you are trusting, you will trust.

Arup says, "Just say to me, so that I can stop worrying about it." No, worrying cannot be stopped that easily. My saying it will not help, you will have to do something; you will have to do what I say. You will have to be a little more practical. You will have to do witnessing.

There were three very hungry tramps, and they came to the house where the governor was cooking rice. He said to them that they could stay the night and whoever had the best dream could have some hot rice.
So the next morning the first tramp said, "I dreamed that I was the king."
The second tramp said, "That's nothing – I dreamed I was God himself."
And the third tramp said, "My dream was very ordinary and I don't stand a chance of winning at all. I dreamed about that hot rice getting cold, so I went down and ate it."

This is what I mean by being practical. So, Arup, be practical. Do what I say. Just my saying it won't help – and the rice is really getting cold. You want me to help create a dream in you, and the rice is getting cold. Just go down and eat the rice.
This will just give you a dream if I say: "Arup, everything is going absolutely beautifully with you. No matter how much your mind is trying, now it is too late. I have got you safely under my wing and there is no way back."
In the first place, I cannot say it because the very desire to be safe and secure is against spiritual growth. I am pushing you into a dangerous realm, I am pushing you into an abyss. You would like to be safely under my wings; now I am throwing you into the very turmoil of existence, with no safety, with no security. I am not a protector, I am a destroyer. I am not your security; if you *really* understand me, I am going to become your dangerous life. You will always be insecure if you have understood me. You will never ask for safety and security. You will abhor safety and security, you will think of them as enemies – they are. You will enjoy being in the open, vulnerable to all that is possible in life. Yes, vulnerable to death too; *all* includes death too. A real life is encountering death each moment. Only unreal, plastic lives are safe.
No, I cannot say that I have got you safely under my wing and there is no way back. You can fall, you can fall from the very last rung. Unless you become enlightened, there is a way back, you can go back: you can deny, you can betray, you can reject. You can fall into the misery again; you can also fall from the very last rung. Until and unless you have crossed the whole ladder, even the last rung, until and unless you are just a nobody, you can fall back. A slight ego, just a tremor of ego, is enough to bring you back. It can again condense, it can again integrate; it can again become a new trip.

Safety is not my way; to be a sannyasin means you are ready to live life without safety. That is the greatest courage, and with that great courage, great bliss becomes possible.

"And you are going to be more and more and more blissful from now on." I am not an Emile Coué; I am not a hypnotist. Yes, you can hypnotize yourself this way – that was the very methodology of Coué. He would tell his patients, "Think, dream, imagine, visualize each night before going to sleep, each morning after the sleep, repeat again and again and again 'I am getting better, I am getting healthier, I am getting happier.' Repeat, go on repeating."

Yes, it helps a little; it creates an illusion around you. But would you like me to help you in creating illusions? My whole approach is that of dehypnosis, it is not of hypnosis at all. I don't want you to be hypnotized by any illusion. I want you to be utterly dehypnotized of all illusions. When you are in a state of disillusionment, utter disillusionment, enlightenment is very close by.

Then Arup says, "Thank you, Osho. I hope it is so..." See! Her mind has already started interpreting: "I hope it is so..." It is not so, she simply hopes. How you can deceive yourself.

"I hope it is so, but sometimes I waver." I am not condemning your wavering, it is perfectly okay to waver sometimes, it is perfectly human to waver sometimes. It is perfectly right, never condemn it; accept it. Don't try to create a false unwavering; that will be of the mind, and will be a deception, and will not lead you anywhere. Let it be as it is. Accept it as it is, and become more and more watchful, become more and more of a witness. Only in that witnessing, will you be safe. Only in that witnessing, will you become more and more blissful every day – not by repeating it. Only in that witnessing, will you stop wavering. Only in that witnessing, will you come to the center of your being, where death exists not, where only life abundant is, where one is drinking the nectar Saraha talks about.

The sixth question:

Osho,
What is it exactly that is obstructing my vision from seeing the obvious? I just do not understand what to do and what not to do. When will I be able to hear the sound of silence?

"What is it exactly that is obstructing my vision from seeing the obvious?" The very desire to see it – the obvious cannot be desired, the obvious is.

You desire, you go away. You start seeking for it. In that very moment you have made it distant, it is no longer obvious, it is no longer close by; you have put it far away. How can you seek the obvious? If you understand it is obvious, how can you seek it? It is just there. What is the need to seek it and to desire it?

The obvious is the divine, the mundane is the sublime, and the trivial is profound. In your day-to-day, ordinary activities, you are meeting God every moment of it, because there is nobody else. You cannot meet anybody else; it is always God in a thousand and one forms. God is very obvious. Only God is! But you seek, you desire, and you miss. In your very seeking you put God very distant, far away. That is an ego trick.

Try to understand it. The ego is not interested in the obvious because the ego cannot exist with the obvious. Ego is not interested at all in the close by; the ego is interested in the distant, faraway. Just think: man has reached to the moon, and man has not yet reached to his own heart. Man has invented space travel but still he has not developed soul travel. He has reached Everest, but he does not bother to go into his own being. The close by is missed and the faraway is sought. Why? The ego feels good; if the journey is hard the ego feels good, there is something to prove. If it is difficult, there is something to prove. To go to the moon the ego feels good, but to go into one's own being will not be much of a claim.

There is an old story...

God created the world. Then he used to live on the earth. You can imagine... His troubles were too many, everybody was complaining, everybody was knocking at odd hours. In the night people would come and they would say, "This is wrong. Today we need rain and it is so hot." And somebody would come just afterward and he would say, "Don't bring rains – I am doing something and it will spoil everything."

And God was getting almost mad. "What to do? So many people, so many desires, and everybody expecting and everybody needs fulfillment, and their desires are so contradictory. The farmer wants the rain and the potter wants no rain because he has made pots and they will be destroyed; he needs hot sun for a few days." And so on and so forth...

Then God called his council and asked, "What to do? They will drive me crazy, and I cannot satisfy them all. Or they will murder me someday. I would like some place to hide."

They suggested many things. Somebody said, "That is not a problem, just go to Everest. That is the highest peak in the Himalayas, nobody will ever reach there."

God said, "You don't know! Just after a few seconds" – for God that *is* just after a few seconds – "Edmund Hillary will reach there with Tensing, and then

the trouble will start. Once they know, then they will start coming in helicop-
ters and buses, and everything will... No, that won't do. It will solve things for
a few seconds." Remember, God's time has a different way. In India we say
millions of years is one day to God, so a few seconds...

Then somebody suggested, "And why not the moon?"

He said, "That too is not very far; a few seconds more and somebody will
reach the moon."

And they suggested faraway stars, but God said, "That is not going to solve
the problem. It's simply a sort of postponement. I want a permanent solution."

Then an old servant of God came close, whispered something in his ear,
and God said, "You are right, that will do."

And the old servant had said, "There is only one place where man will
never reach – hide in man himself." And that is the place where God has been
hiding since then, in man himself. That is the last place that man will ever
think of.

The obvious is the missed because the ego is not interested. The ego is
interested in hard, difficult, arduous things, because there is a challenge. When
you win, you can claim. If the obvious is there and you win, what sort of victory
is this? You are not much of a winner. That's why man goes on missing the
obvious and goes on seeking the distant. How can you seek the distant when
you cannot even seek the obvious?

"What is it exactly that is obstructing my vision from seeing the obvious?"
The very desire is taking you astray. Drop the desire and you will see the
obvious.

"I just do not understand what to do and what not to do." You are not to
do anything. You have just to be watchful of all that is happening around you.
Doing is again an ego trip. Doing, the ego feels good – something is there to
do. Doing is food for the ego; it strengthens the ego. Non-doing, and the ego
falls flat on the ground; it dies, it is no longer nourished.

So just be a non-doer. Don't do anything as far as godliness, truth and the
search for it is concerned. It is not a search in the first place, so you cannot do
anything about it. Just be! Let me say it in another way: if you are in a state
of being, godliness comes to you. Man can never find it; it finds man. Just be
in a silent space – not doing anything, not going anywhere, not dreaming –
and in that silent space suddenly you will find it is there. It has always been
there; you were not silent, so you couldn't see it, you could not hear its still,
small voice.

"When will I be able to hear the sound of silence?" When? You ask a wrong
question. Now or never! Hear it now because it is there, the music is on, the

music is all over. You just need to be silent so that you can hear it. But never say when – when means you have brought the future in, when means you have started hoping and dreaming, when means not now. And it is *always* now, it is always now-time. For existence there is only one time: now, and only one place: here. There, then – drop them!

And the last question:

Osho,
Do you ever feel at a loss with words?

The question is from Rishi. Each time I utter a word I feel at a loss, because that which I want to say cannot be said, and that which has to be conveyed cannot be conveyed. Then you will naturally ask, why do I go on speaking?

I am trying hard. Maybe today I have failed, tomorrow...? Yesterday I failed, today...? I go on speaking in different ways – maybe this way you have not heard, in some other way maybe it will be closer to you. This way somebody has heard, you have not heard; in another way maybe you will be able to hear it. But I am at a loss continually. Words don't come easily because the message is wordless. I am not a priest, I am not trying to give you some dogma, I am not trying to explain some theory to you. Something has happened in me, something has happened to me; I am trying to convey that. I am trying to commune with you.

Words are very awkward. They are very tiny and very small; they cannot contain that which I want them to contain. So each moment I am at a loss. People who don't have any experience are never at a loss; any word will do.

I have heard a beautiful story, meditate over it...

A parish priest was having a few words with his bishop and in the course of conversation said, "It is all right for you, my lord, when you prepare a sermon you can deliver it to several churches in the diocese, but I have to give two new sermons every Sunday."

The bishop replied, "You should be able to give a sermon on almost any subject at a moment's notice, as I can."

"I will take you up on that," said the parson. "Come to my church next Sunday and I will put you to the test."

The bishop agreed and in due course went to the pulpit, to find a card with the single word *constipation* written on it. That was the subject. Without hesitation he started: "And Moses took two tablets and went out onto the mountainside..."

A priest is never at a loss, he has so many scriptures available; he can always find something from his memory. I am continually at a loss because what I want to say to you is not a subject matter; it is my subjectivity. What I want to say to you is my heart; it is not my mind. Unfortunately I have to use the mind because there is no other way. Even to convey the heart, one has to use the mind, hence the absurdity of it. It is very irrational; it is trying to do the impossible. But there is no other way; I am helpless.

But if you ask am I ever at a loss for words? I am, constantly. Each single word, and I hesitate: will it do, how can it do? Knowing it is not going to help, I go on using it; it is a necessary evil. Silence would be better, far better, but when I look at you, then I hesitate. If I become silent it will be even more difficult for you to come closer to me. You cannot understand the words, how will you be able to understand the silence? And if you can understand silence, you will be able to hear that silence in my words too.

If I become silent, then at the most five percent of you will be around me. Those five percent can understand through the words too, because they are listening to my silence, not to my words. So there is no problem for those five percent. But the other ninety-five percent who cannot understand words and cannot understand the silence contained in them will be simply lost. I will not be able to help them at all. Through my words they at least go on hanging around.

In their hanging around there is a possibility that, in some unguarded moment, they may have a contact with me. Some unguarded moment, and in spite of themselves they may come closer to me, they may stumble upon me, some unguarded moment, and I may penetrate into their heart, something may be stirred. It is a perhaps, but it is worth going on.

That five percent will be helped either way, but this ninety-five percent will not be helped by silence. And that five percent also, if I had been silent from the very beginning, would not be here. That five percent shows the way, so that the ninety-five percent by and by will be ninety percent, eighty-five percent, eighty percent...

The day I feel that at least fifty percent of people can understand silence, then words can be dropped. I am not very happy about them, nobody ever was, neither was Lao Tzu, nor was Saraha, nor was Buddha – nobody ever was. But they all had to use words. Not because silence cannot be a communion; silence can be a communion, but for that a very high consciousness is needed.

Once it happened...

Two great mystics of India, Kabir and Farid, met and for two days sat silently together. The disciples were very frustrated; they wanted them to talk, they wanted them to talk so that they could hear something valuable. They were hoping, for months they were hoping, that Kabir and Farid would meet and there would be a great showering, and they would enjoy it, but they were just sitting silently, and the disciples were dozing, yawning, "What to do? What has happened to these two people, because they were never silent before?" Kabir was never silent with his disciples and neither was Farid silent with his disciples, they were continually hammering on their disciples. "Why? What has happened? Have they gone dumb?" – but they could not say anything, it was not appropriate.

After two days, when Kabir and Farid hugged each other and said good-bye – that too in silence – and when the disciples were left with their masters, they jumped upon them. The followers of Kabir said, "What went wrong? For months we have been waiting for Farid to come, and he came, and you never spoke a single word. We were waiting and waiting... We got tired. These two days have been hell!"

And Kabir laughed. He said, "But there was nothing to say, he can understand silence. If I had said anything he would have thought me ignorant, because when silence is there and silence can say it, what is the use of words?"

And the followers of Farid asked Farid, "What happened? Why didn't you speak?"

Farid said, "Are you mad? Speaking with Kabir? We are exactly at the same space, so there is nothing to convey, nothing to say. The moment I looked into his eyes and he looked into my eyes, we recognized. The dialogue finished at the first moment."

"Then for two days... What were you doing for two days?"

Farid said, "We were just enjoying each other, each other's space; we were guests of each other. We overlapped each other, we overflowed each other, we mingled with each other. We danced, we sang, but it all happened in silence. When silence can speak, what is the need of language?"

I am continuously at a loss for words. Each word I utter very hesitatingly, knowing well that it is not going to suffice, it is not adequate. Nothing is ever adequate. Truth is so vast and words are so small.

Enough for today.

CHAPTER 7

don't live lukewarm

It is in the beginning, in the middle and the end,
yet end and beginning are nowhere else.
All those with minds deluded by interpretative thoughts
are in two minds, and so discuss
nothingness and compassion as two things.

Bees know that in flowers honey can be found,
that samsara and nirvana are not two.
How will the deluded ever understand?

When the deluded in a mirror look,
they see a face, not a reflection.
So the mind that has truth denied
relies on that which is not true.

Though the fragrance of a flower cannot be touched,
'tis all pervasive and at once perceptible.
So by un-patterned being-in-itself,
recognize the round of mystic circles.

Truth is, it simply is. It just is. It never comes into existence, never goes out of existence. It never comes, it never goes; it abides. In fact that which abides, we call truth; it remains. That which remains, remains forever, is called truth. It is in the beginning, it is in the middle, it is in the end. In fact there is no beginning, no middle, no end. It is all over.

Looked into deeply, the beginning is in it, the middle is in it, the end is in it; it pervades all, because only it is. It is the same reality that is being expressed in millions of forms. Forms are different, but the substance, the essence, is the same. Forms are like waves and the essence is like the ocean.

Remember, Tantra does not talk about God. To talk about God is a little anthropomorphic. It is to create God in man's image; it is to think about God in human terms – that is creating a limitation. God must be like human beings, true, but he must be like horses also, and he must be like dogs too, and he must be like rocks, and he must be like stars. He must be like all. Yes, man will be included as a form, but man cannot be *the* form.

Just think of God as a horse – it looks absurd. Think of God as a dog – it looks sacrilegious. But we go on thinking of God as man, and it doesn't look sacrilegious. It is the human ego. Man feels very, very happy when he can think in terms of God being like him. In the Bible it is said God created man in his own image – this was certainly written by man. If horses were writing *their* Bible they would not write that, certainly not. They might even write that God created the Devil in man's image, because God... How can God create man in his own image, and man has been so cruel to horses? Nothing in man seems to be divine, ask a horse – maybe the Devil, maybe a representative of Beelzebub, but not God at all.

Tantra drops that whole anthropomorphism. Tantra brings things to their right proportion, puts man in his right place. Tantra is a great vision, it is not centered on man, it is not centered on any partial attitude. It sees reality as it is, in its suchness, in its *tathata,* in its thusness. It does not talk about God. Instead of God, Tantra talks about truth.

Truth is nonpersonal, impersonal. Truth can have the qualities of all, there is no limitation in it. The Bible says: in the beginning God created the world. Tantra says: how can there be any beginning and how can there be any end? And when there is no beginning and no end, how can there be a middle? It is all eternity; it is not time. Tantra is a vision beyond time. In time there is a beginning and there is a middle and there is an end, but in eternity there is no beginning, no middle, no end. It simply is.

Truth is not temporal. In fact time exists in truth as a wave, and space exists in truth as a wave. It is not vice versa: truth does not exist in space, does not exist in time. Time and space exist in truth, they are modes of truth. Just as a horse is a form, a man is a form, so is space a form, a bigger wave, so is time.

Truth is timelessness. Truth is spacelessness. Truth is transcendence.

Truth exists by itself. Everything else exists with the support of truth. Truth is self-evident; nothing else is self-evident. Truth is the very ground of being, the ultimate substratum of existence.

Tantra does not create any ritual, does not create any worship, does not create any temple, does not create the priesthood; they are not needed. Man can stand face to face with truth in direct relationship; no mediator is needed, no priest is needed. The priests go on talking about truth and God and heaven and a thousand and one things, not knowing anything of what they are talking about. Words, mere words! They have not experienced; those words are just empty.

I was reading about a very famous priest who had been feeling unwell for some time; he called in his doctor who gave him a thorough overhaul. "Well," he said, "I will be quite frank with you. I am afraid that your lungs are not in good shape. You ought to spend a few months in Switzerland."

"Oh, dear," replied the priest. "I'm afraid I could not manage it. That will not be possible. My finances won't allow me. I'm a poor man, you know."

"Well it's up to you. It is either Switzerland or heaven."

The priest thought for a while and then said, "Oh, all right then, Switzerland."

Who wants to go to heaven? – not even the priest who continually talks about it. It is a trick to paint death in beautiful colors, but you know all the time it is death. How can you befool yourself?

Gurdjieff used to say that if you want to get rid of religion, live near a priest and you will get rid of religion. Maybe the ordinary human being is deceived, but how can the priest be deceived? He himself is creating the whole deception. No priest is ever deceived. They talk about one thing; they know something else. They say one thing; they do something else.

I was reading about a rabbi...

A Jew, a young man, came to his rabbi. "Rabbi, could I ask your advice on rather an important matter?"

"Certainly," came the reply.

"Well it's like this, I am in love with two girls. That is, I think I am. Now, one is very beautiful but has no money, while the other is rather nice but very plain, although she has plenty of money. What would you do in the circumstances? If you were me, rabbi, what would you do?"

"Well," said the rabbi, "I'm sure that in your heart you love the beautiful one, so I should go ahead and marry her."

"Right!" said the fellow. "Thank you, rabbi. That's what I'll do."

As he prepared to depart, the rabbi said, "Oh, by the way, I wonder if you could give me the address of the other girl?"

The priest, the rabbi, the parson, they know well that whatsoever they are talking about is just nonsense. It is for others, it is meant for others.

Tantra creates no priesthood. When there is no priesthood, religion is pure. Bring in the priest and he poisons it. Bring in the priest and it is bound to be poisoned because the priest has his own investment in it.

A man entered a pub and while he was drinking he saw a drunkard going out of the pub, somehow dragging himself, wavering. Then suddenly the drunkard started making gestures as if he was driving a car, and making the noises of the engine and the honking of the horn.

The newcomer was surprised. He asked the pub owner, "Why don't you tell this poor guy what he is doing?"

The pub owner said, "He always does that, whenever he has taken too much he does that. Now he will do it almost the whole night, he will go around and around in the town; he thinks he is driving a great car."

So the newcomer said, "But why don't you explain it to him?"

He said, "Why should we explain? He gives a dollar per week to keep the car washed."

When you have an investment in somebody's illusion, you cannot destroy that illusion. You would like that the illusion continues. Once the priest comes in, he has his investment in all your illusions: illusions about God, illusions about soul, illusions about heaven, illusions about hell; he now has a great stake. Now he depends on your illusions, he lives on your illusions; he exploits your illusions.

Tantra is disillusionment. It has not created any priesthood. Tantra says it is between you and truth itself, and there should be no one standing between you and truth. Let your heart be open to truth and truth is enough. Nobody is needed to interpret it; you are enough to know what it is. In fact the more you are full of the interpretations, the less is the possibility to know that which is.

Truth is in the beginning, truth is in the middle and truth is in the end. In fact there is no middle, no beginning, no end, it is all one. Truth is not passing, it abides.

This is the first sutra. Saraha says to the king:

> It is in the beginning, in the middle and the end,
> yet end and beginning are nowhere else.

...end and beginning are nowhere else. Now is truth-time, and here is truth-space. This very moment truth is converging here-now. This very moment is the beginning, is the middle, is the end. You need not go into the past to know when existence began, this very moment it is beginning. You need not go into the future to see when existence will end; it is ending this very moment. Each moment is a beginning and the middle and the end, because each moment existence is new. Each moment it is dying and is reborn. Each moment everything goes into the state of non-manifestation and comes back into the state of manifestation.

Now there are rumors in modern physics that this Tantra attitude may be true, may be ultimately true. It may be that each moment everything disappears and comes back again, pops back again, disappears, pops back again. But the interval is so small that we cannot see it. Tantra says that's why it remains fresh, why existence remains fresh.

Except for man everything is fresh, because it is only man who carries the load, the luggage of memory. That's why man becomes dirty, unclean, loaded, burdened; otherwise the whole existence is new and fresh. It carries no past and it imagines no future. It is simply here, totally here. When you are carrying the past, much of your being is involved in the past, a past which is not. And when you are imagining the future, much of your being is involved in the future, which is not, not yet. You are spread very thin, that's why your life has no intensity.

Tantra says to know truth one needs only one thing: intensity, total intensity. How to create this total intensity? Drop the past and drop the future. Then your whole life energy is focused on the small herenow, and in that focusing you are a fire, you are a fire alive. You are the same fire that Moses saw on the mountain, and God was standing in the fire, and the fire was not burning him. The fire was not burning even the green bush, the bush was alive and fresh and young.

The whole of life is fire. To know it you need intensity, otherwise one lives lukewarm. Tantra says there is only one commandment: don't live lukewarm. That is not a way to live; that is a slow suicide. When you are eating, be intensely there. The ascetics have condemned Tantrikas very much; they say they are just eat-drink-be-merry people. In a way they are true, but in a way they are wrong, because there is a great difference between the ordinary eat-drink-be-merry person and a Tantrika.

A Tantrika says that this is the way to know truth: while you are eating, let there be only eating and nothing else, then let the past disappear and the future too; then let your whole energy be poured into your food. Let there be love and affection and gratitude toward food. Chew each bite with tremendous energy and you will not only have the taste of the food but the taste of existence, because the food is part of existence. It brings life; it brings vitality, it brings *prana*. It makes you tick on, it helps you to remain alive; it is not just food.

Food may be the container – life is contained in it. If you taste only food and you don't taste existence in it, you are living a lukewarm life, then you don't know how a Tantrika lives. When you are drinking water, become thirst! Let there be an intensity to it, so each drop of cool water gives you tremendous joy. In that very experience of those drops of water entering your throat and giving you great contentment, you will taste godliness, you will taste reality.

Tantra is not ordinary indulgence; it is extraordinary indulgence. It is not ordinary indulgence because it indulges in existence itself. But, Tantra says, it is through the small things of life that you have the taste. There are no big things in life; everything is small. The small thing becomes big and great if you enter into it utterly, totally, wholly.

Making love to a woman or a man – be the love. Forget everything! In that moment let there be nothing else. Let the whole existence converge on your lovemaking. Let that love be wild, innocent – innocent in the sense that there is no mind to corrupt it. Don't think about it, don't imagine about it, because all that imagination and thinking keeps you thin, spread thin. Let all thinking disappear. Let the act be total. Be in the act – lost, absorbed, gone – and then, through love, you will know what truth is.

Tantra says: it can be known through drinking, it can be known through eating, it can be known through love. It can be known from every space, from every corner, from every angle, because all angles are truth. It is all truth.

And don't think that you are unfortunate because you were not in the beginning when God created the world. He is creating right now! You are fortunate to be here, you can see him creating this moment. And don't think you will miss when the world disappears with a bang; it is disappearing right now. Each moment it is created, each moment it disappears. Each moment it is born, each moment it dies.

So, Tantra says: let that be your life also, each moment dying to the past; each moment being born anew. Don't carry the load. Remain empty. And ...*yet end and beginning are nowhere else*. They are herenow.

> *All those with minds deluded by interpretative thoughts*
> *are in two minds, and so discuss*
> *nothingness and compassion as two things.*

Now there are two ways to describe this experience of truth, this existential experience, which is the experience of suchness. There are two ways to describe it because we have two types of words, the positive and the negative. Saraha's emphasis is on the negative because that was the emphasis of Buddha.

Buddha liked the negative very much for a certain reason. When you describe existence with a positive word, the positive word gives it a certain boundary; all positive words have boundaries. Negative words don't have any boundaries; the negative is unbounded.

For example, if you call existence all, God, absolute, then you are giving a certain boundary. The moment you call it absolute, the notion arises that the thing is finished, that it is no longer an ongoing process. You call it Brahma, then it seems the perfection has arrived, now there is no more to it. When you call it God, you give it a definition, and existence is so vast, it cannot be defined. It is so vast that all positive words fall short.

So Buddha has chosen the negative. He calls it *shunya:* nothingness, zero. Just listen to the word – *nothingness.* Taste it, turn it this way and that, you cannot find any boundary in it. Nothingness – it is unbounded. God? Immediately there is a boundary. The moment you say God, existence becomes a little smaller. The moment you say nothingness, all boundaries disappear.

Buddha's emphasis is on the negative for this reason. But remember: by nothing Buddha does not mean just nothing. When Buddha says *nothingness* he means no-thingness. No thing can define existence because all things are in it and it is bigger than all things. It is more than all the parts put together. Now this has to be understood – it is one of the Tantra attitudes.

You look at a roseflower. You can go to the chemist; he can analyze the flower and he will tell you of what constituents it is made: what matter, what chemicals, what colors. He can dissect it. But if you ask, "Where is the beauty of it?" he will shrug his shoulders. He will say, "I could not find any beauty in it. This is all that I could find: this many colors, this much matter, these chemicals. That's all. I have not missed anything and nothing has been left outside. You can weigh it, it is exactly the same weight as the flower. So nothing has left it. Then you must have been deluded, that beauty must have been your projection."

Tantra says beauty exists, but beauty is more than all the parts put together. The whole is more than the sum of the parts; that is one of the Tantra attitudes, of very great significance. Beauty is more than that of which it is constituted.

Or a small baby, bubbling with joy, giggling, happy – life is there. Dissect the small baby, put the baby on the surgeon's table – what will you find after dissection? There will be no bubbling joy, there will be no laughter, no giggling. There will be no innocence found, there will be no life found. The moment you cut up the baby, the baby is gone, the life disappears. But the surgeon will insist that nothing has left. You can weigh it; the parts weigh the same as the whole baby used to weigh. Nothing has left, it is exactly the same baby – but can you convince the mother that it is the same baby? Are *you* convinced it is the same baby? And if the child belonged to the surgeon himself, would he be convinced it is the same baby, these dead limbs lying on the table?

Something has disappeared. Maybe that something cannot be weighed, maybe that something is not measurable. Maybe that something is not physical, maybe that something is not material, but something has left. The baby will not dance any more, and the baby will not laugh any more, and the baby will not eat and will not drink and will not go to sleep and will not cry and will not be loving and will not be angry; something has left.

Tantra says the total is not the whole. The sum total of the parts is not the whole. The whole is more than the sum total of the parts, and in that moreness is the experience of life.

Nothingness means no-thingness. All things put together will not make existence, existence is more. It is always more than its parts. That's the beauty of it, that's the life of it. That's why it is so tremendously delightful, that's why there is celebration.

So these two – positive and negative words – have to be remembered. Tantra will be using negative words, Buddhist Tantra especially. Hindu Tantra uses positive words. That's one of the differences between Hindu Tantra and Buddhist Tantra. Buddha always uses *no* to describe the ultimate, because he says that once you start giving attributes, those attributes are limiting factors.

So Buddha says: "Go on eliminating: *neti, neti,* go on saying this is not, this is not, this is not, and then that which is left, after all denial, is." So remember that nothingness does not mean emptiness, it means fullness, but indescribable fullness. That indescribableness has been described through the word *nothing.*

All those with minds deluded by interpretative thoughts are in two minds... Saraha says: "Those who are too analytical, interpretative, continuously thinking in categories of mind are always divided, they are split. There is always a problem for them. The problem is not in existence, that problem comes from their own divided mind; their own mind is not one unity."

Now you can ask the scientist also. He says the mind is divided into two parts, the left and the right, and both function differently; not only differently, both function diametrically opposite to each other. The left-sided mind is analytical, and the right-sided mind is intuitive. The left-sided mind is mathematical, logical, syllogistic. The right-sided mind is poetic, artistic, aesthetic, mystic. They live in different categories, and there is only a very small bridge between the two, just a small link.

Sometimes it has happened that in some accident that link was broken and the man became two. In the Second World War there were many cases when the link was broken and the man became two. Then he was not one man. Then sometimes he would say one thing in the morning and by the evening he would completely forget about it and he would start saying something else. In the morning one hemisphere was working, in the evening another hemisphere was working – and these change.

Modern science has to look deeply into it. Yoga has looked very deeply into it: Yoga says, when your breathing changes... For near about forty minutes you breathe through one nostril, and then for forty minutes you breath through the other nostril. Up to now modern science has not thought about it, why the breathing changes and what the implications of it are, but Yoga has thought deeply about it.

When your left nostril is working, your right mind will function; when your right nostril is working, your left mind will function. This is a sort of arrangement inside, so one mind functions only for forty minutes and then it can rest. Somehow man has felt it even without knowing exactly what it is, that after each forty minutes you have to change your work. That's why in the schools, colleges, universities, they change the period after forty minutes. One part of the mind becomes tired. Forty minutes seems to be the ultimate limit; then it needs rest. So if you have been studying mathematics, it is good after forty minutes to study poetry; then you can come back to mathematics again.

This became very clear in the Second World War: that the bridge is very small, very fragile, and can be broken by any accident. And once it is broken the man functions as two, then he is not one man. For forty minutes he is one man, for forty minutes he is another man. If he borrows money from you, after forty minutes he will deny it, he will say, "I have never taken it." And he is not lying; remember he is not lying. The mind that has taken is no longer functioning, so he has no memory of it. The other mind has never borrowed, the other mind will simply, flatly deny: "Have you gone mad? I have never borrowed anything from you."

This happens even in those whose links are not broken. You can watch your own life and you will find a rhythm, continuously. Just a moment before you were so loving toward your wife and suddenly something clicks and you are no longer loving, and you are worried because you are linked; you have a slight memory, a remembrance of just a few minutes before. You were so loving and flowing, and what happened? Suddenly the flow is not there, you are frozen. Maybe you were holding the hand of your wife and the mind has changed and another mind has come in. The hand is in your hand, but suddenly energy is no longer flowing, now you want to leave the hand and escape from this woman. In fact you start thinking, "What are you doing here? Why are you wasting your time with this woman? What has she got?" And you feel very much anxiety also, because just a moment before you were promising, "I will love you for ever." And you become worried because you think this is not right: "Just a moment before I promised and I am already breaking the promise."

You are angry and you want to kill somebody, and just a few minutes later that anger is gone, you are no longer angry. You even start feeling compassion for the other person. You start feeling happy: "It is good that I have not killed him." Watch your mind and you will continuously find this shift; this gear goes on changing.

Tantra says there is a state of unity, when the bridge is no longer a small link but both the minds are really together. This togetherness is the real meeting of the man and the woman, because one part of the mind, the right mind, is feminine; the left mind is masculine. And when you are making love to a woman or a man, when the orgasm happens, both your minds come very close; that's why the orgasm happens. It has nothing to do with the woman, it has nothing to do with anything outside; it is just inside you. Watch…

Tantrikas have been watching the phenomenon of love very deeply because they think – and they are right – that the greatest phenomenon on earth is love, and the greatest experience of humanity is orgasm. So if there is some truth, that truth must be closer in the moment of orgasm than anywhere else. This is simple logic. One need not be very logical about it, it is such an obvious thing: that this is man's greatest joy, so this joy must somehow be opening a door to the infinite, maybe very slightly, very slowly, maybe just a part of it, but something of the infinite enters into it. For a moment the man and the woman are lost, they are no longer in their egos; their capsules disappear.

What happens exactly? You can ask the physiologists too. Tantra has discovered many things. One, when you are making love to a woman and you feel orgasmic and happy, it has nothing to do with the woman; the whole thing is happening within you. It has nothing to do with the woman's orgasm; they are not related at all.

When the woman is having her orgasm, she is having her orgasm; it has nothing to do with you. Maybe you just functioned as a trigger point, but the woman's orgasm is her private orgasm, and your orgasm is your private orgasm. You are both together, but your orgasm is yours; and when you are having your orgasm your woman cannot share your joy. No, it is just absolutely yours. It is private. She can see something is happening – on your face, in your body – but that is just an observation from the outside. She cannot participate in it. When the woman is having her orgasm, you are just a spectator, you are no longer a participant in it.

And even if you are both having orgasms together, then too your orgasmic joy will not be more or less; it will not be affected by the orgasm of the woman, nor will the woman's orgasm be affected by you. You are completely private, totally in yourself, one thing. That means all orgasm, deep down, is masturbatory. The woman is just a help, an excuse; the man is a help, an excuse, but not a must.

The second thing that Tantrikas have been watching is: when the orgasm is happening, it has nothing to do with your sex centers, nothing to do with them, because if the sex centers are cut from the brain you will have orgasm but you will not have any joy. So, deep down, it is not happening at the sex center, it is happening in the brain. Something from the sex center is triggered in the brain, it is happening in the brain, and modern research perfectly agrees with it.

You must have heard the name of the famous psychologist, Delgado. He has devised small instruments, he puts electrodes in the head and those electrodes can be controlled by remote control. You can have a small box of remote control push buttons. You can keep the box in your pocket and any time you want to have a sexual orgasm, you just push a button. It will have nothing to do with your sex center; that button will just stimulate something in your head. Inside the head it will activate those centers which are stimulated by sexual energy when it is released. It will stimulate them directly and you will have a great orgasm. Or you can push another button and you will become immediately angry. Or you can push another button and you will fall into a deep depression. You can have all the buttons in the box and you can change your mood as you like.

When Delgado experimented with his animals for the first time, particularly with mice, he was surprised. He fixed the electrode in his most favorite mouse, who was very well trained; he had been experimenting with him for many days, and a very intelligent mouse... He fixed his electrode in his head and gave a box to the mouse and trained him to push the button. Once he knew that when the button is pushed he has a sexual orgasm, the mouse went mad. In one day, six thousand times... He died, because he would not go anywhere. He would not eat, he would not sleep, he would... He forgot everything. He was just going crazy pushing the button again and again and again.

This modern research into the human brain says exactly what Tantra has been saying. First, the orgasm has nothing to do with the person outside, your woman, your man. Second, it has nothing to do with your sex energy. The woman triggers your sex energy, your sex energy triggers your brain energy; a brain center is triggered, but orgasm happens exactly there in the brain, in the head.

That's why pornography has so much appeal, because pornography can directly stimulate your brain. A beautiful woman or an ugly woman has nothing to do with your orgasm; an ugly woman can give you as beautiful an orgasm as a beautiful woman. But why don't you like the ugly woman? It does not appeal to the head, that's all. Otherwise, as far as orgasm is concerned, both are as capable. The ugliest woman or the most beautiful woman, a Cleopatra, is immaterial. But your head, your brain, is more interested in the form, in the beauty. Tantra says, once we understand this whole mechanism of orgasm, a great understanding can arise.

One step further: modern research agrees up to this point that orgasm happens in the brain. The woman's orgasm happens in the right side of the brain; about that modern research is not yet capable of saying something, but Tantra does. The woman's orgasm happens in the right brain, because that is the feminine center; and the male orgasm happens in the left, that is the male brain. Tantra goes further into this work, and Tantra says when both these sides of the brain come together great joy arises, total orgasm happens.

And these sides of the brain can come together very easily. The less analytic you are, the closer they are. That's why an interpretative mind is never a happy mind. A non-interpretative mind is happier. Primitive people are more joyous than the so-called civilized, the educated, the cultured. Animals are happier than human beings, birds are happier; they don't have the analytical mind. The analytical mind makes the gap bigger.

The more you start thinking logically, the bigger is the gap between the two minds. The less you think logically, the closer they come. The more poetic, the more aesthetic is your approach, the more they will come close and the more possibility there will be of joy, delight, celebration.

And the last point, which I think will take many centuries for science to come to. The last point is that the joy is not happening exactly in the brain either; it happens in the witness who is standing behind both these sides of the brain. Now if the witness is too much attached to the male mind, then the joy will not happen so much. Or if the witness is attached too much to the female mind, then joy will be a little more, but not so much.

Can't you see? – women are happier creatures than men. That's why they look more beautiful, more innocent, younger. They live long, they live more peacefully, more contentedly. They are not worried so much; they don't commit suicide so often, they don't go mad so often. The proportion is double: man goes mad twice as much, man commits suicide twice as often. With all the wars, if you include them also as suicidal and murderous activities, then man has been doing nothing else. Down the centuries he has been preparing for war, killing people.

The feminine mind is more joyous because it is more poetic, more aesthetic, more intuitive. But if you are not attached to any part and you are just a witness, then your joy is utter, ultimate. This joy we have called *anand,* bliss. To know this witness is to become one, absolutely one; then the woman and the man in you disappear completely, then they are lost in oneness. Then orgasmic-ness is your moment-to-moment existence. In that state, sex disappears automatically because there is no need. When a person lives orgasmically twenty-four hours a day, what is the need?

In your witnessing you become orgasmic. Then orgasm is not a momentary thing, it is simply your nature. This is what ecstasy is.

All those with minds deluded by interpretative thoughts are in two minds, and so discuss nothingness and compassion as two things. Saraha says that existence is nothingness. But don't be worried. By *nothingness* we don't mean that it is empty of everything. In fact we mean it is full; it is so full that we call it nothing. If we call it something that will make a demarcation, and it is unbounded, so we call it nothing. But Buddhists have been asked again and again: if it is nothing, then from where does the compassion come? Then why does Buddha talk about compassion?

Saraha says nothingness and compassion are two aspects of the same energy. Nothingness, in existence, means: I have to be nonegoistic. Ego means: I am something. If existence is nothing and I have to go into participation with this existence, if I have to become part of this existence, I have to drop the ego. The ego is making me somebody, is giving me a definition, a limitation. When existence is without any self, it is nothingness, *anatta.* Then I have also to be a nothing; only then these two nothings will be capable of meeting with each other and dissolving into each other. I have to become a no-ego, and in that no-ego is compassion.

With ego is passion; with no-ego is compassion. With ego there is violence, with no-ego there is love. With ego there is aggression, anger, cruelty; with no-ego there is kindness, sharing, affection. So Saraha says compassion has not to be cultivated. If you can live in nothingness, compassion will be flowing out of you of its own accord.

I have heard…

A man went to his bank manager to ask for a loan. After he had taken particulars, the bank manager said, "By rights I should refuse your request, but I will give you a sporting chance. Now, one of my eyes is made of glass, if you can tell me which one it is I will grant you the loan."

The customer looked at him intently for a few moments and then said, "It is your right eye, sir."

"That's correct," said the bank manager – he could not believe it, how he had guessed it. He said, "How did you guess?"

"Well," replied the customer, "it appeared to be more compassionate so I thought it must be a glass eye."

The ego, the calculating, cunning mind, is never compassionate, cannot be. In the very existence of the ego there is violence. If you are, you are violent. You cannot be nonviolent. If you want to be nonviolent, you will have to drop your I, you will have to become a nothingness. Out of nothingness is non-violence. It is not a question of practicing it; it is a question of becoming nobody, then it flows. It is the I that is blocking the flow of your energies; other-wise compassion is easy.

Saraha says nothingness and compassion are not two things. Be nothing and there will be compassion. Or attain to compassion and you will find you have become nothing, a nobody.

This characterization of existence as nothingness is a great step toward annihilation of the ego. This is one of the greatest contributions of Buddha to the world. Other religions go on cultivating, in subtle ways, the same ego. The righteous person starts feeling, "I am righteous"; the moralist thinks, "I am more moral than others." The man who practices religion thinks himself more religious than others. But these are all ego qualities, and they are not going to help, ultimately.

Buddha says that cultivation is not the question, but understanding, aware-ness that there is nobody in you. Have you ever looked inside? Have you ever gone inside and looked around? Is anybody there? You will not find anybody; you will find silence, you will not come across anybody.

Socrates says, "Know thyself." And Buddha says, "If you come to know, you will not find any thyself." There is nobody inside; there is pure silence. You will not hit against any wall, and you will not come across any self. It is empti-ness. It is as empty as existence itself, and out of that emptiness, everything is flowing; out of that nothingness, everything is flowing.

> Bees know that in flowers honey can be found,
> that samsara and nirvana are not two.
> How will the deluded ever understand?

Have you watched it? Around a small, beautiful lake there are many flowers. Frogs may be sitting just by the roots of the flowers, but they don't know that flowers have honey in them. *Bees know that in flowers honey can be found...* Waterfowl, swans, fish and frogs do not know, even when they are living just by the side of the plants. To know that flowers have honey, one has to become a bee. Saraha says the Tantrika is like a bee and the ascetic is like a frog. He lives by the side of the flowers, and he is not at all aware. Not only is he not aware, he denies. He thinks bees are indulgent, that bees are fools, that they are destroying themselves.

Saraha says ascetics are like frogs, and the Tantrika is like a bee. In the phenomenon of sex the sublime is hidden. In the energy of sex there is a key which can open the door of existence. But frogs do not know it. Tantra says it is such an obvious fact that out of sex energy life is born. That means that sex must be at the very core of life. Life comes through sex energy. A new child is born through sex energy, a new being enters into existence, a new guest comes into existence through sex energy. Sex energy is the most creative energy. Certainly, if we look deep into it we may find even greater, more creative possibilities of it.

Tantra says sex is the lowest rung of the sex energy, of libido. If you enter into it with more awareness and you search into it deeply, you will find the highest possibility, *samadhi*, hidden in it.

Sex is like *samadhi* fallen into the mud; it is like a diamond which has fallen into the mud. Clean the diamond; the mud cannot destroy it. The mud is only on the surface; just wash the diamond and again it is shining with all its luster and all its glory.

In sex is hidden the diamond. In love is hidden God. When Jesus says God is love, he may have got this idea somewhere from Tantra, because the Jewish God is not love at all; it cannot come from the Jewish tradition. The Jewish God is a very angry God.

The Jewish God says, "I am very jealous, I am very angry, and if you go against me, I will take revenge." The Jewish God is a very dictatorial God. Love does not fit with the Jewish idea. From where did Jesus get this idea that God is love? Every possibility is it came through the Tantric school of India, that it spread from the Tantrikas. Saraha was here three hundred years before Jesus. Who knows, maybe it was Saraha and Saraha's idea which traveled. There are absolute reasons to think so. There is every possibility of Jesus' coming to India, there is every possibility of messengers spreading from India toward Israel.

But one thing is certain, that it is Tantra which has looked at God as love energy. But Christians missed. Even Jesus gave the hint that God is love – they have missed. They have interpreted it as God-loving; they missed it. Jesus is not saying God is loving, Jesus is saying God is love, God is equal to love. It is a formula: love is equal to God. If you go deep into love you will find God, and there is no other way to find God.

Bees know that in flowers honey can be found, that samsara and nirvana are not two. How will the deluded ever understand? Who are these deluded

people, these frogs? The ascetics, the so-called mahatmas, who go on denying the world because they say God is against the world. This is foolish! If God
is against the world, then why does he go on creating it? He can simply stop it
any moment if he is so against it. If he agreed with your mahatmas, he would
have stopped it long before. But he goes on creating. He does not seem to be
against it, he seems to be absolutely for it.

Tantra says God is not against the world: samsara and nirvana are not two,
they are one. The ascetic fights sex energy, and through that fighting he starts
falling away from God, falling away from life, falling away from the vital source
of life, and then there are perversions – bound to be. The more you fight with
something, the more perverted you become, and then you start finding tricks,
back doors to enter into it again.

So the ascetic, on the surface, fights with sex, fights with life, and deep
down starts fantasizing about it. The more he represses, the more he becomes
obsessed with it; the ascetic is the obsessed person. The Tantrika is a very
natural person; he has no obsessions. But the irony is that the ascetic thinks
that the Tantrika is obsessed, the ascetic thinks that the Tantrikas talk about
sex – "Why do they talk about sex?" – but the real obsession is in the ascetic.
He does not talk about it – or even if he talks about it he only talks to condemn it – but he continually thinks about it. His mind goes on reeling around
and around it.

It is difficult to go against existence. Even if you go, your failure is certain.
Mind will find some way or other.

I have heard...

A Jew was talking to a friend and said, "I prefer to sleep alone; I believe in
celibacy. In fact ever since we were married, my wife and I have had separate
rooms."

"But," said the friend, "supposing during the night you feel that you would
like a little love, what do you do?"

"Oh," replied the other, "I just whistle."

The friend was astonished, but went on to ask, "But supposing it is the
other way round and your wife feels that she would like a little loving – what
happens then?"

"Oh," he replied, "she comes to my door and taps, and when I answer she
says, 'Ikey, did you whistle?'"

Whether you stay in the same room or not, what does it matter? The mind
will find some way – the mind will start whistling. The woman cannot whistle
of course; she is expected not to be so vulgar as to whistle. But she can come

and knock on the door and can ask, "Ikey, did *you* whistle?"

Mind is very cunning. But one thing is certain: you cannot escape the reality of life. If you try to escape, your cunning mind will find ways, and will become more cunning and you will be more in the trap of the mind. I can't see any ascetic ever realizing truth – impossible. He denies life, how can he realize truth?

Truth has to be alive, truth has to be with life, in life. That's why to my sannyasins I never say leave life. I say be in life, be totally in it. There is the door, somewhere in the marketplace.

...that samsara and nirvana are not two, says Saraha, *how will the deluded ever understand?* But the frogs... How will they ever understand? Become a bee!

Let this be a deep remembrance in you, at least for my sannyasins: become a bee, don't become a frog. These flowers of life are carrying the honey of god-liness – collect!

> *When the deluded in a mirror look,*
> *they see a face, not a reflection.*
> *So the mind that has truth denied*
> *relies on that which is not true.*

The mind is like a mirror, it only reflects. It can only give you a shadow experience, never the real, never the original. It is like a lake, you can see the full moon reflected in the lake, but the reflection is not the real moon. If you start thinking that the reflection is the real moon, you will never find the real moon.

Says Saraha: *When the deluded in a mirror look, they see a face, not a reflection.* What is the difference in seeing a face and not a reflection? When you start seeing the face in the mirror, you are deluded; you are thinking, "That is my face." That is not your face; that is just the reflection of your face. In the mirror there can be no real face, only reflections.

The mind is a mirror! It reflects reality, but if you start believing in that reflection you believe in untruth, in the image, and that very belief will become a barrier. Saraha says: "If you want to know the truth, put the mind aside, otherwise it will go on reflecting and you will go on looking at the reflection." Put the mind aside. If you really want to know the real, then go against the reflection.

For example, you see the full moon reflected in the lake. Now where are you going to seek the full moon? Are you going to take a jump into the lake? Are you going to dive deep into the lake to find the moon? Then you will never find it. You may even miss yourself. If you really want to see the real moon, then go against the reflection, just in the diametrically opposite direction, then you will find the moon. Don't go in the mind; go diametrically opposite to the mind.

The mind analyzes; you synthesize. The mind believes in logic. Don't believe in logic. The mind is very calculative, mind is very cunning; you be innocent. Go in the opposite direction. The mind asks for proofs, reasons; don't ask for proofs and reasons. That is the meaning of trust: go in the opposite direction. The mind is a great doubter. If you doubt you go into the mind, if you don't doubt you go against the mind. Doubt not! Life is to be lived, not to be doubted. Life is to be trusted. Go hand in hand with trust and you will find truth; go with doubt and you will go astray.

The search for truth is the search in the opposite direction to the mind because the mind is a mirror, it reflects. To put the mind aside is what meditation is all about; to put the thoughts aside, thinking aside, mentation aside, is what meditation is all about. When you can look into reality without thoughts reflecting it, truth is herenow; then you are truth and *all* is truth. The mind is the great faculty of delusion, illusion, of dreaming.

> *Though the fragrance of a flower cannot be touched,*
> *'tis all pervasive and at once perceptible.*
> *So by unpatterned being-in-itself,*
> *recognize the round of mystic circles.*

A great sutra! *Though the fragrance of a flower cannot be touched...* You cannot touch the fragrance of a flower, it is *...all pervasive and at once perceptible.* You can smell it; you cannot see it but you can smell it, it surrounds you. You cannot touch it, it is not tangible, it is not touchable. If you make tangibility the criterion of truth, then you will say it is not true. Truth is not thinkable. If you think, you will miss.

Truth can be experienced, but cannot be known. Truth can be realized, but not concluded, just as the fragrance of a flower cannot be seen by the eyes and cannot be heard by the ears. If you make it a criterion: "Unless I hear the smell I will not believe, unless I see the smell I will not believe," then you are creating barriers and you will never come to know it.

And by and by, if you don't believe it, if you don't believe at all, you will lose the faculty of smelling it because any faculty that is not used, not trusted, falls out of use, becomes by and by crippled. Trust is a faculty. You have been with doubt so long, married to doubt so long that you say, "I will first need rational proofs – I doubt." So you remain with doubt, and truth can be known only through trust, just as fragrance can be known only by smell. It is there if you smell. If you trust, truth is there.

Shraddha – trust, faith, – simply indicates one thing: that the faculty to know truth is not doubt, is not skepticism. If you insist on doubt, you remain with doubt.

It is *...all pervasive and at once perceptible.* With trust it is immediately there, at once. Not a single moment is lost. *So by un-patterned being-in-itself...* And what is trust? I have never come across such a beautiful definition of trust: *So by un-patterned being-in-itself...* Don't pattern yourself. All patterning is a sort of armoring, all patterning is a sort of protection; all patterning is a way to avoid. Be open, don't be patterned.

So by un-patterned being-in-itself... If you are not patterned, if you are simply open you don't have any armor, you are not protecting yourself by logic, doubt, this and that, you are simply vulnerable, unpatterned, unpro-tected, under the open sky, all doors open. Let friend or foe enter, anybody, but all doors are open. In that openness you are being-in-itself, you are in a state of suchness, you are empty, you are nothingness, and you will recognize what truth is.

...recognize the round of mystic circles. And then you will see that out of this suchness two circles are arising: one is of nirvana, another is of samsara. Two waves are arising in this ocean of suchness: one is of matter, another is of mind – but both are waves, and you are beyond both. Now there is no divi-sion, no distinction. Truth is neither mind nor matter, truth is neither samsara nor nirvana, truth is neither unholy nor holy; all distinctions have disappeared.

If you bring your mind to the ultimate reality, it will not allow you to see the ultimate reality. It will bring something of its own falsities with it.

I was reading an anecdote; meditate over it.

A man arrived at the pearly gates and on being asked his name replied, "Charlie Graball."

"I don't think we have any notice of your coming," he was informed. "What was your occupation in earthly life?"

"Scrap-metal merchant," the visitor said.

"Oh," said the angel, "I will go and inquire." When he returned, Charlie Graball had disappeared. So had the pearly gates.

Charlie Graball, scrap-metal merchant – you carry your habits to the very end.

Maybe mind is useful as far as the man-made world is concerned. Maybe mind is useful as far as thinking about matter is concerned. But to carry this mind to the innermost core of your reality is dangerous; it will disturb there.

Let me say it in this way: doubt is helpful in the world of science. In fact without doubt there would be no science; doubt is the very methodology of science, and because science has become so prevalent, has been so successful in the past, it seems that doubt has become the only methodology to inquire with. So when you go in, you carry doubt – that's not right. When you are going outward, doubt is helpful; when you are going inward, doubt is a barrier. Trust, less and less doubt... If you want to come in, doubt less and less and less, and let there be a moment when there is no doubt left. In that state of no-doubt, you will be at the center. If you want to know the outside world, trust will not be helpful.

That also has happened in the past in the East. We came to know the inner reality through trust, so we thought through trust we can create science also. We were never able to create science. In the East we could not create any great science – nothing to say about it, nothing much, because we entered inside with trust, so we thought trust was the only method to inquire through; that was fallacious. We tried trust on the outside objective things and we failed; the East has been a failure as far as science is concerned. The West has succeeded in science through doubt – now the same fallacy: they think doubt is the only right, valid method to know. It is not. Now, if you try doubt in the inner world you will fail as certainly as the East has failed in scientific growth.

Doubt is good about objects; trust is good about subjectivity. Doubt is good if you are moving further away from your center toward the periphery; trust is good if you are moving toward the center away from the periphery. Trust and doubt are like two wings.

The humanity that is going to be born in future will be capable of doubting and trusting, both together. That will be the highest synthesis: the synthesis of East and West, the synthesis of science and religion. When a man is capable of both doubting and trusting, when doubt is needed, when he is going outward, he doubts, and when trust is needed he puts the doubt aside and trusts. A man who is capable of both will be beyond both, *certainly* beyond both, because he will use both and he will know that he is separate from both – that's transcendence. That beyond-bothness is great freedom. That is exactly what nirvana is: great freedom.

Meditate on these sutras. Saraha is saying great things in simple words, he was showering his great insight on the king. You can also partake of this great insight. You can go very deep into human reality with Saraha.

And always remember, that is the only way to go to the ultimate reality. The human reality is the only way to go to the ultimate reality, because that is where you are. One can proceed only from the place where one is. Sex is your reality;

samadhi can be approached through it. The body is your reality, bodilessness can be approached through it. Outwardness is your reality; inwardness can be approached through it. Your eyes are looking outward; they can be turned inward.

Enough for today.

be a bee, be free!

The first question:

Osho,
I am a frog. I know I'm a frog because I like swimming in murky dark green water
and hopping about in slimy mud. And what is honey anyway? If a frog can be in
an unpatterned state of being, will it become a bee?

Certainly! To be a bee is everybody's possibility; everybody can grow
into being a bee. An unpatterned, alive, spontaneous life, moment-to-
moment life, is the gate to it, the key to it. If one can live not out of the
past then one is a bee, and then there is honey all around.

I know it is difficult to explain this to a frog. The question is right: "What is
honey anyway?" The frog has never known about it. He lives just at the root of
the plant where flowers bloom and bees collect honey, but he has not moved
in that dimension.

By "frog" Saraha means a person who lives out of the past, encaged in
the past, in the memories. When you live through the past you only appar-
ently live, you don't really live. When you live through the past, you live like
a mechanism, not like a man. When you live through the past, it is a repetition, it is a monotonous repetition; you miss the delight, the joy of life and
existence. That's what honey is: the joy of life, the sweetness of just being
herenow, the sweetness of just being able to be. That joy is honey – and

there are millions of flowers blooming all around, the whole existence is full of flowers.

If you know how to collect honey, if you know how to be joyful, you become an emperor; if you don't know, you remain a beggar. These birds singing here – honey is showering. The bee will collect, the frog will miss. This sky, this sun, these people around you – everybody is carrying infinite sources of honey, everybody is flowing with sweetness and love. If you know how to collect it and how to taste it, it is all over the place, godliness is all over the place. The taste of godliness is what Saraha calls honey.

The bee has a few things... And those have to be understood, and they are very dangerous things. One: the bee is never attached to any flower. That is the most profound secret: the bee is not attached to any flower. It has no nuclear family, no wife, no husband. It simply moves wherever any flower invites it. It has freedom.

Man has become confined to the family. Tantra is very much against family, and the insight is great. Tantra says it is because of the family that love has been completely damaged, that the sweetness of life has been completely poisoned. People are clinging to each other, people are trying to possess each other, not to enjoy but to possess. Possession has become the enjoyment. A great shift has happened: you are with a woman not to enjoy her, you are *not* enjoying her; you are with a man not to enjoy the man, you are not enjoying at all, but to possess. Politics has entered, ambition has entered, economics has entered; love is not there.

Love knows no possession. I am not saying you cannot live with a woman for long – you can live for lives together – but there will be no family. By family I mean the legal possession; by family I mean the demand. The husband can demand from the wife, he can say, "You are obliged to give me love." Nobody is obliged to give anybody love. The husband can force the wife to love him. When you can force somebody to love, love disappears; then there is only pretension. Then the wife is fulfilling a duty, then the husband is fulfilling a duty. Duty is not love. Love is honey, duty is white sugar – you will suffer from diabetes sooner or later. White sugar is poison – it is pure poison. Yes, it tastes similar, a little bit like the honey, but it is not honey.

The family is very possessive. The family is against man, it is against society, it is against universal brotherhood. The boundary of the family is your imprisonment. You may not feel it because you have become accustomed to it. Crossing the boundary of a country, have you not felt humiliated? Then you know that the country was not your country, it was a great prison. Getting out and coming in you will know. At the checking post, at the airport, you will know while passing through customs that you are a prisoner. Freedom was bogus, just holy cow dung. But living in a country, if you don't cross the boundary you will never know about it; you will think you are free. You are not free! Yes, the rope is big – you can move around, but you are not free.

And so is the case with the family. If you start crossing the boundary, then you will know you are imprisoned. If you start loving the neighbor then your family will be against you. If you are happy with some other woman, your wife is your enemy. If you are dancing with some other man, your husband is mad at you. He would like to kill you, and just the other day he was saying, "I love you so much, I can die for you." Just cross the boundary, and you will know that you are a prisoner. Never cross the boundary and you can live in blissful ignorance that everything is okay.

It is attachment, it is possessiveness that has destroyed your capacity to go to many flowers, to taste all the flowers. Just think of a bee collecting honey from just one flower – that honey will not be very rich, the richness comes out of the variety. Your life is boring, it is not rich.

People come to me and they say, "I am bored! What should I do?" They are doing everything to get bored and they are thinking as if boredom is happening from somewhere else. Now, you are living with a woman you don't love anymore, but your scriptures say once you have promised, you have to fulfill the promise: be a man who keeps a promise. Once you are committed, you have to fulfill the commitment. Now if you are bored, nothing is surprising – love has disappeared.

It is as if you are forced to eat the same thing every day – how long will you be able to enjoy it? You may have enjoyed it on the first day, yes, the second day, the third day, but then it will start getting on your nerves. Then for ever and ever... Then you will start getting bored, and because man is bored he invents a thousand and one ways to distract his mind: sits glued to the chair before the TV for six hours – what stupidity – or goes to the movie, or listens to the radio, or reads the newspaper, or goes to clubs where bored people just like you gather together. One is trying to somehow distract oneself from the boredom that has happened out of the relationship.

Try to understand. Tantra says: "Be a bee, be free!" Tantra is not saying that if you love a woman then don't be together with her. Be together with her, but the commitment is toward love, not toward the woman; the commitment is toward love, not toward the man. This is a basic difference: you are committed to love, you are committed to happiness. When love is disappearing, when happiness has gone, then say thank you and move on.

Such should be the case with everything in your life. If you are a doctor and you are bored with your job, then you should be capable of dropping it any moment, whatsoever the cost. With risk, life becomes adventure. But you think, "Now I am forty, forty-five, and how can I drop out of the job? And it is going very well financially." But spiritually, psychologically, you are dying. You are slowly committing suicide. Then it is perfectly okay, if you want to destroy yourself and save the bank-balance, it is perfectly okay.

But the moment you feel that the job is no longer a satisfying job, drop out of it! This is the Tantra revolution. The moment you see that something is no longer appealing, has lost the quality of allurement, of enchantment, is no longer magnetic, then don't cling to it. Then say, "I am sorry." Then feel grateful for the past, for all that has happened through the person, through the job, through anything, but remain open in the future. This is the meaning of being a bee. Saraha says: "Only the bee knows that each flower is full of honey."

But I am not saying go to the opposite extreme. There are people who can go to the opposite extreme, and man is so stupid. Just the other day I was reading about a commune in Germany: the Action Analysis Commune. Now there is a rule in their commune that you cannot sleep with the same woman two nights together. Now this is again foolish. It seems man is such an idiot that you cannot help him. If you sleep two nights consecutively with one woman, the commune throws you out.

Now, the one extreme has proved wrong. This is another extreme; it will prove wrong. The first extreme was repressive: you have to sleep with the same woman for years, for your whole life, with the same man, not knowing why, why you continue. The society says so, the state says so, the priest and the politician say so: that on the stability of your nuclear family the whole society depends. This insane society depends on the insane family; the insane family is the unit, the brick, out of which this whole prison is made.

Insane politicians depend on the insane family; insane religions depend on the insane family. They have been repressing you; they don't allow you to move away from the woman or the man or the relationship. They say you have to stay with it, otherwise you are a criminal, a sinner. They make you very afraid of hell and hellfire.

Now, the opposite extreme: that you cannot stay with the same woman the next night again, this too is again repressive. If you want to be with her the next night also, then... Then it will be repression. With the first, love disappeared and boredom entered. With the second, intimacy will disappear and you will feel very alienated, like an island. You will not feel your roots anywhere.

Tantra says just in the middle is the way. Be in that place, be with that person, be in that job where you are enjoying, otherwise change. If you can enjoy one woman for your whole life it is beautiful, it is tremendously beautiful. You are fortunate, because then intimacy will grow, your roots will go into each other, your beings will become intertwined. By and by you will become one person, one soul, and that is a great experience, the highest peak of Tantra will be known through it. But this is not family; this is a love affair. You have gone into the very depth of love.

Now these types of people, this "A. A. Commune," these types of people are dangerous. They think they are doing something very great; they are simply reacting. The society has done something wrong, now they are reacting too much and going to the opposite extreme, which will be again wrong. Man has to be balanced somewhere: first thing.

Second thing: Saraha says, "unstructured, unpatterned state of being." If you live through habit you cannot enjoy life because the habit is of the old. How can you enjoy the same thing again and again and again? Your mind remains the same; then there will be boredom. You can even change the woman and the man, but you are the same, so fifty percent is always the same, there will be boredom.

So first Tantra says never get obsessed with any person, remain free of personalities. Second, Tantra says remain free of your past – then you are a hundred percent free, like a bee. You can fly anywhere; nothing holds you, you have utter freedom.

Don't persist in your past pattern. Try to be inventive, try to be innovative. Be an adventurer, a discoverer; enjoy life through new ways, find new ways to enjoy it. In fact go on finding new ways of doing the same old thing, but find new ways.

There are infinite possibilities. You can come to the same experience from many doors, and each door will give you a different vision. Then life is rich; there is sweetness, there is joy, there is celebration – that is what honey is. Don't be confined to the pattern of a frog. Yes, the frog can hop a little, jump here and there; he cannot fly and cannot know that each flower is carrying divine fragrance. What Saraha means by honey is a poetic metaphor for godliness, that each being is carrying divinity.

People come to me and they say, "We want to know God, where is God?" Now the question is just absurd. Where is he *not!* You ask where he is; you must be dead, blind. Can't you see him: that only he is? In the tree and in the bird, in the animal, in the river, in the mountain, in man, in woman – he is everywhere. He has taken so many forms to surround you, to dance around you. From everywhere he is saying, "Hello!" and you don't listen. From everywhere he is calling you. From everywhere he is inviting you: "Come to me!" but you somehow keep your eyes closed, or you have blinkers on, you don't look anywhere.

You just look in a very narrow way, in a very focused way. If you are looking for money you only look for money, then you don't look anywhere else.

If you are looking for power you look only for power and you don't look anywhere else. Remember, God is not in money, because money is man-made
and godliness cannot be man-made. When I say God is everywhere, remember those things have not to be included which man has made. God cannot be
man-made. God is not in money; money is a very cunning invention of man,
and God is not in power; that too is again a madness of man. Just the very idea
to dominate somebody is insane. Just the very idea that: I should be in power
and others should be powerless is the idea of a madman, a destructive idea.

God is not in politics and God is not in money and God is not in ambition,
but God is everywhere where man has not destroyed him, where man has not
created something of his own. This is one of the most difficult things in the
modern world, because you are surrounded by too many man-made things.
Can't you just see the fact of it?

When you are sitting near a tree, it is easy to feel God. When you are sitting
on an asphalt road... You can go on searching on the asphalt road; you will
not find God. It is too hard. When you are in a modern city, just cement and
concrete buildings all around, in the jungle of cement and concrete you will not
feel God, because man-made things don't grow. That is one of the problems:
man-made things don't grow. They are dead, they don't have any life. God-
made things grow. Even mountains grow! The Himalayas are still growing, still
getting higher and higher. A tree grows, a child grows.

Man-made things don't grow, even the greatest. Even a painting of a Picasso
will never grow, so what to say about a cement, concrete building? Even the
music of Beethoven will never grow, so what to say about technology, about
man-made machines?

Watch! Wherever you see growth, there is God, because only God grows,
nothing else. In everything only God grows. When a new leaf is coming in the
tree, it is God coming out of the tree. When the bird is on the wing, it is God
on the wing. When you see a small girl laughing or a small boy giggling, it is
God giggling. When you see tears flowing from the eyes of a woman or a man,
it is God crying.

Wherever you find aliveness, yes, there is God. Listen carefully, come closer,
feel carefully, be cautious – you are on holy ground.

Tantra says: if you drop your blinkers – that's what Tantra means by "unpatterned life-style" – if you drop your blinkers, if you start opening your eyes as
wide as they are destined to be, suddenly you will see that you can see in all
directions. You have been befooled by society to look only in certain directions;
society has converted you into a slave.

There is a great conspiracy: each small child is damaged. Immediately,
the moment he is born, society starts damaging him. So before he becomes

alert he is a slave and crippled, crippled in a thousand and one ways. When a person is crippled, he will have to depend on the family, on the society, on the state, on the government, on the police, on the army – he will have to depend on a thousand and one things, and because of that dependence he will always be a slave, he will never become a free man. So the society cripples, cripples in such subtle ways. You don't know; before you are able to know anything, you are already crippled.

Tantra says: regain health! Undo whatsoever society has done to you. By and by become alert and start undoing the impressions that society has forced upon you, and start living your life. It is your life, it is nobody else's business, it is *utterly* your life. It is existence's gift to you, a personal gift to you, with your initials on it. Enjoy it, live it! And even if you have to pay much for it, it is worth paying. Even if sometimes you have to pay for your life with your life that too is perfectly good.

Tantra is very rebellious. It believes in a totally different kind of society, which will not be possessive, which will not be money-oriented, which will not be power-oriented. It believes in a different kind of family, which will not be possessive and which will not be life-negative. Our families are life-negative.

A child is born and the whole family tries to kill all joy of life. Whenever the child is joyful, he is wrong; and whenever he is sad and long-faced and sitting in the corner, everything is okay. The father says, "Good! Very good boy." The mother is very happy because he is no trouble. Whenever the child is alive, there is danger, and everybody is trying to kill the joy of the child.

Basically all joy is related to sexuality. The society and the family are so afraid of sex that they cannot allow children to be sexually joyful – and that is the base of all joy. It is very restrictive; children are not allowed even to touch their genital organs, they cannot play with them. The father is afraid, the mother is afraid, everybody is afraid. Their fear comes from their own parents; they are neurotic.

Have you not seen? A child is playing with his genital organs and imme-diately everybody jumps on him: "Stop! Don't do that again!" And he is not doing anything, he is simply enjoying his body, and naturally the sex organs are the most sensitive, most alive, most pleasurable. Suddenly something is cut off in the child. He becomes afraid. Something in his energy is blocked. Now whenever he feels happy he will feel guilty too; now guilt has been put inside him, and whenever he feels guilty he will feel that he is a sinner, he is doing something wrong.

This is my observation of thousands of sannyasins: whenever they are happy, they start feeling guilty. They start looking for the parent who must be somewhere around, and who will say, "Stop! What are you doing?" Whenever they are sad, everything is okay. Sadness is accepted, misery is accepted; joy is denied.

The children are somehow prevented from knowing the joys of life. The father and mother are making love. Children know it; they hear the sounds, sometimes they feel that it is happening, but they are not allowed to participate in it, not even allowed to be there. It is ugly, it is destructive. The children should participate. When the father and mother are making love, the children should play around; they should feel happy with father and mother making love.

They should know that love is a beautiful phenomenon, not anything ugly, nothing to be made private, nothing to hide, nothing to be kept secret. It is not a sin; it is a joy. If the children can see their father and mother making love, thousands of sexual diseases will disappear from the world, because their joy will erupt, and they will feel respectful toward the father and the mother. Yes, one day they will also make love, and they will know that it is a great celebration. If they can see their father and mother making love as if they are praying and meditating, there will be a great impact.

Tantra says that love should be made with such celebration, with such great religious awe, reverence, that the children can feel that something great is happening. Their joy will grow, and there will not be any guilt in their joy. This world can be tremendously happy, but this world is not happy. It is very rare to come across a happy man – very, very rare. And only the happy man is sane; the unhappy man is insane.

Tantra has a different vision, a totally, radically different vision of life. You can become a bee, in freedom you become a bee. A slave, you are a frog; free, you are a bee. Listen to the message of freedom. Get ready to be free of everything that creates bondage. You have to be alert and be aware.

The second question:

Osho,
I am a schoolmaster, a sort of watered-down mixture of priest, politician and scholar – all that you abhor. Is there any hope for me? Also I am fifty-six. Had I best just live out the rest of this life in patience and hope for better luck next time?

No hope for the priest, for the politician, for the scholar, not even in the next life. But you can drop being a priest, being a politician, being a scholar, any moment, and then there is hope, but no hope for the priest, no hope for the politician, no hope for the scholar. I am absolute about that. Even in the next life or next to next – never. I have never heard of any priest ever reaching nirvana, never heard about any politician ever meeting God, never heard about any scholar ever becoming aware, knowing, wise. No, it is not possible.

The scholar believes in knowledge, not in knowing. Knowledge is from the outside, knowing is from the inside. The scholar trusts information. The information goes on collecting, it becomes a heavy load, but nothing grows inside. The inner reality remains the same, as ignorant as before.

The politician seeks power; it is an ego trip. And those who arrive are humble people, not egoists. Egoists never arrive, by their very egoism they cannot arrive. Ego is the greatest barrier between you and existence, the only barrier. So the politician cannot come.

And the priest, the priest is very cunning. He is trying to become a mediator between you and God, and he has not known God at all. He is the most deceptive, the most fraudulent. He is doing the greatest crime a man can do: he is pretending that he knows God, not only that, but that he will make God available to you, that go and follow him and he will take you to the ultimate. He does not know anything of the ultimate. He may know the rituals, how to do the prayers, but he does not know the ultimate. How can he lead you? He is a blind man, and when the blind man leads the blind, they both fall into the ditch.

No hope for the priest, no hope for the politician, no hope for the scholar, but there is hope, Anand Tejas, for you. The question is from Anand Tejas. There is hope for you, every hope for you.

And it is not a question of age. You may be fifty-six, or seventy-six, or a hundred and six – that doesn't matter. It is not a question of age because it is not a question of time. To enter into eternity, any moment is as right as any other moment, because one enters here-now. How does it make any difference how old you are, fifty-six or sixteen? The sixteen-year-old has to enter right now and the fifty-six-year-old has to enter right now; both have to enter right now. The sixteen years are not helpful neither are fifty-six years helpful. There are different problems for both, that I know. When a sixteen-year-old young man wants to enter into meditation or into godliness his problem is different from that of a man who is fifty-six. What is the difference? If you finally weigh them, the difference is quantitative, not qualitative.

The sixteen-year-old has only sixteen years of past; in that way he is in a better situation than the man who is fifty-six; he has a fifty-six year past. He has a big load to drop, many attachments: fifty-six years of life, many experiences, much knowledge. The sixteen-year-old has not that much to drop. He has a little load, less luggage, a small suitcase – just a small boy's suitcase. The fifty-six-year-old has much luggage. This way the younger is in a better situation.

But there is another thing: the old man has no more future. A fifty-six-year-old, if he is going to be alive for seventy years on the earth, has only fourteen years left – no more future, no more imagination, no more dreaming. There is not much space. Death is coming. The sixteen-year-old has a long future: much imagination, many dreams.

The past is small but the future is big for the young; for the old the past is big, the future is small. On the whole it is the same: it is seventy years, both have to drop seventy years. For the young, sixteen years in the past, the remaining years in the future. The future has also to be dropped as much as the past. So finally, in the final reckoning, there is no difference.

There is every hope for you, Anand Tejas, and because you have asked the question, the work has already started. You have become alert about your priest, politician, scholar – that's good. To become aware of a disease, to know what it is, is half the treatment.

And you have become a sannyasin; you have taken a step into the unknown already. If you are going to be with me, you will have to say goodbye to your priest, your politician, your scholar. But I feel confident that you can do it, otherwise you would not have even asked. You have felt that it is meaningless, all that you have been doing up to now is meaningless – you have felt it. That feeling is of tremendous value.

So I will not say just be patient and wait for the next life, no. I am never in favor of postponement; all postponement is dangerous and is very tricky. If you say, "I will postpone – in this life nothing can be done," you are avoiding a situation. Everything can be done. You are simply pretending. It is a trick to save yourself: "Now what can be done? I am so old."

Even on the deathbed, at the last moment, the change can happen. Even when the person is dying, he can open his eye for a single moment, and the change can happen. He can drop the whole past before death comes in and he can die utterly fresh. He is dying in a new way; he is dying as a sannyasin, he is dying in deep meditation. And to die in deep meditation is not to die at all because he will be dying with full awareness of the deathless.

It can happen in a single moment. So please don't postpone, don't say, "Had I best just live out the rest of this life in patience?" No, drop it right now. It is worthless – why carry it, why wait? And if you wait, the next life is not going to be any different. That's why I say there is no hope for the priest and the politician and the scholar. The next life will start from where you end this life: again the priest, again the politician, again the scholar. You will have the next life in continuity with this life. How is it going to be different? It will be the same wheel turning again.

And this time I am available to you. Who knows? – next time I may not be available. This time, somehow, groping in the dark, you have stumbled upon me. Next time, one never knows… This time you took fifty-six years to come to a man through whom revolution is possible. Who knows, next time you may become more burdened – certainly you will become more burdened – the past life's burden, and the next life's burden. You may take seventy years to come, or to find a master.

That's why I say there is no hope for the politician and the priest and the scholar in the future either. But for you there is every hope, because you are not a priest and you are not a scholar and you are not a politician. How can you be? These are things that gather around, but the innermost core remains always free. Don't think of yourself in terms of being a frog, be a bee!

The third question:

Osho,
What role should charity play in the life of a sannyasin?

The question is not from a sannyasin, it is from Philip Martin. The first thing, Philip Martin: become a sannyasin. You should not ask questions about others, that is not gentlemanly; you should ask questions about yourself. Be a sannyasin and then ask. But the question is meaningful, so I am going to answer it anyway. I have the feeling that sooner or later Philip Martin will be a sannyasin; even the question shows some leaning.

First thing: all the religions of the world have emphasized charity, *dhan,* too much. And the reason is that man has always felt guilty with money. Charity has been preached so much to help man feel a little less guilty. You will be surprised: in old English there is the word *gilt,* which means money. In German there is a word *geld* which means money, and *gold* is very close by! *Guilt, gilt, geld, gold* – somehow deep down a great guilt is involved in money.

Whenever you have money you feel guilty. It is natural, because so many people don't have money, how can you avoid guilt? Whenever you have money, you know somebody has become poorer because of you. Whenever you have money, you know somewhere somebody will be starving, and your bank balance goes on becoming bigger and bigger. Some child will not get the medicine needed to survive, some woman will not get the medicine; some poor man will die because he will not have food. How can you avoid these things? They will be there. The more you have money, the more these things will be there erupting in your consciousness; you will feel guilty.

Charity is to unburden you from your guilt, so you say, "I am doing something; I am going to open a hospital, going to open a college. I give money to this charity fund, to that trust…" You feel a little happier. The world has lived in poverty, the world has lived in scarcity; ninety-nine percent of people have lived a poor life, almost starving and dying, and only one percent of people have lived with richness, with money. They have always felt guilty. To help them the religions developed the idea of charity; it is to rid them of their guilt.

So the first thing I would like to say is: charity is not a virtue, it is just a help to keep your sanity intact; otherwise you will go insane. Charity is not a virtue; it is not a *punya*. It is not that you have done something good when you do charity, it is only that you repent for all the bad that you have done in accumulating the money. To me charity is not a great quality, it is repentance, you are repenting. One hundred rupees you have earned, ten rupees you give in charity; it is repentance. You feel a little good, you don't feel that bad; your ego feels a little more protected. You can say to God, "Not only was I exploiting, I was also helping poor people." But what type of help is this? On one hand you snatch one hundred rupees, and on the other hand you give ten rupees – not even the interest.

This is a trick that was invented by the so-called religious people, to help not the poor but the rich. Let it be absolutely clear, this is my attitude: it has been a trick to help the rich, not the poor. If the poor were helped, that was just a consequence of it, a by-product, but that was not the goal of it.

What do I say to my sannyasins? I don't talk about charity; that word seems ugly to me. I talk about sharing, and with a totally different quality in it. Sharing: if you have, you share, not because by sharing you will be helping others, no, but by sharing you will be growing. The more you share, the more you grow, and the more you share, the more you have, whatsoever it is. It is not only a question of money, if you have knowledge, share it; if you have meditation, share it; if you have love, share it. *Whatsoever* you have, share it, spread it all over; let it spread like the fragrance of a flower going to the winds. It has nothing to do with poor people, particularly; share with anybody that is available. And there are different types of poor people.

A rich man may be poor because he has never known any love – share love with him. A poor man may have known love but has not known good food – share food with him. A rich man may have everything and has no understanding – share your understanding with him – he is also poor. There are a thousand and one types of poverty. Whatsoever you have, share it.

But remember, I am not saying that this is a virtue and God is going to give you a special place in heaven, that you will be specially treated, that you will be thought a VIP, no. By sharing herenow you will be happier. A hoarder is never a happy man. A hoarder is basically constipated. He goes on hoarding; he cannot relax, he cannot give. He goes on hoarding, whatsoever he gets, he simply hoards it. He never enjoys it because even in enjoying it you have to share it, because all enjoyment is a sort of sharing.

If you want to really enjoy your food, you will have to call friends. If you really want to enjoy food, you will have to invite guests; otherwise you will not be able to enjoy it. If you really want to enjoy drinking, how can you enjoy it alone in your room? You will have to find friends, other drunkards – you will have to share.

Joy is always a sharing; joy does not exist alone.

How can you be happy alone, absolutely alone? Think! How can you be happy, absolutely alone? No, joy is a relationship; it is togetherness. In fact even those people who have moved to the mountains and have lived an alone life, they also share with existence. Not alone – they share with the stars and the mountains and the birds and the trees; they are not alone.

Just think, for twelve years Mahavira was standing in the jungles alone, but he was not alone. I say to you, on authority, he was not alone. The birds were coming and playing around, the animals would come and sit around, and the trees would shower their flowers on him, and the stars would come, and the sun would rise. The day and the night, and summer and winter, and the whole year round, it was joy. Yes, he was away from human beings – he had to be – because human beings had done so much damage to him that he needed to be away from them so that he could be healed. It was just to avoid human beings for a certain period so they didn't go on damaging him. That's why sannyasins have moved sometimes into aloneness, just to heal their wounds; otherwise people will go on poking their knives into your wounds and they will keep them green, they will not allow you to heal, they will not give you a chance to undo what they have done.

For twelve years Mahavira was silent, standing, sitting, with the rocks and the trees, but he was not alone, he was crowded by the whole existence. The whole existence was merging upon him. Then the day came when he was healed, his wounds cured, and now he knew nobody could harm him. He had gone beyond. No human being could hurt him any longer. He came back to relate to human beings, to share the joy that he had attained there. Jaina scriptures talk only about the fact that he left the world, they don't talk about the fact that he came back into the world. That is only half the story; that is not the full story.

Buddha went into the forest, but he came back. How can you go on being there when you have it? You will have to come back and share it. Yes, it is good to share with trees, but trees cannot understand that much. They are very dumb. It is good to share with animals, they are beautiful. But the beauty of a human dialogue; it is impossible to find anywhere else, the response, the human response. They *had* to come back to the world, to human beings, to share their joy, their bliss, their ecstasy.

Charity is not a good word; it is a very loaded word. I talk about sharing. To my sannyasins I say, share! In the word *charity* there is some ugliness also; it seems that you have the upper hand and the other is lower than you, that the other is a beggar, that you are helping the other, he is in need. That is not good. To look at the other as if he is lower than you: you have and he has not, is not good, it is inhuman.

Sharing gives a totally different perspective. It is not a question of whether the other has or not, the question is that you have got too much, you have to share. When you give charity, you expect the other to thank you. When you share, you thank him that he allowed you to pour your energy, which was getting too much upon you. It was getting heavy, you feel grateful. Sharing is out of your abundance. Charity is for others' poverty, sharing is out of your richness. There is a qualitative difference.

No, I don't talk about charity, but sharing. Share! Whatsoever you have, share, and it will grow. That is a fundamental law: the more you give, the more you get. Never be a miser in giving.

The fourth question:

Osho,
During the meditations my mind still goes five hundred miles per hour. I never experience silence, and whatever witnessing happens is very short, like flashes. Am I wasting my time?

Your mind is mighty slow. Only five hundred miles per hour?! And do you think this is speed? You are mighty slow. Mind knows no speed; it goes so fast, it is faster than light. Light travels 186,000 miles in one second, mind is faster than that. But nothing to be worried about – that is the beauty of the mind, that is a great quality. Rather than taking it negatively, rather than fighting with it, befriend the mind.

You say: "During the meditations my mind still goes five hundred miles per hour." Let it go! Let it go faster! Be a watcher, watch the mind going around so fast, with such speed. Enjoy this, enjoy this play of the mind. In Sanskrit we have a special term for it, we call it *chidvilas,* the play of consciousness. Enjoy it, this play of mind rushing toward stars, moving so fast from here and there, jumping all over existence. What is wrong in it? Let it be a beautiful dance, accept it.

My feeling is that what you are doing is you are trying to stop it – you cannot do that. Nobody can stop the mind. Yes, the mind stops one day, but nobody can stop it. The mind stops, but that is not out of your effort, the mind stops out of your understanding.

Just watch and try to see what is happening, why this mind is rushing; it is not rushing without any reason. You must be ambitious. Try to see why this mind is rushing, where it is rushing. You must be ambitious; if it thinks about money, then try to understand: the mind is not the question. You start dreaming about money, that you have won a lottery or this and that, and then you even start planning how to spend it, what to purchase and what not. Or the mind thinks you have become a president, a prime minister, and then you start thinking what to do now, how to run the country, or the world. Just watch the mind, what the mind is going toward. There must be a deep seed in you. You cannot stop the mind unless that seed disappears.

The mind is simply following the order of your innermost seed. Somebody is thinking about sex, then somewhere there is repressed sexuality. Watch where the mind is rushing, look deep into yourself, find where the seeds are.

I have heard...

The parson was very worried. "Listen," he said to his verger, "somebody has stolen my bicycle."

"Where have you been on it, rector?" inquired that verger.

"Only round the parish on my calls."

The verger suggested that the best plan would be for the rector to direct his Sunday sermon to the Ten Commandments. "When you get to 'Thou shalt not steal,' you and I will watch the faces – we will soon see."

Sunday came. The rector started in fine flow about the commandments, then lost his thread, changed his subject, and trailed off lamely.

"Sir," said the verger, "I thought you were going to..."

"I know, Giles, I know. But you see, when I got to 'Thou shalt not commit adultery,' I suddenly remembered where I had left my bicycle."

Just see where you have left your bicycle. The mind is rushing for certain reasons. The mind needs understanding, awareness; don't try to stop it. If you try to stop it, in the first place you cannot succeed; in the second place, if you can succeed – one can succeed if one makes perseverant effort for years – if you can succeed, you will become dull. No satori will happen out of it.

In the first place, you cannot succeed, and it is good that you cannot succeed. If you can succeed, if you manage to succeed, that will be very unfortunate – you will become dull, you will lose intelligence. With that speed there is intelligence, with that speed there is continuous sharpening of the sword of thinking, logic, intellect. Please don't try to stop it. I am not in favor of dullards, and I am not here to help anybody to become stupid.

In the name of religion many people have become stupid. They have almost become idiots, just trying to stop the mind without any understanding about why it is going with such speed – why, in the first place? The mind cannot go without any reason. Without going into the reason in the layers, deep layers of the unconscious, they just try to stop. They can stop, but they will have to pay a price, and the price will be that their intelligence will be lost.

You can go around India; you can find thousands of sannyasins, mahatmas. Look into their eyes – yes, they are good people, nice but stupid. If you look in their eyes there is no intelligence, you will not see any lightning. They are uncreative people, they have not created anything; they just sit there. They are vegetating, they are not alive people; they have not helped the world in any way. They have not even produced a painting or a poem or a song, because even to produce a poem you will need intelligence, you will need certain qualities of the mind.

I would not suggest that you stop the mind, rather that you understand. With understanding, there happens a miracle. The miracle is that with understanding, by and by – when you understand the causes and those causes are looked into deeply, and through that looking deeply into those causes, those causes disappear – the mind slows down. But intelligence is not lost because the mind is not forced.

What are you doing if you don't remove the causes by understanding? You are driving a car, for example, and you go on pressing the accelerator and at the same time you try to press the brake. You will destroy the whole mechanism of the car, and there is every possibility you will have some accident. This cannot be done together. If you are pushing the brake then leave the accelerator; don't push it any more. If you are pushing the accelerator, don't push the brake. Don't do both these things together, otherwise you will destroy the whole mechanism; you are doing two contradictory things.

You carry on with ambition, and you try to stop the mind? Ambition creates the speed, so you are accelerating the speed, and putting a brake on the mind; you will destroy the whole subtle mechanism of the mind. The mind is a very delicate phenomenon, the most delicate in the whole of existence – so don't be foolish about it. There is no need to stop it.

You say: "I never experience silence and whatever witnessing happens is very short, like flashes."

Feel happy! Even that is something of tremendous value. Those flashes they are not ordinary flashes. Don't just take them for granted. There are millions of people for whom even those small glimpses have not happened. They will live and die and they will never know what witnessing is, even for a single moment. You are happy; you are fortunate.

But you are not feeling grateful. If you don't feel grateful, those flashes will disappear. Feel grateful – they will grow – with gratitude everything grows. Feel happy that you are blessed, they will grow. With that positivity, things will grow.

"...and whatever witnessing happens is very short..." Let it be very short. If it can happen for a single split moment, it is happening, you will have the taste of it, and with the taste, by and by, you will create more and more situations in which it happens more and more.

"Am I wasting my time?" You cannot waste time because you don't possess time. You can waste something that you possess. Time you don't possess. Time will be wasted anyway; whether you meditate or not, time will be wasted. Time is rushing by. Whatsoever you do – do anything, or don't do anything – time is going. You cannot save time so how can you waste time? You can waste only something which you can save. You don't possess time. Forget about it.

And the best use you can have of time is to have these small glimpses, because finally you will come to see only those moments which were moments of witnessing have been saved, and all else has gone down the drain. The money that you earned, the prestige that you earned, the respectability that you earned, has all gone down the drain. Only those few moments when you had some flashes of witnessing, only those moments are saved. Only those moments will go with you when you leave this life. Only those moments can go because those moments belong to eternity, they don't belong to time.

But feel happy it is happening. It always happens slowly, slowly – one drop by one drop a great ocean can become full. It happens in drops, but in the drops the ocean is coming. Just receive it with gratitude, with celebration, with thankfulness. Don't try to stop the mind. Let the mind have its speed. Watch!

The fifth question:

Osho,
How can the sex energy be transformed into *samadhi*?

Tantra and Yoga have a certain map of the inner man. It will be good if you understand that map; it will help you, it will help you greatly. Tantra and Yoga suppose that there are seven centers in man's physiology: the subtle physiology, not in the body. In fact they are metaphors, but they are very, very helpful to understand something of the inner man. These are the seven chakras.

First, and the most basic, is *muladhar*. That's why it is called *muladhar*. *muladhar* means the most fundamental, the basic. *Mul* means the basic, of the roots. The *muladhar* chakra is the center where sex energy is right now available, but the society has damaged that chakra very much.

This *muladhar* chakra has three angles to it: one is oral, the mouth, the second is anal, and the third is genital. These are the three angles of the *muladhar*. The child starts his life with the oral, and because of wrong upbringing, many people remain at the oral, they never grow. That's why so much smoking, chewing gum, continuous eating, happens. This is an oral fixation; they remain in the mouth.

There are many primitive societies which don't kiss. In fact if the child has grown well, kissing will disappear. Kissing shows the man has remained oral; otherwise what does sex have to do with lips? When for the first time primitive societies came to know about civilized man's kissing, they laughed, they simply thought it ridiculous – two persons kissing each other. It looks unhygienic too, just transferring all sorts of illnesses, infections to each other. What are they doing, and for what? But humanity has remained oral.

The child is not satisfied orally; the mother does not give her breast as much as the child needs, the lips remain unsatisfied. So the child will smoke cigarettes later on, will become a great kisser, will chew gum, or will become a great eater, continually eating this and that. If mothers give their breast as much as the child needs, then the *muladhar* is not damaged.

If you are a smoker, try a pacifier – and you will be suddenly surprised – it has helped many people, I give it to many people. If somebody comes and asks me how to stop smoking, I say, "Just have a pacifier, a false breast, and keep it in the mouth. Let it hang around your neck and whenever you feel like smoking, just put the pacifier in the mouth and enjoy it. And within three weeks you will be surprised, the urge to smoke will have disappeared."

Somewhere the breast is still appealing, that's why man is so focused on feminine breasts. There seems to be no reason. Why, why is man so much interested in feminine breasts? Painting, sculpture, film, pornography, everything seems to be breast-oriented. And women are continually trying to hide and yet show their breasts; otherwise the bra is just foolish. It is a trick to hide and show together; it is a very contradictory trick. And now in America, where every foolish thing goes to its extreme, they are injecting chemicals into women's breasts, silicon and other things. They are stuffing breasts with silicon so they become bigger and can get the shape, the shape that ungrown-up humanity wants to see. This childish idea... But man remains somehow oral. This is the lowest state of the *muladhar*.

Then a few people change from oral and they become stuck at the anal, because the second great damage happens with toilet training. Children are forced to go to the toilet at a certain time. Now, children cannot control their bowel movements; it takes time, it takes years for them to come to control. So what do they do? They simply force, they simply close their anal mechanism, and because of this they become anal-fixated.

That's why so much constipation exists in the world. It is only man who suffers from constipation. No animal suffers from constipation, in the wild state no animal suffers from constipation. Constipation is more psychological; it is damage to the *muladhar*, and because of constipation many other things grow into the human mind.

A man becomes a hoarder – a hoarder of knowledge, hoarder of money, hoarder of virtue – becomes a hoarder and becomes miserly. He cannot leave anything. Whatsoever he grabs, he holds it. With this anal emphasis, a great damage happens to the *muladhar*, because the man or the woman has to go to the genital. If they get fixated at the oral or at the anal, they never go to the genital. That is the trick society has used up to now not to allow you to become fully sexual.

Then anal fixation becomes so important that genitals become less important, hence so much homosexuality. Homosexuality will not disappear from the world until and unless anal orientation disappears. Toilet training is a great, dangerous training. Then, if some people become genital – somehow they are not fixated at the oral and the anal and become genital – then there is great guilt created in humanity about sex: sex means sin.

Christianity has thought sex so much a sin that it goes on pretending and proposing and trying to prove a foolish thing: that Christ was born out of a miracle, that he was not born out of a man-woman relationship, that Mary was a virgin. Sex is such a sin; how can Jesus' mother have sex? It is okay for other ordinary people, but for Jesus' mother to have sex? Then how can Jesus, such a pure man, be born out of sex?

I was reading…

There was a young woman who did not seem very well, so her mother took her to the doctor. The mother did all the talking; she was that sort.

"She's pregnant," said the doctor.

"Doctor, I must call you a fool. My daughter has never so much as kissed a man! Have you darling?"

"No, mama, I have not even held a man's hand."

The doctor left his chair, walked to the window, and gazed at the sky. There was a long silence then mother asked, "Is there anything wrong out there, doctor?"

"Not at all, not at all. Only the last time this happened, a star appeared in the east, and I don't want to miss it this time!"

Sex has been condemned so much you cannot enjoy it. That's why energy remains fixated somewhere: oral, anal, genital. It cannot go upward.

Tantra says man has to be relieved, destructured from these three things. So Tantra says that the first great work has to happen in the *muladhar*. For oral freedom screaming, laughing, shouting, crying and weeping are very helpful. That's why my choice of encounter, gestalt, primal and that type of group are helpful in relieving the oral fixation. To relieve you of the anal fixation *pranayam, bastrika,* fast chaotic breathing, is very helpful, because it hits directly on the anal center and makes you able to relieve and relax the anal mechanism. Hence the dynamic meditation is of tremendous value.

And then the sex center: the sex center has to be relieved of the burden of guilt, condemnation. You have to start relearning about it, only then can the damaged sex center function in a healthy way. You have to start relearning to enjoy it without any guilt.

There are a thousand and one types of guilt. In the Hindu mind there is a fear that semen energy is great energy: if even a single drop is lost, you are lost. This is a very constipatory attitude: hoard it. Nothing is lost. You are such a dynamic force; you go on creating that energy every day. Nothing is lost.

The Hindu mind is too obsessed with *virya,* with semen energy: not a single drop should be lost. They are continuously afraid. So whenever they make love, if they make love, then they feel very much frustrated, very much depressed because they start thinking so much energy is lost. Nothing is lost. You don't have a dead quota of energy; you are a dynamo – you create energy, you create it every day. In fact the more you use it the more you have it. It functions like the whole body: if you use your muscles they will grow, if you walk your legs will be strong, if you run you will have more energy to run. Don't think that a person who has never run and suddenly runs will have energy. He will not have energy, he will not even have the musculature to run. Use all that has been given to you by existence and you will have more of it.

So there is a Hindu madness: to hoard. This is on the lines of constipation. And now there is an American madness that is like diarrhea: just throw, go on throwing, meaningfully, meaninglessly, go on throwing. So even a man of eighty years continuously thinks in childish ways. Sex is good, sex is beautiful, but it is not the end. It is the alpha but not the omega. One has to go beyond it, but going beyond it is not a condemnation. One has to go through it to go beyond it.

Tantra has the healthiest attitude about sex. It says sex is good, sex is healthy, sex is natural, but sex has more possibilities than just reproduction. Sex has more possibilities than just fun. Sex is carrying something of the ultimate in it, of *samadhi.*

The *muladhar* chakra has to be relaxed, relaxed from constipation, relaxed from diarrhea. The *muladhar* chakra has to function at the optimum, one hundred percent; then energy starts moving.

The second chakra is *svadhishthan*. That is the hara, the death center. These two centers are very damaged because man has been afraid of sex and man has been afraid of death. So death has been avoided: don't talk about death. Just forget about it, it does not exist. Even if sometimes it exists, don't notice it, don't take any note of it. Go on thinking that you are going to live forever; avoid death.

Tantra says: don't avoid sex and don't avoid death. That's why Saraha went to the cremation ground to meditate, not to avoid death. And he went with the arrowsmith woman to live a life of healthy, full sex, of optimum sex. On the cremation ground, living with a woman, these two centers had to be relaxed: death and sex. Once you accept death and you are not afraid of it, once you accept sex and you are not afraid of it, your two lower centers are relaxed.

Those are the two lower centers, which have been damaged by society, badly damaged. Once they are relieved... The other five centers are not damaged. There is no need to damage them because people don't live in those other five centers. These two centers are naturally available. Birth has happened: the sex center, *muladhar*. Death is going to happen: *svadhishthan*, the second center. These two things are there in everybody's life, so society has destroyed both centers and tried to manipulate man, dominate man, through these two things.

Tantra says meditate while you make love, meditate while somebody dies, go watch, see. Sit by the side of a dying man. Feel and participate in his death. Go in deep meditation with the dying man. And when a man is dying there is a possibility to have a taste of death, because when a man is dying he releases so much energy from the *svadhishthan* chakra. He has to release it because he is dying. The whole repressed energy on the *svadhishthan* chakra will be released because he is dying; without releasing it he will not be able to die. So when a man dies or a woman dies, don't miss the opportunity. If you are close by a dying man sit silently, meditate silently. When the man dies, in a sudden burst the energy will be all over, and you can have a taste of death. That will give you a great relaxation. Yes, death happens, but nobody dies. Yes, death happens, but in fact death never happens.

While making love, meditate so that you can know that something of *samadhi* penetrates into sexuality. While meditating on death, go deep into it so that you can see that something of the deathless enters into death. These two experiences will help you to go upward very easily. The other five centers fortunately are not destroyed; they are perfectly in tune, energy just has to move through them. If these first two centers are helped, energy starts moving. So let death and love be your two objects of meditation.

The last question:

Osho,
Is "Osho" going to be like the Coca-Cola advertisement all over the world?

Why not?
Enough for today.

love is the language

When, in winter, still water by the wind is stirred,
it takes as ice the shape and texture of a rock.
When the deluded are disturbed by interpretative thoughts,
that which is as yet un-patterned turns very hard and solid.

Mind, immaculate in its very being can never be polluted
by samsara's or nirvana's impurities.
A precious jewel deep in mud will not shine,
though it has luster.

Knowledge shines not in the dark,
but when the darkness is illumined,
suffering disappears at once.
Shoots grow from the seed and leaves from the shoots.

He who thinks of the mind in terms of one or many,
casts away the light and enters the world.
Into a raging fire he walks with open eyes.
Who could be more deserving of compassion?

Ah, the beauty of existence, the sheer delight of it, the joy, the song, and the dance! But we are not here. We appear to exist, but we are almost nonexistential because we have lost contact with existence, we have ɔots in it. We are like an uprooted tree: the sap no longer flows; the juɪᴄ ، dried up. No more flowers will come, and the fruits... Not even birds come to take shelter in us.

We are dead because we are not yet born. We have taken physical birth as our birth – that is not our birth. We are still existing as potentialities, we have not become actual; hence the misery. The actual is blissful, the potential is miserable. Why is it so? The potential cannot be at rest, the potential is continuously restless; it *has* to be restless, something is going to happen. It hangs in the air; it is in limbo.

It is like a seed – how can the seed rest and relax? Rest and relaxation are only known by the flowers. The seed has to be deep in anguish, the seed has to continuously tremble. The trembling is: whether he will be able to become actual, whether he will find the right soil, whether he will find the right climate, whether he will find the right sky. Is it going to happen, or will he simply die without being born? The seed trembles inside, the seed has anxiety, anguish. The seed cannot sleep; the seed suffers from insomnia.

The potential is ambitious, the potential longs for the future. Have you not watched this in your own being? You are continuously longing for something to happen and it is not happening; you are continuously hankering, hoping, desiring, dreaming, and it is not happening, and life goes on flowing by. Life goes on slipping out of your hands, and death comes closer and you are not yet actual. Who knows which will come first: actualization, realization, blossoming, or maybe death? Who knows? Hence there is the fear, the anguish, the trembling.

Søren Kierkegaard has said man is a trembling. Yes, man is a trembling because man is a seed. Friedrich Nietzsche has said man is a bridge. Exactly right! Man is not a place to rest, it is a bridge to pass over. Man is a door to go through, you cannot rest at being man. Man is not a being; man is an arrow on the way, a rope stretched between two eternities. Man is a tension. It is only man who suffers from anxiety, the only animal on the earth who suffers from anxiety. What is the cause of it?

It is only man who exists as potentiality. A dog is actual; there is nothing else to happen. A buffalo is actual; there is nothing more, it has already happened. Whatsoever could happen has happened. You cannot say to a buffalo, "You are not yet a buffalo." That will be foolish. But you can say to man, "You are not yet man." You can say to man, "You are incomplete." You cannot say to a dog, "You are incomplete." That will be stupid to say; all dogs are fully complete.

Man has a possibility, a future. Man is an opening. So the constant fear: whether we are going to make it or not, whether we are going to make it this time or not. How many times have we missed before? Are we going to miss again? That's why we are not happy. Existence goes on celebrating; there is great singing, there is great joy, there is great rejoicing. The whole existence is always in an orgy; it is a carnival. The whole existence at each moment is in an orgasm. Somehow man has become a stranger.

Man has forgotten the language of innocence. Man has forgotten how to relate with existence. Man has forgotten how to relate with himself. To relate with oneself means meditation, to relate with existence means prayerfulness. Man has forgotten the very language. That's why we appear like strangers, strangers in our own home, strangers to ourselves. We don't know who we are, and we don't know why we are, and we don't know for what we go on existing. It seems to be an endless waiting: waiting for Godot.

Nobody knows whether Godot will ever come or not. In fact, who is this Godot? Nobody knows even that. But one has to wait for something, so one creates some idea and waits for it. God is that idea, heaven is that idea, nirvana is that idea. One has to wait because one has somehow to fill one's being; otherwise one feels very empty. Waiting gives a sense of purpose and a direction. You can feel good – at least you are waiting. It has not happened yet, but it is going to happen some day. What is it that is going to happen?

We have not even raised the right question – what to say about the right answer – we have not even asked the right question. And remember, once the right question is asked the right answer is not very far away, it is just by the corner. In fact it is hidden in the right question itself. If you go on asking the right question, you will find the right answer through that very questioning.

So the first thing that I would like to tell you today is that we are missing, we are continuously missing, because we have taken the mind as the language to relate with existence. The mind is a way to cut oneself off from existence. It is to put oneself off; it is not the way to put oneself on. Thinking is the barrier. Thoughts are like Walls of China around you, and you are groping through the thoughts, you cannot touch reality. Not that reality is far away; godliness is just close by, just a prayer away at the most. But if you are doing something like thinking, brooding, analyzing, interpreting, philosophizing, then you start falling away and away and away. You fall away from reality more and more, because the more thoughts you have, the more difficult it is to look through them. They create a great fog. They create blindness.

This is one of the fundamentals of Tantra: that a thinking mind is a missing mind, that thinking is not the language to relate with reality. Th
the language to relate with reality? Non-thinking. Words are meanir
reality. Silence is meaningful. Silence is pregnant; words are just c
has to learn the language of silence.

And then something exactly like this happens: you were in your mother's womb, you have forgotten about it completely, but for nine months you had not spoken a single word, but you were together, in deep silence. You were one with the mother; there was no barrier between you and the mother, you didn't exist as a separate self. In that deep silence your mother and you were one. There was tremendous unity; it was not union, it was unity. You were not two so it was not union; it was simple unity. You were not two.

The day you become silent again, the same happens: again you fall into the womb of existence. Again you relate, you relate in a totally new way. Not exactly totally new, because you had known it in your mother's womb, but you had forgotten it. That's what I mean when I say man has forgotten the language of how to relate. That is the way, as you related with your mother in her womb. Every vibe was conveyed to the mother, every vibe of the mother was conveyed to you. There was simple understanding; no misunderstanding existed between you and your mother. Misunderstanding comes only when thinking comes in.

How can you misunderstand somebody without thinking? Can you? Can you misunderstand me if you don't think about me? How can you misunderstand? And how can you understand me if you think? Impossible. The moment you think, you have started interpreting. The moment you think, you are not looking at me, you are avoiding me. You are hiding behind your thoughts. Your thoughts come from your past. I am here, present, I am a statement herenow, and you bring your past.

You must know about the octopus. When the octopus wants to hide, it releases black ink around itself, a cloud of black ink. Then nobody can see it, it is simply lost in its own created cloud of black ink; it is its safety measure. Exactly the same is happening when you release a cloud of thoughts around you: you are lost in it. Then you cannot relate and nobody can relate to you. It is impossible to relate to a mind; you can relate only to a consciousness. A consciousness has no past. A mind is just past and nothing else.

So the first thing Tantra says is that you have to learn the language of orgasm again. When you are making love to a woman or to a man, what happens? For a few seconds – it is very rare; it is becoming even rarer and rarer as man is becoming more and more civilized – for a few seconds, again you are no longer in the mind. With a shock you are cut off from the mind, in a jump you are outside the mind. For those few seconds of orgasm when you are out of the mind, you again relate. Again you are back in the womb, in the womb of your woman or in the womb of your man. You are no longer separate. Again there is unity, not union.

When you start making love to a woman, there is the beginning of a union.

But when orgasm comes there is no union, there is unity; the duality is lost. What happens in that deep, peak experience? Tantra reminds you again and again that whatsoever happens in that peak moment is the language to relate with existence. It is the language of the guts; it is the language of your very being. So either think in terms of when you were in the womb of your mother, or think in terms of when you are again lost in the womb of your beloved and for a few seconds the mind simply does not work.

Those moments of no-mind are your glimpses into *samadhi,* glimpses of satori, glimpses of godliness. We have forgotten that language, and that language has to be learned again. Love is the language.

The language of love is silent. When two lovers are really in deep harmony, in what Carl Jung used to call synchronicity, when their vibes are just synchronizing with each other, when they are both vibrating on the same wavelength, then there is silence. Then lovers don't like to talk. It is only husbands and wives who talk; lovers fall silent.

In fact the husband and wife cannot keep silent because language is the way to avoid the other. If you are not avoiding the other, if you are not talking, the presence of the other becomes very embarrassing. The husband and wife immediately release their ink. Anything will do, but they release the ink around themselves; they are lost in the cloud, then there is no problem.

Language is not a way to relate, it is more or less a way to avoid. When you are in deep love you may hold the hand of your beloved, but you will be silent – utter silence, not a ripple. In that rippleless lake of your consciousness something is conveyed, the message is given. It is a wordless message.

Tantra says one has to learn the language of love, the language of silence, the language of each other's presence, the language of the heart, the language of the guts.

We have learned a language which is not existential. We have learned an alien language – utilitarian of course, fulfills a certain purpose of course – but as far as higher exploration of consciousness is concerned it is a barrier. On the lower level it is okay. In the marketplace of course you need a certain language, silence won't do. But as you move deeper and higher, language won't do.

Just the other day I was talking about the chakras; I talked about two chakras: *muladhar* chakra and *svadhishthan* chakra. *Muladhar* means the base, the root. It is the sex center, or you can call it the life center, the birth center. It is from *muladhar* that you are born. It is from your mother's *muladhar* and your father's *muladhar* that you have attained to this body. The next chakra was *svadhishthan*: it means the abode of the self; it is the death chakra. It is a very strange name to give to the death chakra: abode of the self, *svadhishthan,* where you exist really. Yes, in death!

When you die you come to your pure existence, because only that dies which you are not. The body dies. The body is born out of the *muladhar*. When you die the body disappears, but you? No. Whatsoever has been given by the *muladhar* is taken away by *svadhishthan*. Your mother and father have given you a certain mechanism; that is taken away in death. But you – you existed even before your father and mother had known each other – you have existed always.

Jesus says – somebody asks him about Abraham, what he thinks about the prophet Abraham, and he says – "Abraham? I am, before Abraham ever was." Abraham existed almost two thousand, three thousand years before Jesus, and he says, "I am, before Abraham was." What is he talking about? As far as bodies are concerned, how can he be before Abraham? He is not talking about the body, he is talking about I-am-ness, his pure being – that is eternal.

This name, *svadhishthan*, is beautiful. It is exactly the center that in Japan is known as hara. That's why in Japan suicide is called hara-kiri – to die or to kill oneself through the hara center. This *svadhishthan* takes only that which has been given by the *muladhar*, but that which has come from eternity, your consciousness, is not taken away.

Hindus have been great explorers of consciousness. They called it *svadhishthan* because when you die then you know who you are. Die in love and you will know who you are. Die in meditation and you will know who you are. Die to the past and you will know who you are. Die to the mind and you will know who you are. Death is the way to know. In ancient days in India the master was called the death – because you have to die in the master. The disciple has to die in the master, only then does he come to know who he is.

These two centers have been very much poisoned by society; these are the centers easily available to society. Beyond these two are five more centers. The third is *manipura*, the fourth is *anahata*, the fifth is *vishuddha*, the sixth is *agya*, and the seventh is *sahasrar*.

The third center, *manipura*, is the center of all your sentiments, emotions. We go on repressing our emotions in the *manipura*; it means the diamond. Life is valuable because of sentiments, emotions, laughter, crying, tears and smiles. Life is valuable because of all these things – these are the glory of life. Hence the chakra is called *manipura*, the diamond chakra.

Only man is capable of having this precious diamond. Animals cannot laugh; naturally they cannot cry either. Tears are a certain dimension which is available to man only. The beauty of tears, the beauty of laughter, the poetry of tears and the poetry of laughter are available only to man. All other animals exist with only two chakras, *muladhar* and *svadhishthan*. They are born and they die; between the two there is nothing much. If you are also born and you die, you are an animal; you are not human yet. Many millions of people exist only with these two chakras; they never go beyond them.

We have been taught to repress sentiments, we have been taught not to be sentimental. We have been taught sentimentality does not pay: be practical, be hard. Don't be soft, don't be vulnerable, otherwise you will be exploited. Be hard! At least show that you are hard, at least pretend that you are dangerous, that you are not a soft being. Create fear around you. Don't laugh, because if you laugh you cannot create fear around you. Don't weep; if you weep you show that you are afraid yourself. Don't show your human limitations. Pretend that you are perfect. Repress the third center and you become a soldier, not a man but a soldier – an army man, a false man.

Much work is done in Tantra to relax this third center. Emotions have to be relieved, relaxed. When you feel like crying you have to cry, when you feel like laughing you have to laugh. You have to drop this nonsense of repression; you have to learn expression, because only through your sentiments, your emotions, your sensitivity, do you come to that vibration through which communication is possible.

Have you not seen it? You can say as much as you want and nothing is said; but a tear rolls down on your cheek – and everything is said. A tear can say much more; you can talk for hours and it won't do, and a tear can say all. You can go on saying, "I am very happy," this and that, but your face will show just the opposite. A little laughter, a real authentic laughter, and you need not say anything, the laughter says all. When you see your friend, your face beams, flashes with joy.

The third center has to be made more and more available. It is against thinking, so if you allow the third center you will relax in your tense mind more easily. Be authentic, sensitive, touch more, feel more, laugh more, cry more. And remember, you cannot do more than is needed; you cannot exaggerate. You cannot even bring a single tear more than is needed, and you cannot laugh more than is needed. So don't be afraid, and don't be miserly.

Tantra allows life all its emotions.

These are the three lower centers – lower not in any sense of evaluation. These are the three lower centers, lower rungs of the ladder. Then comes the fourth center, the heart center, called *anahata*. The word is beautiful. *Anahata* means unstruck sound. It means exactly what Zen people mean when they say, "Do you hear the sound of one hand clapping?" Unstruck sound. The heart is just in the middle: three centers below it, three centers above it. The heart is the door from the lower to the higher, or from the higher to the lower. The heart is like a crossroads.

The heart has been completely bypassed. You have not been taught to be heartful. You have not even been allowed to go into the realm of the heart because it is very dangerous. It is the center of the soundless sound. It is the nonlinguistic center, unstruck sound. Language is struck sound, we have to create it with our vocal chords; it has to be struck, it is two hands clapping. The heart is one hand clapping; in the heart there is no word, it is wordless. We have avoided the heart completely; we have bypassed it. We move in such a way in our being, as if the heart does not exist, or at the most as if it is just a pumping mechanism for breathing, that's all. It is not. The lungs are not the heart. The heart is hidden deep behind the lungs. And it is not physical either – it is the place from where love arises. That's why love is not a sentiment, and sentimental love belongs to the third center, not to the fourth.

Love is not just sentimental. Love has more depth than sentiments; love has more validity than sentiments. Sentiments are momentary. More or less the sentiment of love is misunderstood as the experience of love. One day you fall in love with a man or a woman and the next day it has gone, and you call it love. It is not love; it is a sentiment. You liked the woman – liked, remember, not loved – it was a like, just as you like ice cream. It was a like. Likes come and go, likes are momentary; they cannot stay long, they don't have any capacity to stay long. You liked a woman, you loved her, and then finished – the like is finished. It is just like you liked ice cream; you have eaten it, now you don't look at the ice cream at all. If somebody goes on giving you more ice cream, you will say, "Now it is nauseating; stop! I cannot take any more."

Liking is not love. Never misunderstand liking for love, otherwise your whole life you will be just driftwood, you will be drifting from one person to another. Intimacy will never grow.

The fourth center, the *anahata*, is very significant, because it is in the heart that for the first time you were related to your mother. It was through the heart that you were related to your mother, not through the head. In deep love, in deep orgasm, again you are related through the heart, not through the head. In meditation, in prayerfulness, the same happens: you are related with existence through the heart, heart to heart. Yes, it is a dialogue: heart to heart, not head to head. It is nonlinguistic.

And the heart center is the center from where the soundless sound arises. If you relax into the heart center, you will hear *omkar, aum*. That is a great discovery. Those who have entered the heart, they hear a continuous chanting inside their being which sounds like *aum*. Have you ever heard anything like a chanting, which goes on by itself? Not that you do it...

That's why I am not in favor of mantras. You can go on chanting "*Aum, aum, aum,*" and you can create a mental substitute for the heart. It is not going to help; it is a deception. You can go on chanting for years and you can create a false sound within yourself as if your heart is speaking; it is not. To know the heart you are not to chant *aum*, you just have to be silent. One day, suddenly the mantra is there. One day, when you have fallen silent, suddenly you hear the sound coming from nowhere. It is arising out of you from the innermost core; it is the sound of your inner silence. Just as on a silent night there is a certain sound, the sound of the silence, exactly like that on a very, very much deeper level, a sound arises in you.

It arises – let me remind you again and again – it is not that you bring it in; it is not that you repeat "*Aum, aum.*" No, you don't say a single word. You are simply quiet, you are simply silent, and it bursts forth like a spring. Suddenly it starts flowing, it is there. You hear it, you don't say it, you hear it.

That is the meaning when Mohammedans say that Mohammed heard the Koran – that is the meaning. That is exactly what happens at the innermost core of your heart, not that you say it, you hear it. Mohammed heard the Koran; he heard it happening inside. He was really puzzled, he had never heard anything like this. It was so unknown; it was so unfamiliar. The story says that he became ill; it was so weird. When suddenly, sitting in your room, if one day you start hearing inside *aum, aum,* or anything, you will start feeling, "Am I going mad?" You are not saying it, nobody else is saying it – are you going mad?

Mohammed was sitting on a hilltop when he heard it. He came back home trembling, perspiring; he had a high fever. He really became disturbed, he told his wife, "Just bring all the blankets and cover me. I have never had such a trembling; a great fever has come to me."

But his wife could see that his face was illuminated. "What type of fever is this?" His eyes are burning, afire with something tremendously beautiful. A grace has entered with him in the house. A great silence has fallen over the house. Even his wife started hearing something. She said to Mohammed, "I don't think it is a fever, I think God has blessed you. Don't be afraid. What has happened? Tell me!"

His wife was the first Mohammedan; Khadija was her name. She was the first convert. She said, "I can see. God has happened to you, something has happened to you, something is flowing from your heart all over the place. You have become luminous. You have never been like this, something extraordinary has happened. Tell me why you are so worried and trembling. Maybe it is new, but tell me." And Mohammed told her, very much afraid of what she would think, but she became converted; she was the first Mohammedan.

It has always happened so. Hindus say that the Vedas were recited by God himself. It simply means that they were heard. In India we have a word for the holy scriptures, the word is *shruti; shruti* means that which has been heard.

At this center of the heart, the *anahata* chakra, you hear. But you have not heard anything inside you: no sound, no *omkar*, no mantra. That simply means you have avoided the heart. The waterfall is there, and the sound of running water is there, but you have avoided it. You have bypassed; you have taken some other route, you have taken a shortcut. The shortcut simply goes from the third center, avoiding the fourth. The fourth is the most dangerous center because it is the center out of which trust is born, faith is born. The mind has to avoid it. If the mind does not avoid it, then there will be no possibility for doubt. Mind lives through doubt.

This is the fourth center. Tantra says through love you will come to know this fourth center.

The fifth center is called *vishuddha*. *Vishuddha* means purity. Certainly after love has happened there is purity and innocence, never before it. Only love purifies, and *only* love, nothing else purifies. Even the ugliest person becomes beautiful in love. Love is nectar: it cleanses all poisons. So the fifth chakra is called *vishuddha* – *vishuddha* means purity, absolute purity. It is the throat center.

Tantra says only speak when you have come to the fifth center via the fourth – only speak through love, otherwise don't speak. Speak through compassion; otherwise don't speak. What is the point of speaking? If you have come through the heart and if you have heard existence speaking there or godliness running there like a waterfall, if you have heard the sound of godliness, the sound of one hand clapping, then you are allowed to speak. Then your throat center can convey the message, then something can be poured even into words. When you have it, it can be poured even into words.

Very few people come to the fifth center, very rarely, because they don't even come to the fourth, so how can they come to the fifth? It is very rare. Somewhere a Christ, a Buddha, a Saraha comes to the fifth. The beauty even of their words is tremendous, what to say about their silence, even their words carry silence. They speak and yet they speak not. They say and they say the unsayable, the ineffable, the inexpressible.

You also use the throat, but that is not *vishuddha*. The chakra is completely dead. When that chakra starts, your words have honey in them. Then your words have a fragrance; your words have a music to them, a dance. Then whatsoever you say is poetry, whatsoever you utter is sheer joy.

And the sixth chakra is *agya*, *agya* means order. With the sixth chakra you are in order, never before it. With the sixth chakra you become the master, never before it. Before it you were a slave. With the sixth chakra, whatsoever you say will happen; whatsoever you desire will happen. With the sixth chakra you have will, never before it; before it, will does not exist.

But there is a paradox in it. With the fourth chakra ego disappears. With the fifth chakra all impurities disappear, and then you have will – so you cannot harm through your will. In fact it is no longer *your* will, it is the will of existence, and because the ego disappears at the fourth, all impurities disappear at the fifth. Now you are the purest being, just a vehicle, instrumental, a messenger. Now you have will because you are not; now the will of existence is your will.

Very rarely does a person come to this sixth chakra, because this is the last, in a way. In the world this is the last. Beyond this is the seventh, but then you enter a totally different world, a separate reality. The sixth is the last boundary line, the checkpost.

The seventh is *sahasrar. sahasrar* means one-thousand-petaled lotus. When your energy moves to the seventh, *sahasrar*, you become a lotus. Now you need not go to any other flower for honey, now other bees start coming to you. Now you attract bees from the whole earth – or even sometimes from other planets bees start coming to you. Your *sahasrar* has opened; your lotus is in full bloom. This lotus is nirvana.

The lowest is *muladhar*. From the lowest life is born: life of the body and the senses. With the seventh life is born: life eternal, not of the body, not of the senses. This is the Tantra physiology. It is not a physiology of the medical books. Please don't look for it in the medical books; it is not there. It is a metaphor, a way of saying. It is a map to make things understandable. If you move this way, you will never come to that cloudedness of thoughts. If you avoid the fourth chakra, then you go into the head. Now to be in the head means not to be in love; to be in thoughts means not to be in trust; to be thinking means not to be looking.

Now the sutras:

> *When, in winter, still water by the wind is stirred,*
> *it takes as ice the shape and texture of a rock.*
> *When the deluded are disturbed by interpretative thoughts,*
> *that which is as yet un-patterned turns very hard and solid.*

Saraha says: *...in winter...* Listen to each word, meditate on each word. *...in winter, still water by the wind is stirred, it takes as ice the shape and texture of a rock.* A silent lake without any ripples is the metaphor for consciousness. A silent lake without any ripples, waves, no stirring, no wind blowing – that is the metaphor for consciousness. The lake is liquid, flowing, silent; it is not hard, it is not like rock. It is soft like rose flowers; it is vulnerable. It can flow in any direction; it is not blocked. It has flow and it has life and it has dynamism, but nothing is disturbed; the lake is silent, peaceful. This is the state of consciousness.

...in winter... Winter means when desires have arisen. Why call them winter? When desires arise you are in a cold desert land, because they are never fulfilled. Desires are a desert. They delude you; there is no fulfillment in them. They never come to any fruition; it is a desert land and very cold, cold like death. No life flows through desires. Desires block life; they don't help life.

So Saraha says: *When, in winter* – when desires have arisen in you, that is the climate of winter – *still water by the wind is stirred...* And thoughts come, a thousand and one thoughts from every direction; that is the symbol of wind. Winds are coming, stormy winds are coming; you are in a desire state, full of lust, ambition, becoming, and thoughts arise.

In fact, desires invite thoughts. Unless you desire, thoughts cannot come. Just start a desire and immediately you will see thoughts have started coming. Just a moment before there was not a single thought, and then a car passes by and a desire has arisen: you would like to have this car. Now a thousand and one thoughts are there immediately. Desire invites thought. So when there is desire, thoughts will come from every direction, winds will blow upon the lake of consciousness. Desire is cold, and thoughts go on stirring the lake.

When, in winter, still water by the wind is stirred, it takes as ice the shape and texture of a rock. Then the lake starts becoming frozen, it starts becoming solid, rocklike; it loses fluidity, it becomes frozen. This is what, in Tantra, is called the mind. Meditate over it. The mind and consciousness are not two things but two states, two phases of the same phenomenon. Consciousness is liquid, flowing; mind is rocklike, like ice. Consciousness is like water. Consciousness is like water, mind is like ice; it is the same thing. The same water becomes ice, and the ice can be melted again; through love, through warmth, it can be melted again and will become water.

And the third stage is when water evaporates and becomes invisible and disappears; that is nirvana, cessation. Now you cannot even see it. Water is liquid, but you can see it; when it evaporates it simply disappears, it goes into the unmanifested. These are three states of water and these are three states of mind too. Mind means ice, consciousness means liquid water, nirvana means evaporation.

When the deluded are disturbed by interpretative thoughts, that which is as yet un-patterned turns very hard and solid. The lake is un-patterned. You can pour water into any vessel, it will take the shape of the vessel. But you cannot pour ice into any vessel; it will resist, it will fight.

Two types of people come to me. One, who comes like water, his surrender is simple, very innocent, childlike, he does not resist. Work starts immediately, no need to waste time. Then somebody comes with great resistance, with fear; he is protecting himself, armoring himself. Then he is like ice, it is very difficult to give him liquidity. He fights all efforts to make him liquid. He is afraid he may lose his identity. He will lose solidity, that's true, but not identity. Yes, he will lose the identity that solidity has, but that solidity is bringing misery and nothing else.

When you are solid you are like a dead rock. Nothing can flower in you, and you cannot flow. When you are flowing you have juice. When you are flowing you have energy. When you are flowing you have dynamism. When you are flowing you are creative. When you are flowing you are part of existence. When you have become frozen you are no longer part of this great flow, you are no longer part of this great ocean; you have become a small island, frozen, dead.

When the deluded are disturbed by interpretative thoughts, that which is as yet un-patterned turns very hard and solid. Be mindful! Be more and more in the state of unpatternedness, unstructuredness. Be without character, that's what Tantra says. It is very hard even to understand, because down the centuries we have been taught to have characters. Character means a rigid structure, character means the past, character means a certain enforced discipline. Character means you are no longer free, you only follow certain rules. You never go beyond those rules; you have solidity. A man of character is a solid man.

Tantra says drop character, be fluid, more flowing, live moment to moment. It does not mean irresponsibility; it means greater responsibility because it means greater awareness. When you can live through a character you need not be aware, character takes care. When you live through a character you can fall asleep easily. There is no need to be awake, the character will continue in a mechanical form. But when you don't have any character, when you don't have any hard structure around you, you have to be alert each moment. Each moment you have to see what you are doing. Each moment you have to respond to the new situation.

A man of character is a dead man. He has a past, but no future. A man who has no character... And I am not using the word in the same sense as when you use it about somebody: that he is characterless. When you use that word *characterless* you are not using it rightly, because whomsoever you call characterless has a character. Maybe it is against society, but he has a character; you can depend on him too.

The saint has a character, so does the sinner; they both have characters.

You call the sinner characterless because you want to condemn his character; otherwise he has a character. You can depend on him. Give him the opportunity and he will steal; he has a character. Give him the opportunity and he is bound to steal. Give him the opportunity and he will do something wrong; he has a character. The moment he comes out of jail he starts thinking, "What to do now?" Again he is thrown in jail, again he comes out... No jail has ever cured anybody. In fact jailing a person, imprisoning a person, makes him even cleverer, that's all. Maybe you won't be able to catch him so easily next time, but nothing else; you just give him more cleverness. But he has a character.

Can't you see? A drunkard has a character, and a very, very stubborn character. A thousand and one times he thinks not to drink anymore, and again the character wins and he is defeated. The sinner has a character, so has the saint.

What Tantra means by characterlessness is freedom from character. The character of the saint and the character of the sinner both make you solid like rocks, ice. You don't have any freedom, you can't move easily. If a new situation arises you cannot respond in a new way. You have a character, how can you respond in a new way? You have to respond in the old way. The old, the known, the well practiced – you are skilled in it. A character becomes an alibi; you need not live.

Tantra says: be characterless, be without character. Characterless-ness is freedom.

Saraha was saying to the king, "Sir, I am characterless. You want to put me back into my old solidity of being a scholar, a pundit in the court? You want to put me back into my past? I have dropped out of it. I am a characterless person. Look at me. Now I don't follow any rules, I follow my awareness. Look at me, I don't have any discipline; I have only my consciousness. My only shelter is my consciousness. I live out of it. I don't have any conscience; my consciousness is my only shelter."

Conscience is character, and conscience is a trick of the society. The society creates a conscience in you so that you need not have any consciousness. It makes you follow certain rules for so long; it rewards you if you follow, it punishes you if you don't follow. It makes you a robot. Once it has made the mechanism of conscience in you, it can be free of you. Then you can be trusted, you will be a slave your whole life. It has put a conscience in you just as if Delgado had put an electrode in you; it is a subtle electrode, but it has killed you. You are no longer a flow, no longer a dynamism.

Saraha says to the king, "I am unstructured, sir. I have dropped out of all patterns. I don't have any identity any longer. I live in the moment."

Mind, immaculate in its very being can never be polluted
by samsara's or nirvana's impurities.
A precious jewel deep in mud will not shine,
though it has luster.

Says Saraha: *Mind, immaculate...* When the mind has no thoughts; that is when the mind is pure consciousness: when the mind is a silent lake without any ripples, no interpretative thoughts, no analytical thoughts, when the mind is not philosophizing but just is.

Tantra says: walking, walk; sitting, sit; being, be! Exist without thinking. Let life flow through you without any blocks of thoughts. Let life flow through you without any fear. There is nothing to fear; you have nothing to lose. There is nothing to fear, because death will take only that which birth has given to you. It is going to take it anyway, so there is nothing to fear.

Let life flow through you. *Mind, immaculate in its very being can never be polluted by samsara's or nirvana's impurities.* And Saraha says, "You think I have become impure so you have come to help me and bring me to the world of the pure people? I am now in an immaculate state of mind. I am no longer solid ice. Nothing can pollute me any longer because no thought can create a ripple in me. I have no desire."

That's why – a tremendous saying – he says *...polluted by samsara's or nirvana's impurities.* No, it is not possible, not even nirvana can pollute me, what to say about samsara. This arrowsmith woman cannot pollute me, neither can this cremation ground pollute me, nor can my mad activities pollute me; nothing can pollute me. I am beyond pollution. I am no longer in a state where pollution is possible. Even nirvana cannot pollute me. What does he mean when he says even nirvana, even nirvana's impurities? Saraha is saying, "I don't desire the world, I don't desire even nirvana."

To desire is to be impure. Desire is impure, what you desire is irrelevant. You can desire money – it is impure. You can desire power – it is impure. You can desire God – it is impure. You can desire nirvana – it is impure. Desire is impure; the object does not matter, what you desire is meaningless. Desire – the moment desire comes, thoughts come. Once the climate of cold winter is there, the desire, then winds start blowing. If you start thinking how to attain to nirvana, how to become enlightened, you will be inviting thoughts, your lake will be stirred. Again you will start becoming frozen in pieces; you will become solid, rocklike, dead. You will lose the flow – and flow is life, and flow is existence, and flow is nirvana.

So Saraha says: "Nothing can pollute me, don't be worried about me. I have come to a point, I have attained to a point where impurity is not possible."

A precious jewel deep in mud will not shine, though it has luster. You can throw me into mud, into dirty mud, but now dirty mud cannot make me dirty. I have attained to that precious jewelness, I have become a precious jewel now; I have understood who I am. Now you can throw this jewel into any mud, any dirt; maybe it will not shine, but it cannot lose its preciousness, it will still have luster. It will still be the same precious jewel.

A moment comes when you look into yourself and you see your transcendental consciousness, then nothing can pollute you.

Truth is not an experience; truth is experiencing. Truth is not an object of awareness; truth *is* awareness. Truth is not outside; truth is your interiority.

Says Søren Kierkegaard: truth is subjectivity.

If truth is like an object, you can get it and lose it; but if truth is you, how can you lose it? Once you have known, you have known; then there is no going back. If truth is some experience, it can become polluted, but truth is experiencing, it is your innermost consciousness. It is you. It is your being.

> *Knowledge shines not in the dark,*
> *but when the darkness is illumined,*
> *suffering disappears at once.*

Saraha says: *Knowledge shines not in the dark...* The darkness of the mind, the darkness of a structured being, the darkness of ego, the darkness of thoughts, a thousand and one thoughts, the darkness that you go on creating around yourself like an octopus – and because of that darkness that you go on creating, your innermost jewel shines not; otherwise it is a lamp of light. Once you stop creating this ink around you, this black cloud around you, then there is illumination.

And *...suffering disappears at once.* This is the Tantra message, a great, liberating message. Other religions say you will have to wait. Christianity says, Islam says, Judaism says, you will have to wait for the last judgment day, when everything will be reckoned with: what good you have done, what bad you have done, and then you will be rewarded or punished accordingly. You have to wait for the future, for the judgment day.

Hindus, Jainas and others say you have to balance your bad acts with good acts: bad karma has to be dropped and good karma has to be evolved. You will have to wait for that too. It will take time. For millions of lives you have been doing millions of things, good and bad. To sort it out, to balance it, is going to be almost impossible.

The Christian and the Judaic and the Mohammedan judgment day is easier. At least you will not have to reckon with everything you have done. God will

take care, he will judge – that is his business. But Jainism and Hinduism say
you have to look into your bad karmas, drop the bad, replace it with good; that
too it seems will take millions of lives.

Tantra is liberating. Tantra says: ...*suffering disappears at once.* The moment
you look into yourself – that single moment of inner vision – suffering disappears because suffering had never really existed. It was a nightmare, that's why
you are suffering; it is not because you have done bad karmas. Tantra says you
are suffering because you are dreaming. You have not done anything, neither
good nor bad.

This is tremendously beautiful. Tantra says that you have not done anything; existence is the doer. The whole is the doer, how can *you* do anything?
If you have been a saint, it was the will of existence; if you have been a sinner,
it was its will. You have not done anything. How *can* you do? You are not separate from the will of existence, how can you do? You don't have any separate
will; it is the will of existence, it is the universal will.

So Tantra says you have not done anything good or bad. It has to be looked
into, that's all; you have to see your innermost consciousness. It is pure, eternally pure, unpolluted by samsara or nirvana. Once you have seen that vision
of your pure consciousness, all suffering stops, immediately, at once. It does
not take even a split second.

Shoots grow from the seed and leaves from the shoots.

And then things start changing. Then the seed is broken. The seed, Tantra
says, is the ego; once the seed of the ego is broken... The closed seed is ego;
the broken seed is egolessness. You put the seed in the earth; it cannot grow
unless it disappears, unless it breaks open, dies. Ego is like an egg, hidden
behind it is the possibility of growth.

The seed, once broken, becomes egolessness. Then shoots come. Shoots
are no-thoughts, no-desires, no-mind. Then leaves come. Leaves are knowing, experiencing, illumination, satori, *samadhi.* Then flowers come. Flowers
are *sat-chit-anand:* being, consciousness, truth. And then the fruit, the fruit is
nirvana, utter disappearance into existence. Once the seed is broken, everything follows. The only thing to be done is to put the seed into the earth, to
allow it to disappear.

The master is the earth and the disciple is the seed.

The last sutra:

> *He who thinks of the mind in terms of one or many,*
> *casts away the light and enters the world.*

Into a raging fire he walks with open eyes.
Who could be more deserving of compassion?

He who thinks of the mind in terms of one or many... Thinking is always divisive; it divides. Thinking is like a prism – yes, mind is like a prism. A pure white ray enters into the prism and is divided into seven colors; a rainbow is born. The world is a rainbow. Through the mind, through the prism of the mind, one single ray of light, one single ray of truth enters and becomes a rainbow, a false thing. The world is a false thing.

The mind divides. It cannot see the whole, it always thinks in terms of duality. Mind is dualistic. Or, mind is dialectical, it thinks in terms of thesis-antithesis. The moment you talk about love, hate is present. The moment you talk about compassion, anger is present. The moment you talk about greed, the opposite, charity, is present. Talk about charity and greed is present; they go together. They come in one package; they are not separate. But the mind continuously creates that.

You say beautiful and you have said ugly too. How can you say beautiful if you don't know what ugliness is? You have divided. Say divine and you have divided, you have said profane. Say God and you have proposed the Devil too. How can you say God without the Devil there? They go together.

The mind divides, and reality is one, indivisibly one. Then what to do? The mind has to be put aside. Don't look through the prism. Push away the prism and let the white light, the oneness of existence penetrate your being.

He who thinks of the mind in terms of one or many, casts away the light and enters the world. If you think of one or many, dual or nondual, if you think in concepts, you have entered the world, you have cast away the light. There are only two possibilities: either cast away the mind or cast away the light. It is your choice.

A man came once to Ramakrishna. He was praising Ramakrishna very highly, and he was touching Ramakrishna's feet again and again, and he was saying, "You are simply great, you have renounced the world. You are such a great man. How much you have renounced."

Ramakrishna listened, laughed and said, "Wait! You are going too far, the truth is just the opposite."

The man said, "What do you mean?"

Ramakrishna said, "I have not renounced anything. *You* have renounced. You are a great man."

The man said, "Are you kidding, I have renounced? I am a worldly man, I indulge in things, a thousand and one greeds are there. I am very ambitious;

I am very money-oriented. How can I be called great? No, no, you must be joking."

And Ramakrishna said, "No. There were two possibilities before me, and two were the possibilities before you. You have chosen the world and renounced God; I have chosen God, renounced the world. Who is the real renouncer? You have renounced the greater, more valuable, and chosen the meaningless. I have renounced the meaningless and chosen the valuable. If there is a great diamond and a stone, you have chosen the stone and renounced the diamond; I have chosen the diamond and renounced the stone – and you call me a great man, a great man of renunciation? Have you gone mad? I am indulging in God. I have chosen the precious one."

Yes, I too agree with Ramakrishna, Mahavira, Buddha, Jesus, Mohammed, Saraha, they have not renounced. They have indulged; they have *truly* indulged. They have *really* enjoyed; they have celebrated existence. We who are running after ordinary stones, we are the great renouncers.

There are only two possibilities: either to renounce the mind and choose the light, or renounce the light and choose the mind; it is up to you.

He who thinks of the mind in terms of one or many casts away the light and enters the world. Into a raging fire he walks with open eyes. Who could be more deserving of compassion? Saraha says, "Sir, you have come to help me. You think you are compassionate toward me. Certainly your whole kingdom will think that way: that the king has gone to the cremation ground, how much is his compassion for Saraha. You think you have come because of compassion? You make me laugh. In fact it is I who am feeling compassion for you, not otherwise. It is I who am feeling sorry for you. You are a fool."

Into a raging fire he walks with open eyes. Your eyes appear to be open, but they are not open. You are blind. You don't know what you are doing – living in the world, do you think you are enjoying? You are just in a raging fire.

Exactly that happened when Buddha left his palace and left the boundaries of his kingdom, and told his driver, "Now go back. I am going into the jungle; I have renounced."

The old driver said, "Sir, I am old enough, I am more aged than your father; listen to my advice. You are doing something utterly foolish. Leaving this beautiful kingdom, this palace, a beautiful wife, all the luxuries for which each human being hankers. Where are you going and for what?"

Buddha looked back at that marble palace and he said, "I see there only fire and nothing else, a raging fire. The whole world is burning with fire. I am not renouncing it because there is nothing to renounce in it. I am trying just to escape from the fire. No, I don't see any palace and I don't see any joy there."

Saraha says to the king: *Into a raging fire he walks with open eyes. Who could be more deserving of compassion?* You think, sir, you have come because of compassion to help me? No, the situation is just the reverse; I feel compassion for you. You are living in a raging fire. Beware! Be alert! Be awake! And get out of it as soon as possible, because all that is beautiful, all that is truthful, all that is good, is known and experienced only through the no-mind. Tantra is a process of creating no-mind in you.

No-mind is the door of nirvana.

Enough for today.

just far out baby!

The first question – it is from Prabha:

Osho,
Hingle de je, bipity jang dang – do run nun, de jun bung. Hingle de jibbity dangely ji.

This is wonderful, Prabha! This is beautiful, this is just far out, baby. I am driving you sane. Just a step more, and the enlightenment...

The second question:

Osho,
Is prayer useful? If so, teach me how to pray. I mean, prayer to receive God's love, to feel his grace.

First, prayer is not useful, not at all. Prayer has no use, no utility. It is not a commodity. You cannot use it; it is not a thing. It is not a means to anything else, how can you use it?

I can understand the questioner's mind. The so-called religions have been teaching people that prayer is a means to God. It is not. Prayer *is* God. It is not a means toward anything; to be prayerful is the end in itself. When you are prayerful, you are divine. Not that the prayer leads you toward the divine; in prayerfulness you discover your divinity.

Prayer is not a means. It is the end unto itself.

But this fallacy has persisted down the centuries in man's mind. Love is also a means, so is prayer, so is meditation. All that is impossible to reduce to means has been reduced, and that's why the beauty is lost.

Love is useless, so is prayer, so is meditation. When you ask, "Is prayer useful?" you don't understand what the word *prayer* means. You are greedy, you want God, you want to grab God. Now you are finding ways and means to grab, and God cannot be grabbed.

You cannot possess God. You cannot contain God. You cannot interpret God. You cannot experience God. Then what can be done about God? Only one thing: you can be God. Nothing else can be done about it because you *are* God. Recognize it or not, realize it or not, but you are God. Only that can be done which is already there; only that can be done which has already happened. Nothing new can be added – only revelation, only discovery.

So the first thing: prayer is not a utility. The moment you use prayer, you make it ugly. It is a sacrilege to use prayer, and whosoever has said to you to use prayer has been not only irreligious but anti-religious. He does not understand what he is saying. He is talking nonsense.

Be prayerful, not because it has some utility but because it is a joy. Be prayerful, not because through it you will arrive anywhere, but through it you are, through it you start being. Through it you are present, without it you are absent. It is not a goal somewhere in the future; it is a discovery of the presence that is already there, that is already the case.

Don't think in terms of things, otherwise prayer becomes part of economics, not part of religion. If it is a means, then it is part of economics. All means are part of economics; ends are beyond economics. Religion is concerned with the end, not with the means. Religion is not concerned at all with reaching somewhere. Religion is concerned only with one thing: to know where we are.

To celebrate this moment is prayer. To be herenow is prayer. To listen to these birds is prayer. To feel the presence of people around you is prayer. To touch a tree with love is prayer. To look at a child with deep respect, with reverence for life, is prayer.

So first thing: don't ask, "Is prayer useful?" And then the second thing you say: "If so, teach me how to pray." If you start with *if*, prayer cannot be taught. The very beginning with if is the beginning of doubt – if is not part of a prayerful mind. Prayer needs trust; there is no if. It is so, it is absolutely so.

When you can trust the unknown, the invisible, the unmanifest, then there is prayer. If you start with if, then prayer will be at most a hypothesis. Then prayer will be a theory, and prayer is not a theory. Prayer is not a thing, not a theory; prayer is an experience. You cannot start with if. The very beginning goes wrong, you have taken a step in the wrong direction.

Drop ifs and you will be in prayer. Drop *all* ifs. Don't live life through hypothetical things: "If this is so, if there is God, then I will pray." But how can you pray if God is just an "if"? If God is just "as if," then your prayer will also be just "as if." It will be an empty gesture. You will bow down, you will utter a few words, but your heart will not be there. The heart is never with ifs.

Science works through ifs. Religion does not work through ifs.

You are asking: "If there is love, then teach me love." If there is love! Then nothing has stirred in your heart. Then the spring has not come and that breeze, which is called love, has not touched you,. You must have heard somebody else talking about love. You must have read in some book, you must have been reading romantic poetry. The word *love* has come to you but there has not been a single moment of love experience. So you ask, "If there is love, then teach us" – but with *if* love cannot be taught.

Have you never experienced any moment of love, prayer, beautitude? I have never come across a single human being who is so poor. Have you not ever listened to the silence of the night? Have you not ever been thrilled by it, touched by it, transformed by it? Have you never seen a sun rising on the horizon? Have you never felt a deep interrelationship with the rising sun, have you not felt more life in you, pouring from everywhere? Maybe for a moment... Have you never held the hand of a human being and something started flowing from you to him and from him to you? Have you never experienced when two human spaces overlap and flow into each other? Have you never seen a roseflower and smelled the fragrance of it, and suddenly you were transported into another world?

These are moments of prayer. Don't start with if. Gather all the moments of your life which were beautiful, they were all moments of prayer. Base your temple of prayer on those moments, let that be the foundation, not if. The bricks of if are false. Build the foundation with certainties, with absolute certainties – only then, *only* then is there a possibility of your ever entering into the world of prayer. It is a great world; it has a beginning, but it has no end. It is oceanic.

So please don't say, "If so." It *is* so! And if you have not yet felt it is so, then look into your life and find some certainties about beauty, about love, about experiences which go beyond the mind. Collect all those.

The ordinary habit of the mind is not to collect them, because they go against the logical mind. So we never take note of them. They happen, they happen to everybody. Let me repeat: nobody is so poor, they happen to the poorest man. Man is made in such a way, man is in such a way they are bound to happen. But we don't take note of them because they are dangerous moments. If they are real, then what will happen to our logical mind? They are very illogical moments.

Now, listening to a bird, and something starts singing within you – this is very illogical. You cannot find out how it is happening, why it is happening, why it should be so. The mind is at a loss. The only course left for the mind is not to take note of it, forget about it. It is just a whim, maybe some eccentric moment, maybe you have gone temporarily mad. The mind interprets these things like this: "It was nothing, just a mood. You were emotional, you were being sentimental, that's all; there was no authentic experience in it."

This is the way to deny. Once you start denying then you don't have any moments to base your life of prayerfulness upon. Hence the question, "If so…"

My first suggestion is: go into your life; remember all those moments. You must have been a small child collecting seashells on a beach, and the sun was showering on you, and the wind was salty and sharp, and you were in tremendous joy. No king has ever been so joyful; you were almost at the top of the world, you were an emperor. Remember, that is the right brick to base upon.

You were a small child running after a butterfly – that was the moment of prayer. For the first time you fell in love with a woman or a man, and your heart was churned and stirred, and you started dreaming in a new way. That was the moment of prayer: your first love, your first friendship.

Gather from your past a few certainties about something that goes beyond the mind, which the mind cannot interpret, which the mind cannot dissect, which is simply transcendental to the mind. Collect those transcendental moments – even a few will do – but then there will be no if. Then you move with certainty, it is not a hypothesis. Then there is trust. If it could happen to you when you were a child, why can't it happen to you now? Why not? Gather those moments of wonder, when you were thrilled.

Just the other day I was reading about a man, a very simple man, a very old man. The English philosopher, thinker, Doctor Johnson, was staying with the old man. In the morning when they were taking their tea, the old man said, "Doctor Johnson, you may be surprised to know that when young I also tried to become a philosopher."

Doctor Johnson asked, "Then what happened? Why could you not become a philosopher?"

The man laughed and he said, "But cheerfulness again and again erupted into my life" – cheerfulness. "Because of that cheerfulness I could not become a philosopher. Again and again, I tried hard to repress it."

I like that answer. Those moments of cheerfulness are moments of prayer. A philosopher cannot pray, a thinker cannot pray, because all thinking starts with if, all thinking starts with doubt. Prayer starts with trust.

That's why Jesus says: "Only those who are like small children, only they will be able to enter into the kingdom of my God." Those whose eyes are full of wonder, for whom each moment is a moment of surprise, those whose hearts are still open to be thrilled, only they. So first drop if, and collect some certainties. That is the first lesson about prayer.

The second thing you say: "...teach me how to pray." There is no how. Prayer is not a technique. Meditation can be taught; it is a technique, it is a method. Prayer is not a method, it is a love affair. You can pray, but prayer cannot be taught. It happened once...

Some of Jesus' disciples asked him, "Master, teach us to pray and teach us how." And what did Jesus do, do you know? He acted exactly the way a Zen master is supposed to act: he simply fell on the ground, on his knees, and started praying.

They were puzzled; they looked... They must have shrugged their shoulders: "We have asked him to teach, and what is he doing? He is praying, but how can his praying help us?"

Later on they must have asked, and Jesus said, "But that is the only way; there is no technique."

Jesus prayed – what else could he do? If they had been a little more alert they would have sat silently by the side of Jesus, holding his hands or touching his robe: contact high. Something would have happened there.

I cannot teach you prayer, but I am prayer. I need not fall on my knees to pray, I am prayer. Just imbibe my being, drink me, my presence, as much as you can, and it will teach you what prayer is. Every morning I am teaching you what prayer is. Every moment when you come to me I am teaching you what prayer is. I am in prayer. Just be a little open. Just open your doors and let my breeze pass through you. It is an infection. Prayer is an infection.

I cannot teach you how to pray, but I can make you prayerful. Get more in tune with my presence. Don't keep these questions inside your mind because they will be the barriers. Just be vulnerable, and it will happen. One day suddenly, you will see the heart is singing and something is dancing within you, some new energy, as if in a dark night a sudden ray of light has entered your being.

That is prayer – you cannot do it, you can only allow it to happen. Meditation can be done; prayer cannot be done. Meditation is more scientific that way, it can be taught. But prayer – prayer is absolutely unscientific, it is a matter of the heart. Feel me, and you will feel prayer. Touch me, and you will touch prayer. Listen to me and you are listening to words which are full of prayer.

Then sometimes sitting silently, let there be a dialogue, a dialogue with existence. You can call existence God or father or mother; all are okay. But don't repeat any ritual. Don't repeat the Christian prayer, and don't repeat the Hindu prayer, don't repeat the *Gayatri Mantra* and don't repeat *namokar.* Don't repeat any mantra, Indian, Tibetan, Chinese, don't repeat! Create your own mantra, don't be a parrot. Can't you say something to existence on your own? And don't rehearse it, don't prepare for it. Can't you face existence directly as a small child faces his father or mother? Can't you say something to existence? Can't you say hello?

Let prayer happen, don't prepare for it. A prepared prayer is a false prayer, and a repeated prayer is just a mechanical thing. You can repeat the Christian prayer; you have crammed it, it has been forced upon you. You can repeat it in the night and fall asleep, but it will not make you aware because it has not been done as a response.

I have heard...

A great mathematician used to pray every night with a single word: he would look at the sky and would say, "Ditto."

What is the point of repeating every day the same as yesterday? What are you doing when you are repeating the same prayer again and again? Ditto is better. Why bother God every day with the same repetition? Say something if you have something to say. If you don't have something to say, just say, "I don't have anything to say today."

Or just be silent – what is the need of saying? But be true, at least between you and the whole, let there be truth; that's what prayer is. Open your heart.

I have heard...

Moses was passing through a forest and he came across a man, a shepherd, a poor man, a dirty, poor man with rags for clothes. He was praying – it was prayer time and he was praying.

Moses, just out of curiosity, stood behind him and listened. He could not believe what sort of prayer this was, because he was saying, "God, when I die, allow me into your paradise – I will take care of you. If you have lice, I will remove them." He had lice, so certainly he says, "If you have lice, I will remove them. I will give you such a good bath, and I will cook food for you, and I cook

really good things. I will take care of your sheep. I will prepare milk for you."
...and this and that. "And I can do good massage too."

Then it was too much. When he came to lice, it was too much. Moses just
shook him and said, "What nonsense are you talking, you will remove lice. So
God has lice?"

The poor man was disturbed. He said, "I don't know exactly because I have
never seen him. But all that I know is what I know about myself: I have lice."

Moses said, "Stop! Never pray in this way. This is sacrilege, you will fall
into hell."

The man started trembling and perspiring. He said, "But I have been doing
this my whole life; whatsoever comes to my mind, I say. I don't know... Teach
me the right way."

And Moses teaches him the right way to pray, and the poor shepherd goes
with his sheep. Then suddenly God thunders all over the forest, and God is
very angry. He says to Moses, "You are mad! I have sent you into the world to
bring people to me, and you are throwing my people away from me. A lover –
he was a lover. He was one of the best prayers, and you have broken his heart,
you have broken his trust. Go and apologize, and take your prayer back."

And Moses goes and falls at the feet of the shepherd and says, "Excuse
me, forgive me. I was wrong, you are right. God approves of you; my prayer
has to be taken back."

That's exactly how it should be. Let your prayer grow, let it happen. Yes,
whenever you are feeling like having a chitchat with God, wait for those
moments. There is no need to repeat it every day – there is no need. When the
feeling comes, let it be out of your feeling. Don't make a ritual out of it.

Sometimes taking a bath, sitting under the shower, and you suddenly feel
the urge to pray, let it be there. It is perfectly good; your bathroom is perfectly
good, there is no need to go to any church. In that moment when the urge is
there, your bathroom is the church. Let the prayer be there, have a little chitchat, and you will be surprised how beautiful it is. When it comes out of the
heart it is heard, it is responded to.

Sometimes making love to your woman, suddenly an urge arises to pray.
Pray that very moment. You cannot find a better moment than that; you are
closest to existence, you are closest to life energy. When the orgasm is showering on you, pray. But wait; don't make it a ritual. That is the whole Tantra
attitude: let things be spontaneous.

And the last thing you say: "I mean, prayer to receive God's love, to feel
his grace." Again your question is wrong: "I mean, prayer to receive God's
love." You are greedy! Prayer is to love God. Yes, love comes from God a

thousandfold, but that is not the desire. That is the outcome of it – not the result but the consequence. Yes, love will come like a flood. You take one step towards God and God takes a thousand steps toward you. You give him one drop, offer him one drop of your love, and his whole ocean becomes available to you. Yes, that happens, but that should not be the desire; the desire is wrong. If you simply want God's love, and that's why you are praying, then your prayer is a bargain. Then it is business, and beware of business.

In a small school somewhere in the United States, the teacher asks the boys, "Who was the greatest man in human history?"

Of course an American says, "Abraham Lincoln," and an Indian says, "Mahatma Gandhi," and an English boy says, "Winston Churchill," and so on and so forth.

And then a small Jewish boy stands up and says, "Jesus," and he wins, he wins a reward.

But the teacher asks him, "You are a Jew, why did you say Jesus?"

He said, "I know all the time in my heart it is Moses, but business is business."

Don't make prayer a business. Let it be a pure offering. Just give it out of your heart, don't ask anything in return. Then much comes – a thousandfold, a millionfold, existence flows toward you. But again remember, it is a consequence, not a result.

The third question:

Osho,
You mentioned Jung's idea that men need two types of women. Historically,
a lot of men seem to feel this way, while very few women seem to need more
than one man at a time. Can there be something to this idea in male psychology?
If so, why?

The question is from Anand Prem. First thing: she says, "Historically, a lot of men seem to feel this way…" History is just bunk. History was created by men – no woman has written history. It is male-oriented, it is male-dominated, it is male-managed. It is a false history.

Man has tried to condition woman in such a way that he can exploit her easily and she cannot even rebel. Slaves always have to be hypnotized in such a way that they cannot rebel. Man has conditioned the woman's mind in such a way that she thinks the way man wants her to think.

You say, "Historically, a lot of men seem to feel this way..." – because men are freer, they are the masters. Women have lived like slaves; they have accepted the slavery. You have to throw off that slavery completely; you have to come out of it.

Just the other night I was reading that in the sixth century there was a great Christian conference of all the great Christian leaders to decide whether women have souls or not. Fortunately they decided that women do have souls, but only by one vote. It is not much of a victory. By the majority of one vote – just one vote less and historically you would not have any soul – it is not much, this soul.

Man has crushed the whole psychology of women. Whatever you see is not really the psychology of women; it is man-made psychology, man-created psychology in women. The freer you are, the more you will also feel the same way, because men and women are not really so different as they have been thought to be. They *are* different: their biology is different, and certainly their psychology is different, but they are not unequals. Their similarities are more than their dissimilarities.

Just think, a man eating the same thing every day gets fed up; and a woman, will she get fed up with it or not? She will also get fed up. What is the difference between the two? Boredom is as natural to man as to woman, and unless a sexual relationship evolves into a spiritual friendship, it is going to be boring.

Let it be very clear to you: a sexual relationship in itself cannot be a lasting affair, because as far as sex is concerned it is a momentary thing. Once you have made love to a woman, you are really finished with her; you are no longer interested in her. Unless something more than a sexual relationship arises between you, something higher, some spiritual contact is made... It can be made through sex, it *should* be made, otherwise sexual relationship is just physical. If something spiritual, something like a spiritual marriage happens, then there will be no problem. Then you can stay together, and whether you are a man or a woman you will not think of other women or other men. It is finished; you have found your soul mate.

But if the relationship is only physical, then the body gets tired, bored. The body needs a thrill, the body needs the new, the body needs sensation. The body is always hankering for something new.

An ATS driver, after a long journey across Salisbury Plain, arrived at her destination, a remote camp, at midnight. The sergeant of the guard showed her where to leave the lorry, and then said, "Where will you sleep tonight?"

The girl explained that the only thing she could do was to kip down in the cab. It was a cold night and the sergeant thought for a moment and said, "If you like you can have my bunk, I'll sleep on the floor."

The offer was accepted with thanks. After the girl had turned in, she felt very sorry for the sergeant lying down there on the hard cold floor, and leaning out said, "This isn't right – why don't you get up here and squeeze in alongside of me?"

This being done, the sarge said, "Well, how's it to be? Do you want to sleep single or married?"

The girl giggled and said, "I think it would be nice if we slept married, don't you?"

"Right, I'm not fussy, we'll sleep married then," he said, turning his back on her and going off to sleep.

Marriage bores. That's why you see so many bored faces all around the world. Marriage is a tremendous boredom. Unless something spiritual happens in it, which is rare, men start looking outside. Women will also look outside, but they have not been free. That's why you find so many women prostitutes, but not so many male prostitutes. Yes, they exist in London I think, a few, but male prostitutes are just almost nonexistent. Why?

Prostitution is a by-product of marriage, and unless marriage disappears prostitution is going to remain. It is a by-product; it will go only with marriage. Now, your so-called mahatmas have been trying to stop prostitution, and these are the people who go on forcing marriage. They don't see the absurdity of it: prostitution exists because of marriage. In animals there is no prostitution because there is no marriage. Have you ever found any animal prostituting itself? There is no problem. Why should prostitution exist at all?

That ugly thing exists because of one other ugly thing: marriage. But there are not so many male prostitutes because women have not been free; they have been repressed completely. They have not even been allowed to have their sexual joy. They are not even *supposed* to have it. Only bad women are supposed to have sexual joy, not good women, not ladies, only women. Ladies are not supposed to have any joy; they are far superior.

This is not real history, this is managed history, this is arranged history. If you go on for thousands of years enforcing an idea, it becomes almost real. It is not true psychology. To know the true psychology, you will have to give women total freedom, and then see. You will be surprised, they will be far ahead of men.

You can watch them: a man almost always goes on wearing the same gray dress. Women...? Every day they need a new sari. I watch their mind. If they are given total freedom, they will be far ahead of men. Men can go on... You can see, their clothes are not very colorful, and something like fashion does not exist as far as man is concerned. What fashion: the same gray official suit, the same tie; they don't have much of a wardrobe. But women... The whole market exists for them. They are the real consumers.

Man is the producer; woman is the consumer. Ninety percent of the things in the market exist for women. Why? They want new things more; they want new experiences, new thrills more. Maybe because their sexuality has been repressed it is a diversion of their energy, and because they cannot have a new husband, a new sari is a substitute, a new car is a substitute, a new house is a substitute. They put their energy somewhere else, but this is not reality.

Women have been so corrupted and destroyed that it is very difficult to decide what their real psychology is. Don't listen to history. History is an ugly record, it is a record of long slavery; at least *women* should not listen to history. They should burn all history books, they should say that history has to be written again. You will be surprised that when you impose a certain idea, the mind starts functioning that way. Mind starts imitating ideas. It has been a long hypnosis the woman has lived in.

But I am not saying that society should be just like animals. I am saying that sex should be a jumping board. If your relationship is defined by sex only and it has nothing more in it, then marriage will create prostitution. But if your marriage is deeper than your body, then there is no need.

Each single human being, man or woman, is such an infinite space. You can go on exploring, go on exploring, there is no end to it. Each human being, man or woman, each day is so alive and so new: new leaves coming up, new flowers blooming, a new climate, new moods. If you love, if you are really intimate, you will never find the same old woman with you, and you will never find the same old man. Life is such a tremendous dynamism.

But you don't love; you are stuck with the body. You don't look in, you don't look at the inner sky which is constantly changing. What more change do you need? But you don't look at that. Of course the body is the same, then it loses excitement. When excitement is lost, your life becomes boring. When you become bored you start seeking help, because you are getting neurotic. Your life is a drag. You go to the psychoanalyst – in the past you used to go to the priest, now you go to the psychoanalyst – you ask for help, something is going wrong. You don't enjoy life, there is no delight; you start thinking of committing suicide. If you move with excitement, then you become criminals; if you stay with society, with the establishment, then you become bored. It is a great dilemma: you are not allowed to move anywhere. Between these two horns you are crushed and killed. Either, live with the establishment then you will live a bored life, or go anti-establishment, but then you look like a criminal, then you start feeling guilty.

Women have to come to absolute freedom, and with the freedom of women, man will also be free – because you cannot be really free if you are keeping somebody as a slave. A master is a slave of the slave. Man is not really free, because he cannot be. Half of humanity is forced to remain slaves – how can man be free? His freedom is just so-so, just superficial. With the freedom of women, man will also be free.

And with freedom there is a possibility to enter into a deeper relationship. If that doesn't happen then there is no need to remain bored; then there is no need to remain clinging to each other.

A man who had felt unwell for some time went to his doctor and asked for a checkup. The doctor gave him a going over and said, "Either you pack up smoking, drinking and sex, or you'll be dead in twelve months."

After a while the man went back and said, "Look, I'm so bloody miserable I might just as well be dead. Please can I smoke just a little?"

"Very well, just five filter-tips a day," said the medico, who was a very abrupt man.

Some weeks later the man was back again: "Look here, I do miss my pint. Please...?"

"Alright, two halves a day then, and no spirits."

Time went by, and the patient approached the doctor for the third time. Seeing the man, the doctor said, "Yes, yes, but only with your wife – no excitement!"

Life needs excitement. If you cannot allow it to have spiritual excitement, it will need physical excitement. Give it a higher excitement and the lower excitements disappear, they are not needed. Don't give it a higher excitement and the lower is the only available excitement.

Man has tried to keep himself open. Jung is tricky, and what Jung is saying is the old crap. This has always been said by men: that a man needs two women at least. One: the mother type, the wife type, another: the mistress, the inspiration. If man needs two women, then women also need two men, the father type and the Don Juan.

But what I am trying to say is that even in the twentieth century men like Freud and Jung are still as male chauvinistic as ever, there is not much difference. Women have to think for themselves; men cannot be of much help. They have to come to their own understanding, and now there is opportunity to come to their own understanding.

But Anand Prem's question is not basically about women; it is about her own mind. She is a clinging type, and that clinging is also because of the historical conditioning. The woman clings too much because she is afraid about insecurity, about safety, about finance, about this and that. She is too afraid;

she has been made afraid. That is the trick of the man: to make the woman afraid. When the woman is afraid she can be easily dominated. You cannot dominate somebody who is not afraid – so create fear.

First man creates fear in women about their virginity. He creates great fear that virginity is something very valuable. Down the centuries he has created that fear, so every girl is afraid: if she loses her virginity all is lost. Through that fear she cannot relate to people, she cannot make friendships, she cannot move in freedom. She cannot have a few experiences before she decides whom to choose. The fear: she has to be virgin.

Look at the distinction: they have not told the boys, "You have to be virgin." They say, "Boys are boys." And girls are not girls? Girls are girls too. Why are boys, boys? Virginity is not asked from the boys, they are given freedom.

Through virginity, a great conditioning... And once a woman becomes too afraid of losing her virginity... Think: up to the twentieth year of age, twenty years she has been protecting her virginity, twenty years of conditioning – she will become frigid. Then she will *never* enjoy. Then she will never be able to flow in love, she will never have any orgasm. Down the centuries, millions of women have not had any orgasm; they don't know what orgasm is. They simply suffer, they are simply means for the man. This is a great degradation.

But if virginity is too important, and there is twenty years of conditioning that one has to be a virgin and always on guard, then it will be very difficult to drop that habit. How can you suddenly drop it after twenty years of conditioning? Just one day it is the honeymoon and you have to drop it. How can you drop it? You can only pretend. But deep down you think your husband is a criminal, a beast, an ugly man, because he is doing something which you know is a sin. You never allowed any other man... Love is sin, and this man is doing that.

No wife is ever capable of forgiving the husband. In fact in India particularly, no woman respects the husband, cannot – *shows* all respect but cannot respect. Deep down she hates the man because this is the man who is dragging her into sin. How can you respect the husband when he is the sinner? Without him you were a virgin; with him you have fallen. That's why the society teaches so much: "Respect the husband," because the society knows naturally the woman will not be able to respect him, so respect has to be forced: respect the husband, because if things go naturally, she will hate this man. This is the man who is preparing hell for her.

And out of this sin children are born. How can you love your children? Born out of sin, you will hate them too, deep down in the unconscious. The very presence of the children will remind you again and again of the sin that you have committed. The whole of society has suffered because of this foolishness.

Love is virtue, not sin. To be capable of more love is to be more virtuous; to be capable of enjoying love is a basic quality of a religious man. These are my definitions.

Anand Prem is a great clinger, and she thinks that whatsoever is true about her is true about all women. In a way she is right because all other women have been conditioned in the same way, but it is not true. Neither about other women nor about you, Anand Prem, is it the truth.

Become capable of being individuals, then you will have some taste of freedom. A woman is never thought of as an individual. When she is small she is a daughter, when she is young she is a wife, when she becomes a little older she is a mother, still older she is a grandmother, but she is never herself: sometimes a daughter, sometimes a wife, sometimes a mother, sometimes a grandmother, but never herself – always in relation to somebody else.

Individuality is needed as a basic requirement. A woman is a woman. Her being a daughter is secondary, her being a wife is secondary, her being a mother is secondary. A woman is a woman; her womanhood is primary. When women start becoming individuals, there will be a totally different world: more beautiful, more joyous.

Now there is boredom and jealousy, nothing else. You are bored with the woman, the woman is bored with you; you are jealous, she is jealous. Why does this jealousy come as a shadow of boredom? Boredom brings it. Too many people come to me and they want not to be jealous, but they don't understand why jealousy comes, they don't understand the mechanism of it.

Listen, when you are bored with a woman, you know deep down that she must be bored with you too. That's natural. If she is bored with you, then she must be looking for some other man somewhere – the milkman, the postman, the driver, whosoever is available – she must be looking somewhere. You know when *you* are bored you start looking at other women, so you know; this is a natural inference. Jealousy arises. So you become jealous – she must be looking – then you start finding ways to see whether she is looking or not. Naturally, how can she avoid looking? There are so many men, and she is bored with you. It is her life; her whole life is at stake.

The woman is jealous; she knows that the husband is bored. Now he is not so delighted as he used to be; now he does not come running home with joy. Now he simply tolerates her. In fact, he is more interested in his newspaper than he is interested in her. He immediately gets irritated – small things and he becomes very, very angry and rough. All that softness, that honeymoon softness, has gone. She knows he is bored; he is no longer interested in her.

Then suddenly, certainly she knows, her instinct knows, he must be becoming interested somewhere else – jealousy. Then if some day he comes home happy, she is worried; he must have been with some woman, otherwise why is he looking so happy? If he goes for a holiday, or if he goes for some business trip, she is worried. If he starts going too often for business trips, it becomes more certain. Jealousy poisons the relationship, but it is part of boredom.

If you are not bored with the person, you will not be jealous because you will not have that idea in your mind. It is not, in fact, because of the other's interest in the other; it is because of your interest in the other that you become jealous, that jealousy arises.

Of course women are more jealous because they are less free, their boredom is more fixed. They know the man goes out; he has more possibilities, opportunities. They are encaged in the home, imprisoned in the home with the kids; it is difficult for them to have as much freedom. They feel jealous. The more they feel jealous, the more they cling. Fear arises: if the man leaves them, what will happen? A slave becomes more attached to his safety than to his freedom. A slave becomes more attached to his security than to his freedom. That's what has happened. It has nothing to do with feminine psychology, Prem. Yes, I understand it has happened to woman. It is an ugly phenomenon. It has to be dropped; it should not be so in the future if men and women become a little more aware. Both are living in hell.

The squire and his lady were chief patrons of the Agricultural Show, and after the opening ceremony they dutifully walked round, mixing with the tenants and peasantry, and looking at the exhibits.

But his lordship spent so much time in the beer tent that her ladyship wandered off to admire the prize bull. Never was a male animal so splendidly equipped.

"My, but that's a fine beast you have there, Giles," she said to the yokel in charge.

"Yes, my lady, he be champion, and father o' champions."

"Go on, tell me about him."

"Well, ma'am, this here bull went to stud three hundred times last year."

"Indeed? Well, go over to his Lordship will you, my good fellow, and tell him there's a bull here went to stud three hundred times in one year, will you."

Giles dutifully trotted up to the squire and gave the message.

"Very interesting indeed," was his lordship's comment, "Always the same cow, I presume?"

"Oh, no indeed, sir, three hundred different cows."

"Aha! Go and tell her ladyship that, will you."

Animals are so happy because they don't have any institution to live in. Mind you, I am not against marriage; I am for a higher marriage. I am against *this* marriage because this marriage has created prostitution. I am for a higher marriage.

If you can find the intimacy, spiritual intimacy with a man or woman, then there will be a natural togetherness; no law is needed to enforce it. Then there will be a spontaneous joy in being together. While it lasts, good; when it disappears, there is no point in being together, no point at all. Then you are crushing each other, killing each other, then you are either a masochist or a sadist; you are neurotic.

If my idea some day prevails – which seems very difficult, because man has become so accustomed to dead roles that he has forgotten how to live – if some day life prevails and man becomes courageous enough to live dangerously, then there will be real marriages. Then you will find many soul mates together. There will be no prostitution.

Of course the larger part of humanity will go on changing partners, but nothing is wrong in it. The only problem that arises again and again in the minds of men and women is: what about kids? That is not a big problem. My conception is that of a commune, not of a family; families have to disappear. Communes should exist.

For example, this is a commune. Kids should belong to the commune, and the commune should take care of the kids. The mother should be known: who the mother is, but the father should not be known; there is no need. That was the original state of humanity, matriarchal. Then society became patriarchal: the father became important, and with the father came a thousand and one illnesses. The greatest illness has been private property; it came with the father, and society will suffer from private property until the father disappears.

A commune, where kids belong to the commune, where the commune can take care of them... The mother will look after them, but the mother can trust one thing: that she can move from one man to another, there is no problem in it. The kids should be taken care of; even if she dies, the commune is there.

And when the property belongs to the commune and not to any individual, there will be real communism. Even in Soviet Russia real communism does not exist. It cannot exist with the father; it is impossible. Private property came with the family, with the nuclear family: father, mother, kids – then private property came. Private property can go only when this nuclear family disappears and a totally new concept, of commune, arrives. It is possible now. The world has come to that state of consciousness where communes can exist, and through communes, communism. It is not otherwise. Not that communism comes first; it is not possible. If communism comes first, it will bring only dictatorship. It will bring only an ugly society as has happened in Soviet Russia or is happening in China.

First let there be communal life as far as sex is concerned, then property will disappear. Property is part of sexual possession. When you possess a woman, you possess property; when you possess a man, you possess property – you have to possess property. When you don't possess any human being, who bothers to possess property? Then property is to be used, there is no need to possess. It is easier to use it without possessing it, because people who possess cannot use it – they are always afraid, they are miserly.

Property can be used more freely, but first the family has to disappear. I am not saying that all families will disappear. Non-spiritual families will disappear; only spiritual families will remain. But it is good, because why should those people who are not spiritual enough be forced to remain bored? Why should they be forced to remain in a relationship which does not lead to any joy, why? This is criminal.

The fourth question:

Osho,
I used to think that I am pretty aware, pretty surrendered. That image still crosses my mind, but I don't really believe in it. And all this makes me wonder that maybe all your talk of awareness and surrender is just to drive us crazy like a carrot in front of a donkey, and that none of it really exists – and that makes me feel angry, stupid and indifferent all at once.

The carrot exists and the donkey does not. Now it is up to you to choose. You can be a donkey, then the carrot does not exist. If you look at the carrot, the carrot exists and the donkey disappears. Naturally if you think the carrot does not exist, you will feel angry, stupid and indifferent, because you will be the donkey. Rather than thinking that the carrot does not exist, why don't you look inside yourself? Do *you* exist?

My whole emphasis is: enlightenment exists; *you* don't exist. Awareness exists; ego does not exist. That is my whole emphasis.

But still the choice is yours; it is up to you. If you want to choose misery, then misery is possible only with the ego. Then you have to choose the ego, then you have to choose the donkey. Then you have to go on believing that the carrot does not exist. But it exists! And once you start feeling the carrot, you will start seeing that the donkey is disappearing; it was just an idea. With the carrot there is bliss. With the ego there is only hell. Choose whatsoever you want to choose.

The fifth question:

Osho,
Before I met you, I was miserable and totally unaware. Now I am miserable with
some degree of awareness. What's new?

Can't you see it? That "some degree of awareness" – do you think it is
valueless? That is the first ray, and the sun is not far away. If you catch hold
of the ray, if you move in the direction the ray is coming from, you will reach
to the very source of light.

If only one ray exists in darkness, it is enough proof of light, of godliness.
Don't call it "some degree of awareness."

But I understand. We have lived unaware so long, we have lived unconsciously so long, we have lived like machines so long, that even when a little
awareness comes our old habits are so heavy, so big.

There was once a young woman who joined the ATS and went for her
medical. The doctor had her strip off, and then called over his assistant. "Look
at that: the biggest navel I've ever seen in all my career."

The young doctor looked and said, "By George, girl, that's a huge navel.
Can I take a photograph of it for the medical press?"

The girl was fed up and could not understand what all this was in aid of.
"You'd have a big navel if you'd been in the Salvation Army for as many years
as I have."

This only heightened the mystery. "The Salvation Army? What's that got
to do with it?"

"I carried the banner for ten years!"

You have been carrying the banner for millions of lives, so the navel has
become very big. The unconsciousness is all your biography; all that you
know about yourself is nothing but unconsciousness. So even when a ray of
light enters, first you cannot trust it – maybe you are looking at a dream, illusion, projection? Maybe there is some trick in it? Even if you trust it, it looks
so small against your great past, that you cannot trust that it is going to help
in any way.

But let me tell you one thing: a small candle is more powerful than all the
darkness upon all the planets. Darkness has no power; darkness is impotent.
A small candle is potential – because it *is!* Darkness is just an absence.

A man came to the surgery covered with blood and bruises. "What is the
matter?" said the doctor.

"It's my wife – another of her nightmares."

"Don't talk daft man! She might have kicked you, but not these injuries!"

"Listen, doc, she had one of her nightmares. She shouted out, 'Get out, quick, my husband is coming home!' And me being only half awake, naturally I jumped straight out of the window."

It is a long, old habit of being unconscious. But look at that "some degree of awareness," focus yourself on it – that is your hope. Through that small ray the door opens. Can't you see it? You ask me what is new?

The sixth question:

Osho,
I am a Catholic Christian. I love your talks, but when you say something which goes against my religion then I am terribly upset.
What should I do?

There are three things: first, only listen to that which suits you, don't listen to that which goes against you. That's what many are doing. Otherwise it is going to be a rough journey. But when you are here listening, it is difficult – how to avoid that? In fact before you know it is against you, you have listened to it.

Then you need to do something which professors know how to do, pundits, scholars know how to do. When you listen to something which goes against you, first think that it is trivial: it does not matter, it is not very relevant, it does not change your mind. It is a small thing. Maybe a little difference in the details, but basically Osho agrees with you – keep that in mind.

It happened...

A woman went to the doctor and complained she could not get passionate. The doctor examined her and told her that if she would follow his special diet she would get very randy. This was agreed, but after a few weeks she was back and said, "There's something gone wrong. Last night I got so passionate I chewed my boyfriend's ear off."

"Oh, don't worry about that trifle," said the doctor, "it's only protein, no carbohydrates."

This is the first way, that only in small details... It is nothing very important, you need not worry. That will help you and you will not get so upset.

The second thing is: interpret. That's what Saraha goes on saying. Be interpretative! Interpret it in such a way that it comes closer to your idea. That can always be done; a little skill is needed, a little logic, a little play with words, that's all. It is not much of a problem; you can manage it. If you have really been a Catholic it will not be difficult at all.

Listen to this…

The Irish navvies were digging the road outside a house full of made-up floozies. A parson came along, pulled down his hat and went in. Says Pat to Mike, "Did you see that? Just what you'd expect with one of them parsons."

Soon after a rabbi arrived, turned up his collar, and in he went. Says Mike to Pat, "Is it not a terrible thing that the priest of God's own people should go in there?"

Lastly a Catholic priest arrived, wrapped his cloak round his head and dived quickly into the bawdy house.

"Pat, isn't that dreadful now? To think that one of the girls must have been taken ill!"

This is an interpretation. When the rabbi goes, it is something else; when the parson goes, it is something else; when the Catholic priest arrives… You can change the interpretation, there is no problem with it: now some girl seems to be ill. This is the second way to avoid me.

And the third way is: think, "This guy here is mad." That is the surest of all; if nothing else works, that works. Just think, "This man is mad – only a madman can say things against Catholicism." That will help you, and will not upset you at all.

The newly appointed priest thought he'd walk this vast parish and meet the flock. One day he followed a dusty track for miles to find a devout family with fourteen children.

"Good day, Connelly! You're a credit to Ireland: the biggest family in the parish."

"Good day, father. But this is not the biggest family in the parish: that's Doylan, over the hill."

It was a tired priest who greeted Doylan and his sixteen children, "God bless all these eighteen little Catholics," he said.

"Sorry, father, but this is a Protestant family."

"Then I'll go at once," said the priest, "for it's nothing but a dirty sex maniac that ye are."

If I go with you, think, "This man is great"; if I don't go with you, think, "This man is mad" – that will help you. These are the tricks others are playing and not getting upset. Now you know the secrets, you can do that too. But if your whole effort is not to get upset, then why are you here? My whole effort here is to make you as upset as possible. Then why go with me at all? Unless I upset you, I cannot transform you. Unless I destroy you, I cannot create you. Unless I am very drastic, there is no way, no hope for you.

It is my compassion that I go on hammering on your head – because that is the only way. And I have to hammer too much. What can I do? You have such thick heads. Something upsets you because something true comes into your vision; otherwise it will not upset you.

Always remember, anything upsetting you is valuable. Think over it, meditate over it; allow it to have its whole say, contemplate over it. Let it be there, long present in your being so that you can look at it from all the angles possible, because something upsetting simply means that something has made you aware that whatsoever you have been believing up to now is just a lie. Only truth upsets. Only truth destroys because only truth can create.

I am a chaos, and if you are really going to be with me, you have to pass through chaos.

That's what Saraha says, that's what Tantra is all about: destructuring, taking your character away, taking your ideology away, taking your mind away. It is surgical. I am helpless. I have to do it, and I know it is a very thankless job.

The last question:

Osho,
What is samsara?

Samsara is this story...

The London fog was swirling over the Thames as a young tramp settled himself on the embankment for the night. Suddenly he was roused by a gentle voice, and looking up saw a beautiful brunette alighting from her chauffeur-driven Rolls Royce.

"My poor man," she said, "you must be terribly cold and wet. Let me drive you to my home and put you up for the night."

Of course the tramp didn't refuse this invitation and climbed into the car beside her. After a short drive the car stopped before a large Victorian mansion and the brunette stepped out, beckoning the tramp to follow her. The door was opened by the butler – into whose charge the lady gave the tramp – with instructions that he should be given a meal, a bath and a comfortable bed in the servants' quarters.

Some while later, as the brunette was preparing to retire, it occurred to her that her guest might be in need of something, so slipping on her negligee, she hurried along to the servants' wing. As she rounded the corner a chink of light met her eye, indicating that the young man was awake. Knocking softly on the door she entered the room and inquired of the young man why he was not sleeping.

"Surely you are not hungry?"

"Oh no, your butler fed me royally."

"Then perhaps your bed is not comfortable?"

"But it is – soft and warm."

"Then you must need company. Move over a little."

The young man, overjoyed, moved over – and fell into the Thames.

Enough for today.

about Osho

Osho's unique contribution to the understanding of who we are defies categorization. Mystic and scientist, a rebellious spirit whose sole interest is to alert humanity to the urgent need to discover a new way of living. To continue as before is to invite threats to our very survival on this unique and beautiful planet.

His essential point is that only by changing ourselves, one individual at a time, can the outcome of all our "selves" – our societies, our cultures, our beliefs, our world – also change. The doorway to that change is meditation.

Osho the scientist has experimented and scrutinized all the approaches of the past and examined their effects on the modern human being and responded to their shortcomings by creating a new starting point for the hyperactive 21st Century mind: OSHO Active Meditations.

Once the agitation of a modern lifetime has started to settle, "activity" can melt into "passivity," a key starting point of real meditation. To support this next step, Osho has transformed the ancient "art of listening" into a subtle contemporary methodology: the OSHO Talks. Here words become music, the listener discovers who is listening, and the awareness moves from what is being heard to the individual doing the listening. Magically, as silence arises, what needs to be heard is understood directly, free from the distraction of a mind that can only interrupt and interfere with this delicate process.

These thousands of talks cover everything from the individual quest for meaning to the most urgent social and political issues facing society today. Osho's books are not written but are transcribed from audio and video recordings of these extemporaneous talks to international audiences. As he puts it, "So remember: whatever I am saying is not just for you...I am talking also for the future generations."

Osho has been described by *The Sunday Times* in London as one of the "1000 Makers of the 20th Century" and by American author Tom Robbins as "the most dangerous man since Jesus Christ." *Sunday Mid-Day* (India) has selected Osho as one of ten people – along with Gandhi, Nehru and Buddha – who have changed the destiny of India.

About his own work Osho has said that he is helping to create the conditions for the birth of a new kind of human being. He often characterizes this new human being as "Zorba the Buddha" – capable both of enjoying the earthy pleasures of a Zorba the Greek and the silent serenity of a Gautama the Buddha.

Running like a thread through all aspects of Osho's talks and meditations is a vision that encompasses both the timeless wisdom of all ages past and the highest potential of today's (and tomorrow's) science and technology.

Osho is known for his revolutionary contribution to the science of inner transformation, with an approach to meditation that acknowledges the accelerated pace of contemporary life. His unique OSHO Active Meditations™ are designed to first release the accumulated stresses of body and mind, so that it is then easier to take an experience of stillness and thought-free relaxation into daily life.

Two autobiographical works by the author are available:
Autobiography of a Spiritually Incorrect Mystic,
St Martins Press, New York (book and eBook)
Glimpses of a Golden Childhood,
OSHO Media International, Pune, India (book and eBook)

OSHO international meditation resort

E ach year the Meditation Resort welcomes thousands of people from more than 100 countries. The unique campus provides an opportunity for a direct personal experience of a new way of living – with more awareness, relaxation, celebration and creativity. A great variety of around-the-clock and around-the-year program options are available. Doing nothing and just relaxing is one of them!

All of the programs are based on Osho's vision of "Zorba the Buddha" – a qualitatively new kind of human being who is able *both* to participate creatively in everyday life *and* to relax into silence and meditation.

Location
Located 100 miles southeast of Mumbai in the thriving modern city of Pune, India, the OSHO International Meditation Resort is a holiday destination with a difference. The Meditation Resort is spread over 28 acres of spectacular gardens in a beautiful tree-lined residential area.

OSHO Meditations
A full daily schedule of meditations for every type of person includes both traditional and revolutionary methods, and particularly the OSHO Active Meditations™. The daily meditation program takes place in what must be the world's largest meditation hall, the OSHO Auditorium.

OSHO Multiversity
Individual sessions, courses and workshops cover everything from creative arts to holistic health, personal transformation, relationship and life transition, transforming meditation into a lifestyle for life and work, esoteric sciences, and the "Zen" approach to sports and recreation. The secret of the OSHO Multiversity's success lies in the fact that all its programs are combined with meditation, supporting the understanding that as human beings we are far more than the sum of our parts.

OSHO Basho Spa
The luxurious Basho Spa provides for leisurely open-air swimming surrounded by trees and tropical green. The uniquely styled, spacious Jacuzzi, the saunas,

gym, tennis courts...all these are enhanced by their stunningly beautiful setting.

Cuisine
A variety of different eating areas serve delicious Western, Asian and Indian vegetarian food – most of it organically grown especially for the Meditation Resort. Breads and cakes are baked in the resort's own bakery.

Night life
There are many evening events to choose from – dancing being at the top of the list! Other activities include full-moon meditations beneath the stars, variety shows, music performances and meditations for daily life.

Facilities
You can buy all of your basic necessities and toiletries in the Galleria. The Multimedia Gallery sells a large range of OSHO media products. There is also a bank, a travel agency and a Cyber Café on-campus. For those who enjoy shopping, Pune provides all the options, ranging from traditional and ethnic Indian products to all of the global brand-name stores.

Accommodation
You can choose to stay in the elegant rooms of the OSHO Guesthouse, or for longer stays on campus you can select one of the OSHO Living-In programs. Additionally there is a plentiful variety of nearby hotels and serviced apartments.

www.osho.com/meditationresort
www.osho.com/guesthouse
www.osho.com/livingin

more books and eBooks by OSHO media international

The God Conspiracy:
The Path from Superstition to Super Consciousness

Discover the Buddha: 53 Meditations to Meet the Buddha Within
Gold Nuggets: Messages from Existence

<u>OSHO Classics</u>
The Book of Wisdom: The Heart of Tibetan Buddhism.
The Mustard Seed: The Revolutionary Teachings of Jesus
Ancient Music in the Pines: In Zen, Mind Suddenly Stops
The Empty Boat: Encounters with Nothingness
A Bird on the Wing: Zen Anecdotes for Everyday Life
The Path of Yoga: Discovering the Essence and Origin of Yoga
And the Flowers Showered: The Freudian Couch and Zen
Nirvana: The Last Nightmare: Learning to Trust in Life
The Goose Is Out: Zen in Action
Absolute Tao: Subtle Is the Way to Love, Happiness and Truth

The Tantra Experience: Evolution through Love
Tantric Transformation: When Love Meets Meditation

<u>Pillars of Consciousness</u> (illustrated)
BUDDHA: His Life and Teachings and Impact on Humanity
ZEN: Its History and Teachings and Impact on Humanity
TANTRA: The Way of Acceptance
TAO: The State and the Art

Authentic Living

Danger: Truth at Work: The Courage to Accept the Unknowable
The Magic of Self-Respect: Awakening to Your Own Awareness
Born With a Question Mark in Your Heart

OSHO eBooks and "OSHO-Singles"

Emotions: Freedom from Anger, Jealousy and Fear
Meditation: The First and Last Freedom
What Is Meditation?
The Book of Secrets: 112 Meditations to Discover the Mystery Within

20 Difficult Things to Accomplish in This World
Compassion, Love and Sex
Hypnosis in the Service of Meditation
Why Is Communication So Difficult, Particularly between Lovers?
Bringing Up Children
Why Should I Grieve Now?: facing a loss and letting it go
Love and Hate: just two sides of the same coin

Next Time You Feel Angry...
Next Time You Feel Lonely...
Next Time You Feel Suicidal...

OSHO Media BLOG
http://oshomedia.blog.osho.com

for more information

www..com

a comprehensive multi-language website including a magazine, OSHO Books, OSHO Talks in audio and video formats, the OSHO Library text archive in English and Hindi and extensive information about OSHO Meditations. You will also find the program schedule of the OSHO Multiversity and information about the OSHO International Meditation Resort.

http://OSHO.com/AllAboutOSHO
http://OSHO.com/Resort
http://OSHO.com/Shop
http://www.youtube.com/OSHO
http://www.Twitter.com/OSHO
http://www.facebook.com/pages/OSHO.International

To contact OSHO International Foundation:
www.osho.com/oshointernational,
oshointernational@oshointernational.com